£25.

Father Mathew
and the
Irish Temperance Movement
1838-1849

Father Mathew

and the

Irish Temperance
Movement
1838-1849

COLM KERRIGAN

CORK
UNIVERSITY
PRESS

First Published in 1992 by
Cork University Press
University College
Cork
Ireland

British Library Cataloguing in Publication Data
Kerrigan, Colm
Father Mathew and the Irish Temperance Movement 1838-1849.
1. Title
178

ISBN 0 902561 60 X

Typeset in Ireland by Tower Books, 13 Hawthorn Ave., Ballincollig,
Co. Cork;
Printed in Ireland, by Colour Books of Baldoyle, Dublin

Contents

Acknowledgements   vii

Introduction   1
Ireland in the Eighteen Thirties   9
Father Mathew   37
The Temperance Crusade   57
Drinking and Crime   86
Teetotallers and Repealers   107
Reasons and Superstitions   132
The Catholic Clergy   153
Conclusion   168

Notes and References   187
Bibliography   225
Index   245

Acknowledgements

I must acknowledge my debt to David Tierney who ten years ago convinced me of the need for a book on Father Mathew's temperance crusade, and I am also indebted to Bernard Canavan who has encouraged me to persist with the work over the years. Father Nessan, OFM Cap., offered me useful guidance at the outset and, more recently, I have had the benefit of several informative letters on Father Mathew and his work from John Quinn. I am grateful to Elizabeth Malcolm, Sean Connolly, Thomas Bartlett and David Johnson for useful comments on an earlier attempt to explore some of the ideas in Chapter 4, and to Oliver MacDonagh for his helpful remarks on Chapter 5.

I wish to thank the staff of the British Library, especially those at the Newspaper Room at Colindale. My thanks are also due to the staff of the National Library of Ireland, the State Paper Office, Dublin and the Public Record Office at Kew. The help of the staff at the Department of Irish Folklore, University College, Dublin has been valuable, as has that of Patricia McCarthy at the Cork Archives Institute and Mrs Brigid Dolan, who guided me through the Haliday Pamphlet collection at the Royal Irish Academy. Father O'Cuill, OFM Cap., was helpful to me with Father Mathew's draft correspondence, and I greatly appreciate the hospitality shown me at the Capuchin Franciscan Friary in Church Street, Dublin, during my visits there.

I have been fortunate in having members of my family in Ireland who were always willing to take me to places around the country that had associations with Father Mathew: my sisters Mella Burke and Mary Kerrigan, my brother Finbar Kerrigan and my brother-in-law Colm Burke. Finally, I wish to thank the following people without whose help this book could not have been completed: Jean M. Kerrigan , Noel Kerrigan, John H. Pierce, Vivienne Crouch, David H. Fahey, Joe O'Halloran, Shirley MacNeill, Chris Lloyd, Henry Watton, H. David Behr, David Webb and Rosemary Taylor.

Introduction

It is difficult to understand the neglect of Father Mathew's temperance crusade by historians, bearing in mind its enormous impact on Irish life at the time and the great amount of material that has survived about it. Police and magistrates in the southern counties of Ireland submitted detailed reports on the progress of the crusade in their districts at the beginning of 1840 in reply to a circular from the Chief Inspector of Constabulary in Dublin. These replies (the Temperance Reports) have survived in the original handwriting of the police officers and magistrates, as have the printed replies to another circular three years later, when magistrates and county inspectors of constabulary were asked to comment on various aspects of Repeal agitation, then at its height, including the connection between temperance and Repeal (the Repeal Reports). Sir Robert Peel, Daniel O'Connell and Lord Morpeth were among the prominent figures of the day whose opinions on Father Mathew and his work have survived, and few of the many travellers who passed through Ireland in the eighteen forties failed to record their impressions of the temperance movement and its celebrated and undisputed leader. Statistical evidence that could be used to assess the effect of the movement on the lives of Irish people at the time is available in parliamentary returns on drink consumption, drunkenness and crime.

Father Mathew's voluminous draft correspondence has survived where, in appalling handwriting, he has left us little that betrays his own inner life but much that can help us understand what he was trying to do and the problems he encountered.

Newspapers reported Father Mathew's visits to towns and villages throughout Ireland from the end of 1839 and he got equally good press coverage when he took his crusade to Scotland and England and for the early part of his mission to the United States between 1849 and 1851. By May 1840, within six months of Father Mathew's decision to travel from Cork to spread the campaign by personal visits around the country to administer the pledge, his first biographer, Father Birmingham of Borrisokane, had placed his completed manuscript with his publisher.[1]

Besides an account of Father Mathew's work in Cork and his early

journeys outside that city up to and including that to Dublin in March
1840, Birmingham's book contained observations on several issues that
were later to become subjects of controversy. These included the state
of drunkenness before the advent of Father Mathew, the effect of the
temperance crusade on the economy, the attitude of the Catholic clergy
to his work and the nature of the commitment entailed in taking the
total abstinence pledge. As these observations were based on his attending many of Father Mathew's meetings — he had actually reported some
of these meetings for the *Dublin Evening Post* — and from his having
had 'long and frequent conversations' with him, they may be taken to
represent Father Mathew's own views at the time and to this extent the
book is of value. But in his reverence for his subject, his enthusiasm
for the success of the cause of temperance and his uncritical acceptance
of the claims made on its behalf, Birmingham sets the pattern for future
works on Father Mathew's life and work.

Birmingham's short book contained two pages of biographical detail
on Father Mathew's life before he took up the cause of temperance. In
1863, seven years after Father Mathew's death, the first full length
biography appeared, written by John Francis Maguire. Maguire had
known Father Mathew for many years and had been a firm supporter
of his temperance work. Indeed, Maguire's own career from local jour-
nalist to member of parliament at Westminster was assisted to some extent by his association with the temperance movement in that the
newspaper he founded to report on temperance matters grew into the
influential *Cork Examiner* in the eighteen forties. It may have been his
debt to temperance that prevented him from formulating the kind of
critical assessment of Father Mathew's life and work that should have
been possible by one who witnessed so many of the events he wrote about
and was on such intimate terms with the subject of his biography. Though
the many anecdotes he relates in his long book bear witness to the com-
plex character of his subject, he is reluctant to form any but the most
favourable judgements of Father Mathew in all his dealings. Even on
Father Mathew's debts, an issue with which he was particularly well informed, having worked on a committee to try to solve them, Maguire
refused to blame him for the obvious organisational and administrative
ineptitude which permitted the debts to mount up, preferring instead
to attribute blame to the careless parishes which did not pay for their
medals or to Lady Elizabeth Mathew, who declined to leave to her nephew
the legacy he was expecting.[2]

Sister Mary Francis Clare's biography of Father Mathew was published eleven years after Maguire's and had the declared aim of encouraging boys to take the pledge. It contained little that was not already covered by Maguire and the tone was more hagiographical. She disagreed strongly with Maguire's suggestion that Father Mathew's miracles could have been 'performed by natural causes'. She had intended, she wrote in her Introduction, to give an account of his miracles in her book, 'but for the present this plan is abandoned'. This was a pity, for two reasons. Many of those who claimed to have been healed by Father Mathew would still have been alive at the time she was writing and their testimony would have been of interest. Her account would also have been of particular significance because of her own commitment to the reality of miracles — she believed herself to have been miraculously healed at Knock.[3]

In 1878 J.H. Olivier's *Vie du Père Mathew* came out in France, based almost entirely on *'la belle et riche'* biography by Maguire, a French translation of which had appeared in Brussels in 1868.[4]

For the centenary of Father Mathew's birth in 1890 his brother's grandson, Frank Mathew, wrote a book in which he 'tried to show him as he was known to his nearest relatives, to trace the cause of his success, and the connection of the temperance movement with the history of his times'. His explanation of Father Mathew's mission and its connection with other events in mid-nineteenth-century Ireland falls a long way short of his declared aim, although it could hardly be otherwise in so short a book and by a writer who was not a historian. His brief sketch of Father Mathew's personality in the context of the well-known Mathew family is, on the other hand, most illuminating. To his credit, he was not inhibited by family ties from acknowledging that his grand-uncle, in addition to inheriting some of the family's endearing characteristics like a passion for hospitality, had also taken on some of its less admirable traits like wilfulness and bad temper.[5]

Another literary figure, Katharine Tynan, wrote a biography of Father Mathew which came out in 1908. She acknowledged Frank Mathew's 'enthralling biography' as well as that of Maguire and proceeded to quote liberally from both. One of her few observations not based on their works was that Ireland was then 'becoming temperate under the influence of the Gaelic League'. A biography in Irish the previous year, based almost entirely on Maguire's work, had drawn attention to Father Mathew's efforts to promote sobriety and self respect and to provide reading rooms for teetotallers as forerunners of the work of the Gaelic League.[6]

No book was to be written on Father Mathew for nearly forty years, when, in the nineteen forties, two were ready at almost the same time. In a note at the beginning of his *Father Theobald Mathew* Father Rogers enumerated the deficiencies in Maguire's biography and in the course of his own book makes amends for many of them, including the correction of Maguire's faulty account of how Father Mathew took up the cause of temperance in the first place. There is evidence in Rogers' book, too, of the considerable amount of research from manuscript and printed sources that he considered was necessary for the long overdue revision of Maguire's work. As a historian's attempt to present an adequate picture of the effects of Father Mathew's work on the people of Ireland at the time, however, two essential sources were neglected. The first were the Temperance Reports of 1840 which provide a rich source of information on the movement at this early stage of its development, when enthusiasm was high. The second neglected source was the contemporary press. As early as page 55 in his book Rogers remarked that to follow Father Mathew's progress around Ireland would have been 'a most wearisome, almost an impossible task'. But newspaper accounts of Father Mathew's visits to towns and villages up and down the country were often detailed and colourful and offer the historian endless insights into how the movement was received and perceived by contemporaries. Father Rogers' frugal use of this source caused him to rely too heavily on recorded opinions of notable people of the day or on books by visitors to the country whose competence to make judgements on Irish events was often limited by inadequate knowledge of Ireland and its problems, history and traditions.[7]

A few weeks before Father Rogers' book was put on sale by Browne and Nolan Ltd., another Dublin publisher, Messrs. Gill and Son Ltd., had received the manuscript that was to become Father Augustine's *Footprints of Father Theobald Mathew O.F.M. Cap.* Father Augustine had written an introduction to Sean Ua Ceallaigh's Irish language biography of Father Mathew in 1907 and his own book, delayed by wartime restrictions on paper and by the appearance of Father Rogers' book, did not come out until 1947. In the intervening 40 years he had been collecting material on Father Mathew's life and work but it was not until 1933 that he decided to write a full-length work. As the title of his book suggests, Father Augustine traced his fellow Capuchin's life from cradle to grave, drawing on material used by Maguire and other biographers, correcting and supplementing it where necessary from a wide variety of sources, including newspapers favourably disposed towards the movement. The vast amount of information contained in the book is of interest but it does not meet the author's stated aim of writing a biography that would be 'critical, definitive and interpretative'. For while it may be considered definitive in that most known facts about what Father Mathew did and where he did it were included, and interpretative in that a religious interpretation is given throughout, it cannot be seen as a critical work.[8]

The book's main weakness is its failure to see Father Mathew and his temperance crusade in anything but the most glowing light. Such a vision could only be sustained by inadequate attention to the same two sources that had been neglected by Father Rogers. From the Preface to his work it is clear that Father Augustine did not himself examine the Temperance Reports in any detail but relied on a study of them by another Capuchin, Brother (later Father) Nessan, whose thesis 'The Life and Times of Father Mathew' had been accepted by University College Cork in 1939. Familiarity with the Temperance Reports would have convinced him of the variety of opinions about the temperance crusade that were current at the time, something that does not come across in his book. There was also a variety of views expressed in the press about the value of Father Mathew's work. Not every newspaper of Catholic and Liberal tendency was as favourably disposed to Father Mathew's activities as the *Cork Examiner* and the *Dublin Evening Post*, nor was hostility as evident everywhere among Tory newspapers as that shown by the *Limerick Standard* or the *Dublin Evening Mail*. The latter expressed open hostility to the temperance crusade, yet neither the newspaper nor its criticisms were mentioned by Father Augustine. It is as if any criticism of Father Mathew's work, much less a criticism of his personality, would somehow detract from the portrait of saintliness the author was trying to construct.

My own interest in the subject goes back twelve years when I came across a reference to a series of meetings Father Mathew held in Commercial Road in London's East End in 1843, when crowds of up to 50,000 were said to have attended. Sceptical at first that such large crowds could have been assembled for a temperance gathering in the days before mass communications, I found, on reading the newspapers of the day, that such numbers had indeed been present and that thousands of them had taken the pledge, part of a total of 600,000 who had done so during his stay in England that summer. One report quoted the landlord of the George on Commercial Road as saying that Father Mathew could stay as long as he liked in the area because business was never better.[9]

A walk along Commercial Road revealed that the George was still in business nearly a century and a half after the prospective teetotallers crowded into it to have one last drink — the 'farewell to whiskey' — before pledging themselves to Father Mathew to abandon it forever. The site of his meetings was occupied by a church and school. No plaque or notice of any kind marked the spot where thousands of Irish immigrants appeared before him in batches, their faces, as Jane Carlyle described them, 'exhibiting such concentrated wretchedness'. Later, visiting some of the scenes of his greatest meetings in Ireland — the Old Court House in Limerick, Eyre Square in Galway, Beresford Place in Dublin — I was aware of a similar absence of any sign or notice to commemorate them.[10]

Newspaper reports of his meetings in London and other English cities and dissatisfaction with the biographies already referred to led me to undertake a systematic reading of newspaper accounts of his meetings in Ireland, Scotland, England and the United States from 1838 to 1851, a task that took me five years of Saturdays to complete. In the meantime, two articles appeared which, abandoning the biographers' preoccupation with the saintliness of Father Mathew's life, concentrated on the significance of his temperance crusade in the history of modern Ireland.

In 'Fr Mathew: Apostle of Modernisation' H.F. Kearney expressed regret that Father Mathew had been mentioned by Irish historians only in the context of the Repeal movement. His reading of the Temperance Reports led Kearney to find in Father Mathew's crusade a parallel with a modified version of the Lynch-Vaizey theory of a dual economy — a money economy in the towns with a tenuous influence on the subsistence economy elsewhere. For while the Temperance Reports from rural areas did indeed show examples of revivalism and superstition, those from the towns where the movement was strongest show evidence for a commitment to the 'virtues of thrift and self-help'. The movement, that is, was seen as encouraging social and economic as well as moral improvement, and could thus be seen as a force for the modernisation of Ireland.[11].

In Elizabeth Malcolm's 'Temperance and Irish Nationalism' the discussion of Father Mathew and his work returned again to the familiar context of their association with the Repeal and Young Ireland movements, though her treatment of this association raised issues not touched on by Father Mathew's biographers or by historians of nineteenth-century

Ireland. It was not surprising then, that when her major work on the Irish temperance movement appeared in 1986 a considerable amount of attention was given to Father Mathew's work. Her short but detailed examination of the early stages of the crusade took full account of the Temperance Reports as well as the hostility voiced by the *Dublin Evening Mail* and the reservations of the traditional temperance movement. Other aspects of the crusade looked at in considerable depth within the confines of a single chapter include the numbers who took the pledge, Father Mathew's relationship with clergymen in the Catholic church and with Protestants, the effects of his crusade on drink consumption, how his debts influenced the progres of the crusade and the controversial subject of modernisation.[12]

While Kearney and Malcolm have given a relevance to Father Mathew's campaign against drink that will make it difficult to dismiss by future historians of the period, their work has raised almost as many questions as it has answered about the details of the campaign and its significance. The present work is an attempt to explore some of these questions and offer some tentative answers.

It begins with an account of Ireland in the eighteen thirties, with particular attention to those aspects of Irish life that might be seen as relevant to a study of Father Mathew's work. These include the problems associated with drinking and the attempts of the early temperance advocates to overcome them. Father Mathew's life before he took up the temperance cause is next examined, for, while this is not a biography, some appreciation of the personality of the man who was so central to the rise and progress of the campaign is essential to an understanding of it. His biographers, especially those who knew him, were the main source for this, although newspaper sketches of his personality and the accounts of travellers to Ireland who met him have also been of value. There follows a description of the crusade to various parts of the country, based largely on the Temperance Reports and on newspapers, national and local. Further chapters examine particular aspects of the campaign that are problematic. These include the claims made for the effect of Father Mathew's work on drink consumption and on crime, for which British Parliamentary Papers were the main source, and the connection of the crusade with the Repeal and Young Ireland movement, based on the Temperance Reports, the Repeal Reports, newspapers and the great amount of literature on Daniel O'Connell's campaign against the Union. Chapter Six looks at the extent to which Father Mathew's reputation for miraculous cures may have helped the movement and the following chapter considers whether his work was helped or hindered by Catholic bishops and priests at the time. Finally, the effects of the Famine on the temperance movement are examined as well as the long-term significance of Father Mathew's crusade in the history of modern Ireland.

CHAPTER 1

Ireland in the Eighteen Thirties

There is disagreement about whether the Irish population growth in the late eighteenth century was caused by the fertility arising out of an early age for marriage or by a drop in the level of mortality. But 'the most important feature of these years is not in question, namely, that rapid population growth occurred in Ireland between 1780 and 1830 due to some combination of low death rate, high marriage rates and high fertility of marriage'. The high regard with which children were held in Ireland must also be taken into account. A recent writer has pointed out that, in the absence of the state taking care of the old and the sick, parents would have seen their children as 'a form of social insurance which they could cash in when they became economically dependent'. The widespread use of the potato in the late eighteenth century is important whichever explanation is given most weight. In one it was the potato which facilitated early marriage by making subdivision viable — more people could subsist on a smaller space — while in the other explanation it was the 'universal acceptance' of the potato as the staple food throughout most of Ireland that was suggested as the cause of the reduction in mortality. This dependence on the potato, especially among the rural population, continued during the early nineteenth century, despite the risks of failure and famine. Visitors noticed that the whole class of small farmers and labourers subsisted almost entirely on potatoes. The additional income some families obtained from spinning wool, cotton and flax (these were predominantly female occupations) was as precarious as cultivating the potato. Both 'were inherently unstable economic endeavours: they answered paupers' immediate needs while reinforcing their ultimate impoverishment'.[1]

Visitors to Ireland in the years before the Famine were often struck by the sharp distinction 'between the wretched hovel and the gentleman's house', as Sir John Burgoyne put it in 1831. 'In Ireland', Gustave de Beaumont wrote in his book which came out eight years later, 'there are only the rich and the poor.' He was not strictly accurate in this, nor in his observation on the same page that the man 'who has not a spot of ground to cultivate dies of Famine', but in both exaggerations he identified fundamental points about the condition of the country at the time. The first was the presence of an enormous number of people living in various stages of impoverishment, whose misery may have made them all seem alike to a traveller, but among whom there were in reality important differences. De Beaumont's second observation suggests a key to these differences, namely the importance of land, or, more specifically, the nature of the system of tenure under which land was held.[2]

The Commissioners appointed to investigate the conditions of the poor in Ireland noted in their Third Report in 1836 that families engaged in agriculture in Ireland constituted about two-thirds of the population, compared with just over a quarter in England and Wales. Land in Ireland was the property of landlords, most of whom were descendants of the English and Scottish beneficiaries of the 'settlement' of Ireland in the sixteenth and seventeenth centuries. About half of the substantial landlords lived on their estates, leasing land to farmers. While most tenant farmers paid their rent in cash either to a landlord, to a larger farmer or to a middleman, cottiers, who rented smaller pieces of land on a year-to-year basis for cultivating potatoes and sometimes other crops, often paid for it in whole or in part by means of labour services equivalent to an agreed amount of money. De Beaumont complained that farm implements were not provided by landlords and that this led to a poor quality of cultivation. As the tenant had no guarantee of being able to benefit from any improvements he might make to the land he leased (except in parts of Ulster, where 'tenant right' existed), he had no incentive to invest any more labour than was necessary to the upkeep of his holding. Going through Clare in 1842 Kohl saw fields 'in the most disorderly state, and evidently tilled in the most negligent manner'.[3]

Bicheno, on the other hand, noted the great care that country people put into the cultivation of their potato crop, but, like most travellers, was appalled at the physical condition of the cabins they lived in, 'composed of stones and mud rudely put together . . . floors formed of clay, uneven and full of holes, containing dirty water, through which the pigs and ducks trample'. Barrow, who travelled through part of Ireland in 1835, reproduced several sketches of cabins in his book. These varied from 'wretched mud hovels' to the apparently neat and comfortable stone and thatch 'Better sort of Connaught cabin'. Bicheno, who thought the cabins couldn't be all that unwholesome when their occupants seemed to enjoy such good health, received a revealing answer to his question about why pigs, goats, a cow and poultry lived with a family in a cabin. They have a right, he was told, because they pay the rent. A more sophisticated explanation is that, rather than poverty, it was the cultural pattern, going back to Celtic times, whereby the 'well-being and fertility of the cattle were linked to those of the family' that led to the continuation of the custom of keeping animals in cabins. But the custom was then in decline, and even the one room windowless, smoky, earthen-floored cabin that travellers loved to dwell on was not everywhere the norm; there is evidence that on some estates there were slate roofed houses with windows and chimneys and that a small number of them even had wooden floors.[4]

'Except for their rags, they have no national dress', wrote Kohl, one of the many travellers to comment on the attire of the impoverished Irishman of the period, dressed in thread-bare friezecoat, a garment once made from the exclusively Irish-produced coarse grey cloth, but by the 'thirties mostly made from imported fabric. Often the coats worn by Irish small farmers, 'patched and mended until the original fabric was unrecognizable' were the cast-offs of the poor of England or Scotland. Women, it appears, were able to present themselves in a more dignified appearance, with their traditional hooded cloaks of black, blue, grey, red or scarlet. De Beaumont believed that English paupers were better clothed than Irish labourers. Certainly the borderline between the dress of the poorer tenants, cottiers and labourers on the one hand and the beggars on the other was often thin. When Elizabeth Smith came from India to Ireland to occupy the property her husband had inherited in county Wicklow, she was met by what she took to be a contingent of beggars. 'Them's the tenants', she was informed by 'the only one amongst them with a whole coat'. Appearances, also, may have been deceptive: all may not have been as impoverished as they pretended. Quite apart from tenants not wishing to look too prosperous in case they were presented with a demand for an increase in rent, Binns recorded the stories of one 'beggar' who said he could give his daughter £30 and another who had several sums of money out at interest.[5]

If the outward signs of poverty — dirty cabins, tattered clothes, plain food — often convinced travellers that the condition of the Irish poor was worse than it really was, these same outward signs could lead to misunderstandings about rural Irish society and its problems. As landless labourers and small tenant farmers dressed alike, they were lumped together as the 'Irish poor' although their actual circumstances were quite distinct. The romantic notion of early marriages among the children of tenant farmers, facilitated by the sub-division of holdings and subsistence farming of potatoes, may have had its origin in this same confusion. Recent work on the farming community in county Cavan in the pre-Famine period found no evidence that farms were getting smaller between 1800 and 1845, and suggests that it was the plight of the landless cottiers that gave unperceptive visitors the impression of increasing impoverishment among all sections of the Irish countryside. While the system of sub-letting was clearly in decline by the eighteen thirties it was still a cause of concern even to well-informed visitors. The custom should be abolished, wrote W.W. Simpson, an English land valuator who knew Ireland well. His reason — and this was in 1840 — was that draining and other improvements to estates were always out of the question for sub-tenants as they would always lack the capital and the energy needed.[6]

The good health Bicheno noticed was real, for, despite poor cabins and poor clothing, the rural population, in the absence of potato failure, enjoyed a balanced and nourishing diet, although it is true that in some areas, particularly in the south and west, there was regular hardship in the summer months, when the potatoes of the old season were used up and new ones were not ready for digging. Irish agriculture was also successful enough to export food to England and to provide capital for food processing industries like corn milling and bacon curing. But as few other profitable outlets for Irish agricultural capital existed in Ireland, much of it tended to go to England for investment. Even in Ulster, the one part of Ireland where industrialisation was comparable to England, the majority of the population were engaged in agriculture, with only ten per cent living in towns of 2,000 or more. The Poor Law Commissioners estimated that for 30 weeks of the year 585,000 men in Ireland were unemployed, who, with their dependants, constituted nearly two and a half million people in need. What was at the root of Ireland's problems, one of the Commissioners rightly noted, was 'the want of some mode of employment which may compete with the land for a portion of the population'. Eager to work but finding none, thousands emigrated, with variations in the numbers leaving in the years between 1830 and the Famine influenced by the potato crop in particular years or clusters of years.[7]

In his novel *The Black Prophet* William Carleton put the blame for the country's evils at the door of the middleman. The novel was set in an earlier period, but the middleman remained a despised figure, John Keenan seeing him in 1840 as one of the main causes of Irish 'wretchedness'. Recent research has drawn attention to the positive contribution of middlemen to the development of the Irish town, and even de Beaumont's condemnation of landlords as the real authors of Irish misery needs qualification. The consolidation of farms in the transition from tillage to pasture farming that the demands of the market required did not always lead to a decrease in the need for labour, and, while the encumberances of the more improvident landlords did render their heirs unable to improve the conditions of their tenants, some tenants were able to turn their landlord's problems to their own advantage. Those of the second Marquis of Donegall, for example, managed to secure or renew longer leases at a time when their financially embarrassed landlord was in need of ready cash.[8]

The concept of the 'dual economy' formulated more than thirty years ago to characterise the modern 'money' economic system which was said to prevail in the maritime eastern part of Ireland contrasted with the subsistence economy in operation in the rest of the country, with 'slight and tenuous' connections between the two, has been much criticised, most usefully by Mokyr, who has seen the value of the concept and has modified it in his own work. The subsistence economy did exist and was less commercialised, but it was interrelated with the 'money system' in a variety of ways, to a greater or lesser degree in different parts of the country. With bartering as common as financial transactions in farmers' dealing with labourers in the middle of the decade, Mokyr found it unsurprising that the country as a whole should be underdeveloped commercially and financially. The traditional form of society may also have inhibited approval for those 'entrepeneurial activities' that modern economists feel might have enabled the country to adapt to new conditions and 'to reorganize its agricultural structures to meet changing circumstances'.[9]

As there was no Poor Law in operation in Ireland until the end of the decade, voluntary agencies provided what care there was for those unable to find work and unwilling to emigrate. These were mostly located in the cities and towns, where so many of the unemployed and unemployable gathered. When Robert Lowery was in Dublin in 1839 he noticed that the city seemed full of beggars, most of them able-bodied men. They were not confined to Dublin, as Thompson, in the same year, found all public places crowded with them, offering 'the most painful evidence of the number and variety of the ills to which nature is subject'. While public charity may have been largely confined to the towns, private charity was not: the Poor Law Commissioners calculated that between 1 million and 2 million was given annually by farmers and cottiers to the poor who called on them begging.[10]

Lowery was impressed by the beggars' wit and humour and Binns admired the capacity of the Irish poor for immediately grasping the drift of questions put to them. But compliments on their intelligence often had a sting in the tail. Trollope's view of the working class of Ireland as more intelligent than those of England is often quoted, but less well known is his remark a few sentences later that the Irish were 'perverse, irrational and but little bound by the love of truth'. Often, too, a tribute to their intelligence was followed by one of sadness or surprise that a people apparently so gifted should be content, or appear to be content 'with filth, rags, disorder, wretched accommodation and very inferior diet'. Lady Chatterton was enthusiastic about the amount of talent, imagination and 'tender and delicate feeling' she found among 'the common people' in 1838, and wondered 'that such a people should be content to dwell in smoky hovels, when, if they choose to exert themselves and employ the energies which I think they possess, their condition might be improved!' Exasperation at trying to make sense of Ireland's problems is perhaps most evident in Kohl's book. Having agreed with de Beaumont's view that the privations of the Irish poor were the worst in the world, having shown the income of a large landowner to have been many thousand times more than that of the men who tilled his soil, and having accepted that the country was the victim of an unjust administration, he then goes on to claim that 'a main root of Irish misery lies in the indolent, fickle, extravagant, and inactive character of the people'. Samuel Wilderspin, the pioneer of infant schools, admired not only their 'native quickness' but also their great patience, 'and with these two qualities what might not be accomplished?' Having visited hundreds of 'the lowest cabins' near Dublin he found the occupants 'delighted to receive information on all subjects except *one*'.[11]

That one subject was of course religion. The Established Church in Ireland had, together with Dissenters, about a million and a half members, while the remaining six and a half million people were Catholics, who, despite Catholic emancipation and the concessions granted by the Whig administration in the second half of the decade, continued, with justification, to feel that, in proportion to their numbers, they had an unfair share of power in the country. In Ireland, de Beaumont noted, as 'religion marks the race, Protestantism is regarded as a species of nobility', and Lowery, an English Chartist, noted that everything in Ireland was viewed 'through the medium of religious prejudices. Whatever the Catholics undertook the Protestants opposed, and whatever the Protestants commenced was resisted by the Catholics. I had marked our English sectarianism, but from it no Englishman could have any conception of the bitterness of religious intolerance in Ireland.' But even here the picture was not as bleak as that painted by visitors. Even in a town with a reputation for segregation like Bandon, an analysis of manuscript returns in connection with the 1834 Religious Census suggests 'significant social interaction among members of the Church of Ireland, Roman Catholic Church and the Presbyterian Meeting'.[12]

The town of Bandon was a product of the settlement of Munster in the sixteenth and seventeenth centuries but most towns and villages in Ireland were either of medieval origin, like Carlow, Drogheda or Sligo, or the product of the landlord system of the eighteenth century, with all the towns in county Monaghan, for example, 'landlord inspired' although, as has been shown in the case of Castlecomer in county Kilkenny, the direct participation of the landlord in the actual development of the town may have been no more than the granting of a lease on terms favourable to building. The wide variety of activities carried out in Irish towns, mostly related to agriculture, were catalogued by Samuel Lewis in his *Topographical Dictionary*, and a modern historian, who has checked Lewis' entries about mills, factories and the like with other sources has confirmed that Lewis' accounts can be trusted. Kohl's description of a typical Irish town in the early eighteen forties would hold good for the 'thirties except that the workhouse would not yet have been built: 'a number of goodly buildings, a similar number of ruined dwelling houses, a suburb-quarter of miserable huts, some new well-built national and infants schools, some old and some quite modern Catholic churches, a fever hospital, an extensive fortress-looking workhouse, and lastly, perhaps, some barracks for soldiers'. Such towns, of course, could only prosper if the agricultural community surrounding them prospered and Burgoyne in 1831 found them languishing, though 'in situations suited by nature for business and commerce'. Some did thrive, though, and many middle class Catholic merchants made substantial fortunes in towns and cities during the period. Some of this was spent on philanthropic ventures, providing schools, libraries and schemes for self improvement mostly but not entirely for the urban poor.[13]

The national schools Kohl indicated as a feature of a typical Irish town were the product of a system of education, introduced in 1831, whereby children of all creeds would receive instruction in the same schools. While all religious denominations had reservations about the new system to begin with, the schools set about confronting the high levels of illiteracy that prevailed in large areas of the country, especially in Connaught and Munster. In these provinces and in the counties of Donegal and Louth, more than six people in every ten over the age of five were unable to read or write. Though the majority of the population in the South and West of the country were Irish speaking, the native language was already in decline and not solely because of its neglect by the national schools. Irish, the language of the oral culture of the countryside, was becoming the language of the poor, while English, the language of the towns, was associated with the written culture, with commerce and prosperity: it was the language of advancement. At the same time as the Irish language was in decline there was a revival of interest by scholars in the antiquities of Ireland, spearheaded by Edward O'Reilly, John O'Donovan and Edward O'Curry, which was to lead in the following decades to an increased knowledge of and pride in the country's past.[14]

Archbishop MacHale of Tuam opposed the national school system, not because of the neglect of the Irish language he held so dear, but because he saw the secularisation of education as a first step towards the destruction of Catholicism in Ireland. MacHale, because of his uncompromising views on this and other subjects, was perhaps the best known of the 26 bishops who were responsible for the direction of more than 2,000 parish priests and curates in a manner that, in its organisation and discipline, was beginning to resemble that exercised by the hierarchy in modern Irish Catholicism. Parish clergy in the countryside had been campaigning for many years, with varying degrees of enthusiasm, against traditional beliefs and observances that were at variance with the form of Catholic teaching the hierarchy wished to see practised throughout Ireland. In this they had considerable success, although they were rather less successful in their opposition to traditional rural activities, like faction fighting and violent agrarian disturbances. Nevertheless, priests made a considerable contribution to imposing orderly habits on a population without the assistance to their efforts that might have been available had Irish work patterns been regulated by something like that which prevailed in industrialised societies at the time.[15]

Religious observances were not carried out then as strictly as in modern Ireland. Mass attendance was quite low in Irish speaking areas but, considering the distances that had to be travelled in some parts of the countryside to reach a church and the reluctance of many of the poor to attend mass in ragged clothes, the overall picture of mass attendance for the country was reasonably good and particularly good in the towns. Some of the older priests had been educated on the continent but by 1840 most of those engaged in parish work were more likely to have been trained as priests at Maynooth. Between a fifth and a sixth of serving priests belonged to one or other of the traditional religious orders, most assisting in urban parishes like, for example, the Dominicans in Galway. One of these regular clergy, as they were called, was Dr. Spratt, a Dublin Carmelite, who became a well-known social reformer. While Irish bishops appreciated the assistance of these regulars at a time when there was a scarcity of priests in the country they were nevertheless subject to many restrictions, including some relating to the administration of the sacraments. Most suspicions about the regulars among the secular clergy, however, centred on the former draining money away from needy parishes.[16]

Contemporaries were impressed by the high esteem in which priests were regarded by their parishioners, a regard that sometimes extended to crediting priests with miraculous powers of healing. Visitors were impressed with the way priests associated themselves with the conditions of the poor. De Beaumont found that 'the Catholic clergy were the only persons in Ireland who loved the lower classes, and spoke of them in terms of esteem and affection. This fact alone would explain the power of the priests in Ireland.' De Tocqueville found that those he dined with in Carlow, besides showing pronounced political leanings and hostility towards landlords, had 'a love of the people and confidence in them'.

That priests' identification with popular demands could be attributed to them having the same humble origin as those they championed has been questioned by recent work suggesting that priests came from a higher stratum of society than most of their parishioners. And the fact that priests depended on their parishioners for their incomes does not seem to have prevented them from consistently condemning popular pursuits like faction-fighting and popularly approved forms of social protest like agrarian outrages. Any explanation of the power of priests must surely take account of the plight of so many of the poorer section of the Irish people at the time, a plight calculated to excite the sympathy of any sensitive and educated person living close to them, and a condition that must have convinced the priests that any improvement of the spiritual condition of their charges was unlikely if not impossible until the basic necessities of life were assured.[17]

O'Connell had succeeded in enlisting the active support of the Catholic clergy in the campaign for Catholic emancipation, to the extent that, as early as 1826, the Duke of Wellington had heard from Henry Goulburn, then Chief Secretary in Ireland, that the priests were ruling the country. Bicheno noted in 1830 that as the gentry were losing influence the priests were gaining it. 'They are becoming the lords paramount in politics as well as in religion.' When Catholic emancipation was achieved the Irish bishops wanted their priests to withdraw from politics. Many of the political issues of the time, however, like those of tithe, education and the needs of the poor, had a religious dimension so it is not surprising that clerical engagement in politics continued. There was considerable political involvement in the various political societies formed by O'Connell in the eighteen thirties, giving him not only important verbal support but assisting him in distributing his addresses throughout the country and permitting the doors of churches as centres for collections to enable him to carry on his political work. The culmination of this co-operation was the massive clerical support for Repeal in the next decade. Nor could the priests reasonably be accused of *causing* the discontent. Nobody would listen to O'Connell if the Irish people were clothed and fed, wrote an English visitor in 1837, following a short tour of the Irish Midlands the previous year, and another opponent of Repeal, Count Cavour, noticed that Ireland was peaceful when the Government was seen to have been respecting Irish beliefs. Barrow insisted on seeing priests as 'political partisans' and Inglis condemned one at Mitchelstown for 'irritating the passions of the lower classes, and endeavouring to widen the breach, which unhappily now subsists, between the aristocracy and the people'. A few years later, with Repeal agitation reaching its peak, Madden wrote of priests as 'ranting intemperately in favour of *ultra*-democratic government as the noisiest and most reckless of the Chartists'.[18]

Following failure to defeat the Coercion Act of 1833 (introduced to deal with agitation over the tithe question in Ireland) and the heavy defeat for his motion for the Repeal of the Union with Britain, O'Connell saw little hope of finding a constitutional remedy for Ireland's grievances. In return for supporting the Whigs in bringing down Peel's Tory government O'Connell nevertheless gained many concessions for Ireland. These included a partial settlement of the Tithe question, the appointment of a Catholic Attorney General for Ireland as well as many Catholic magistrates.[19]

Thomas Drummond was the Under Secretary whose energies did most to ensure that the Government's Irish policies were carried out, although he was ably supported by the Chief Secretary, Lord Morpeth (later to return to Ireland as the Earl of Carlisle) and the Lord Lieutenant, Lord Mulgrave, later to be appointed ambassador to France. Drummond's role in bringing all police in Ireland under unified government control in the 1836 Police Act has been exaggerated at the expense of Lord Morpeth, who steered the bill through parliament, according to the most recent history of police in England and Ireland. His courage in telling landlords in 1838 that property had its duties as well as its rights has not been questioned. Agrarian outrages still occurred, and Drummond showed his impartiality by sparing no effort to bring those responsible to justice, while at the same time understanding the conditions that caused the crimes. On an individual and family level many still preferred private vengeance to legal proceedings, but the expansion of the role of the Crown Solicitor helped to initiate more cases in the courts that had previously been ignored and witnesses in trials received better protection. Indeed, it was this impartiality in the administration of justice that was the most significant feature of the late eighteen thirties: the law, if not always obeyed, was at least respected, and the government, if not always respected, was at least thought of by the majority of people as at least trying to be fair.[20]

*   *   *

A German traveller in Ireland in 1828 wrote of the tradition of drinking parties 'of which the sole and avowed object was desperate drinking'. The fashion for such drinking bouts among the gentry was indeed in decline by then, but six years later John Edgar told the Select Committee on Drunkenness that he blamed the higher classes for the sanction they had given to the use of 'spirituous liquors'. For by now whiskey had become the usual drink of all social classes, having replaced ale and cider as the favourite alcoholic drink for the majority of the population, and, in the form of whiskey punch, had become more popular than brandy with the gentry. The whiskey was produced in more than 80 distilleries scattered fairly evenly among the larger towns throughout the country, except that there were seven each located in the counties of Cork and Dublin. It was retailed by some 400 spirit dealers and sold in more than 20,000 licensed premises situated mainly in the cities and towns. In the town of Westport, county Mayo, for example, Binns found one spirit shop for every eight houses, but in the rest of the barony there were only six for a population of 30,000. While there would have been unlicensed premises — shebeens — in rural areas, often run by widows with no other means of support, the figures seem to bear out Bishop Doyle's impression in 1829 that excessive drinking prevailed mostly in the towns.[21]

The more habitual drinkers in the large towns and cities were likely to have been caught up in the iniquitous truck system widespread throughout Great Britain at the time, when, for example, the man who spent all or most of his wages on drink was more likely to get taken on the following Monday than the man who spent his money on his family. Edgar complained to the Select Committee on Drunkenness that many people in Belfast got paid in public houses where they were expected to drink at least one glass of spirits 'as a compensation to this house' which led to many of them staying on drinking for the night. The Poor Law Commissioners also noted the lack of sobriety in Belfast, deploring the system then going out of use, where workers were given a note for work done, to be cashed in a public house. Dunlop found the carpenters union met in public houses in the north of Ireland and the rooms were given free in expectation of the money spent on drink. Not surprisingly, tradesmen throughout the country had a reputation for drunkenness.[22]

Country people came to town for fairs and markets 'where friendships were renewed over several drinks' and bargains were consolidated with a treat of whiskey, but, in general their drinking practices were to a considerable extent determined by breaks in their daily routines. Weddings, patterns and wakes were accepted occasions for drinking bouts. For wakes in particular, lack of money was not a deterrent. Lady Chatterton's book on her travels in Ireland in 1838 contains the pathetic story of a sick girl whose mother was unable to afford 4d. to spend on broth recommended by the doctor as nourishment to keep her alive, but whose father, when she died from her illness, was able to raise 30 shillings 'to wake the corpse'. John McCarthy recalled cases of widows and children who had been nearly ruined through providing extravagant wakes. He also remembered seeing a man carried away dead from a funeral fight, where whiskey had been provided by one of the portable shebeens that followed fairs, markets and funerals.[23]

To be able to offer hospitality with a plentiful supply of whiskey was a matter of pride among all classes. 'It was considered the rankest breach of hospitality', wrote S.C. Hall, 'to suffer a guest to leave a house sober.' This may have been an exaggeration, but Hall and his wife wrote elsewhere of a man they knew in West Cork whose daily intake 'was five and twenty tumblers of whiskey punch, of the ordinary strength' and Thackeray's coachman in Cork, before he took the pledge, used to have 20 glasses of punch a day. He may have needed it as protection against the cold and damp: several people in Sligo told Binns that they drank 'from the want of clothing and the comfortless condition of their homes'. Witnesses before the Poor Inquiry, however, did not think that keeping warm through insufficiency of clothing or want of a fire caused people to drink, except perhaps when travelling or when standing in the cold and wet waiting for an employer to take them on.[24]

Explanations for excessive drinking by the poor tended to focus on their misery. Dr. Speer felt that 'in the entire mass of misery of the poor, whiskey is thought to form the principal remedy; they conceive it to be a cure for all complaints, and all weathers; in warm weather it allays their thirst; when cold it heats them; when wet it dries them; in sorrow they fly to it as a charm and a blessing, and in its intoxicating draughts their misery is forgotten'. They drank not from any love of debasement, the *Galway Vindicator* claimed, but because they were 'forced to seek an unnatural excitement, relief from constant, ever-present, and ever-provoking misery'. Thomas Davis took this line of explanation further. He thought that the Irishman, in his intoxication 'had flung off his chains, and his duties, too; he had lost sight of his own miseries' even though this abandonment led to even greater privations for himself and his family. William Channing, an American temperance advocate, saw two important causes of intemperance as the burden of care and toil laid on many people at the time and the lack of self-respect that the state of society, with its hideous inequalities, induced 'among the poor and laborious'. Contemporary evidence would suggest that it was the second of these causes that was most relevant to Ireland. Channing continued, 'Just so far as wealth is the object of worship, the measure of man's importance, the badge of distinction, so far there will be a tendency to self-contempt and self-abandonment among those whose lot gives them no chance of its acquisition.'[25]

As a further cause of intemperance Channing mentioned the love of excitement and John Francis Maguire, looking back on those days,

TABLE 1.1

BEER PRODUCTION IN IRELAND 1831-39

1831	746	1834	1,027	1837	900
1832	771	1835	915	1838	967
1833	841	1836	1,016	1839	907

Figures are in thousands of standard barrels.

Source: George B. Wilson, *Alcohol and the Nation* (London, 1940), p. 369.

TABLE 1.2

GALLONS OF LEGAL SPIRITS CONSUMED IN IRELAND 1831-39

(Percentage movements in brackets)

1831	8,710,672	
1832	8,657,756	0.7 decrease
1833	8,168,596	5.6 decrease
1834	9,708,416	18.9 increase
1835	11,381,223	17.2 increase
1836	12,248,772	7.6 increase
1837	11,235,635	8.3 decrease
1838	12,296,342	9.4 increase
1839	10,815,709	12.0 decrease

Source: *Return of the Total Number of Gallons of Spirits distilled and charged with duty . . . 1800-1845.* P.P. 1846 (361) xliv, p. 427.

TABLE 1.3
ILLICIT DISTILLATION, IRELAND, 1832-39

	Number of detections	Number of stills seized	Number of people convicted
1832	5,455	974	1,042
1833	8,223	1,549	1,926
1834	8,192	1,524	2,194
1835	4,904	956	1,248
1836	3,323	590	903
1837	3,136	395	682
1838	3,298	368	593
1839	1,359	168	227

Source: *Report from the Select Committee . . . appointed to consider the consequences of extending the Functions of the Constabulary in Ireland to the Suppression or Prevention of Illicit Distillation . . .* P.P. 1854 (53) X pp. 290, 269.
Report of the Commissioners of Inland Revenue . . . and complete tables . . . P.P. 1870 (C.82) XX p. 390.

described the Irish people as a 'warm, fiery, passionate and impulsive race, easily excited' and argued that if they had been a 'dull, sullen and lethargic race', like the Dutch or Russians, their drinking would not have brought such ruin and misery upon them. Crude national stereotypes aside, this was an attempt to explain how Ireland had such a reputation for drunkenness when *per capita* consumption of alcohol was much lower than in many other countries.[26]

There were a large number of small breweries in Ireland — as many as 240 in 1837 — but the two largest producers were Guinness's in Dublin and the Cork brewery of Beamish and Crawford. While some beer was drunk in the countryside, most was consumed in the cities and towns, and, as the vast majority of the population lived in the countryside at this time, beer statistics are clearly of limited value as indices of drinking. The figures in Table 1.1 are further limited in their use as they relate to production rather than consumption of beer. No figures exist to record the movement of beer between England and Ireland, so the actual amount consumed in Ireland may have been smaller or greater than shown in the figures. Assuming an equal amount moved both ways, the actual quantity drunk was relatively small — about one barrel per year among eight people in Ireland compared with one barrel per year for every person in England. While the figures show an increase of 21.6 per cent in production in 1839 over 1831 it will be noticed that there was no increase at all after 1834. Furthermore, there was an increase in beer production between 1831 and 1839 in every country in Europe for which figures are available, including England, Scotland and Belgium.[27]

Table 1.2 shows the amount of spirits on which duty was paid for consumption in Ireland from 1831 up to 1839, the year when Father Mathew first took his mission outside Cork and the first year in which the figures for spirit consumption on a national scale could have been significantly influenced by his temperance work. At first sight the figures suggest an enormous increase in spirit drinking in the decade, with a percentage increase of 24.2 between 1831 and 1839, or, if 1838 is taken as the last full year before the temperance work of Father Mathew began to influence the figures, the percentage increase up to that date was 41.2. The figures, however, need to be put in perspective.

It can first of all be noted that for every gallon and a half of legal spirits drunk in Ireland in 1836, for example, two and a half gallons were drunk in Scotland. In the United States, Denmark and Sweden the consumption of spirits per head of population was even higher.[28]

Concentrating on the figures for Ireland, several factors combine to indicate that the increase in drinking was not as great as the figures suggest. In the first place there was an increase in population during the period of about a third of a million people. If population increase is taken into account the percentage increase up to 1839 would be adjusted to 18.9 per cent and that up to 1838 would stand at 35.9 per cent.[29]

There was also an increase in illegal distilling in the early part of the decade (Table 1.3) brought about jointly by an increase in the rate of duty from 2/10d. to 3/4d. during 1830 and an exceptionally low price for barley in 1833, followed by relatively low prices in 1834 and 1835. The duty increase led to legal spirits bought in licensed premises being dearer, while cheap barley meant that the alternative, illegally distilled spirits, could be produced even more cheaply than in other years. Irish temperance advocates who gave evidence to the Select Committee of Drunkenness and Irish distillers before the Revenue Commissioners were agreed about the increase in illicit distillation in 1834. While temperance reformers had a tendency to exaggerate the amount of liquor in use and the distillers were anxious to secure a reduction in the rate of duty by convincing the Commissioners that a high rate of duty caused an increase in illicit distillation, their evidence must be treated with caution. It is, however, substantiated by the large number of detections, stills seized and people convicted for distilling offences in 1833 and 1834. Detections and convictions, of course, depended on the vigilance of the Revenue Police and the integrity of magistrates in convicting the offenders. The vigilance and efficiency of the Revenue Police is likely to have been less in the early part of the decade before they were reorganised and given proper training in 1836. It is likely, therefore, that the figures for spirits consumed for the early part of the decade were augmented by the illicit product to a far greater extent than those for the later years. Parties of Revenue Police increased from 57 in 1833 to 70 in 1838 and the number of stipendiary magistrates had increased to 54 by 1839. That this increased and better trained force, assisted by a more professional magistracy, was able to detect and convict a much smaller number of illegal distillers at the end of the decade than in the earlier years would seem further evidence for the actual decline of illicit distilling in the later part of the eighteen thirties. Two further factors contributed to this decline. The rate of duty on legal spirits was reduced to 2/4d. in 1834, at which rate it stayed fixed down to 1840, and the price of barley began to rise again from 1836. While legal whiskey became cheaper to buy in the middle of the decade, poteen became more expensive to produce. By the end of the decade Otway was able to report that in the west, at any rate, illicit distillation had been 'in a great measure suppressed by the vigilance of the excise service'.[30]

It is likely, therefore, that the apparently large increase in drinking in Ireland during the eighteen thirties that is suggested by the figures for legal spirits alone, needs considerable modification when an increase in population and a reduction in illicit distillation are taken into account. But however much weight is given to these factors, they could do no more than suggest a smaller percentage increase. That there was nevertheless a considerable increase would appear to remain true.

*   *   *

At the first annual meeting of the Hibernian Temperance Society (formerly the Dublin Temperance Society, established in 1829) in April 1830, one of the resolutions passed was 'that the unhappy propensity

of our Countrymen to the use of Ardent Spirits is one of the chief causes
of Pauperism, Disease and Crime, prevalent in Ireland'. That it was individual weakness rather than political, social or economic factors that
might have been responsible for drunkenness was further suggested by
Lord Cloncurry at the same meeting. 'I have labourers at seven shillings
a week', he said, 'well clad, their gardens in good order, their cottages
clean and comfortable: I have had tradesmen at a guinea, themselves
and their families in squalid misery.' The chairman of the meeting, P.C.
(later Judge) Crampton emphasised that the temperance movement was
not connected with party or sect and that it 'embraces persons of all
classes and conditions'. From this it will be clear that the early temperance
societies, though not political in the party or sectarian sense, were conservative in their approach to the social evil which they saw as destruc-
tive of the established order in Ireland, an order in which many of the
temperance campaigners played prominent and influential roles. James
Henry blamed whiskey for one of the murders perpetrated by the combinations in Dublin. More extraordinary than the conservative origins
of a movement that was later to produce such radical changes in attitudes
to drinking were the means by which they were to pursue their object.
It was not the drunkard who was to be confronted and frightened or
coaxed into sobriety, but the moderate drinker who was to be persuaded
to change his ways. In their belief that in the reform of the temperate
lay the cure to drunkenness they were following the approach to
temperance adopted by the movement which had become active during
the previous decade in America, particularly in the New England
states.[31]

It was Dr. John Edgar, a Presbyterian minister from Belfast, who first
thought of introducing temperance societies to Ireland, having been convinced of their value by Rev. Joseph Penney, one of Edgar's former fellow
students who had emigrated to America and had become involved in
temperance work there. Announcing his commitment with the dramatic
gesture of pouring the remainder of a gallon of whiskey into the court
before his house, he proceeded to have a letter published in the *Belfast
Newsletter* in August 1829, where, following the American approach,
moderate drinkers were encouraged to stop drinking spirits, for, it was
argued, the system of drink manufacture and distribution as it then stood
could not have been maintained by the drunkard alone. But the moderate
drinker was not only making the drink trade viable, he was placing himself
in danger. The moderate drinker may begin with the prudent use of

spirits, but this leads inevitably to habitual use 'and that habitual use is the high road to absolute drunkenness'. Not only is moderate habitual drinking the parent of drunkenness 'but in numberless instances it impairs the mind, and shortens the life, and ruins the soul'. The 'influential part of society', Crampton said at the Hibernian Temperance Society meeting referred to already, can influence the rest of society by good example, or rather by the absence of bad example. By sanctioning ardent spirits 'they are the unconscious abettors of intemperance — they are accessories before and after the fact. Their daily habits are a daily temptation to the weak and unthinking: they represent ardent spirits as a salutary stimulant; they make its use amiable, respectable, and even fashionable: they thus lend the weight of influence and of public opinion to vice.'[32]

George W. Carr, an Independent clergyman in New Ross, had been in communication with Edgar and actually succeeded in setting up a temperance society in the town shortly before Edgar established the Ulster Temperance Society in Belfast in the autumn of 1829. Members of these and other temperance societies at this time took a pledge undertaking to abstain from distilled spirits except for medicinal purposes and, in every way they could, to discountenance the use of spirits in the community. The numbers who belonged were estimated to have been 3,500 by 1830 and 15,000 the following year. The temperance message was put across in sermons, meetings and through the distribution of tracts. By the end of 1836 Alexander Mayne, who worked with Edgar in the Ulster Temperance Society for some years, was estimated to have been responsible for the distribution of no less than 25,000 temperance tracts. Most of the early temperance campaigners in the north of Ireland were Presbyterian or Methodist ministers or Evangelical clergymen within the Established Church, while in the south a significant role was played by Quakers and by professional people other than clergymen. A Quaker, Dr. Harvey of Meath Hospital, encouraged Dr. Cheyne, Physician General to the Army in Ireland, to publicise his writings on the diseases that arose from intemperance. Many of the early temperance advocates were already involved in other charitable or philanthropic work. In Dublin two of the best known figures in the antislavery movement, Richard Webb and James Haughton, were also prominent in the promotion of temperance, and in Cork the meetings of a temperance society founded there in 1831 took place in a room where the local antislavery society took breakfast. Jane Ann Carlisle, who founded temperance societies in

Cootehill, county Cavan, and Dublin and was later responsible for the Band of Hope, had noticed, while a prison visitor in Dublin, that many of the women prisoners had fallen to their state because of drink.[33]

There was some Catholic involvement in the promotion of temperance in the 'anti-spirits' period, although it seems to have been generally independent of the temperance societies. This was partly at least through suspicions of proselytism, suspicions that were given fuel by the presence of 'missionaries' to Ireland like Dr. Urwick, a Congregationalist minister, in prominent positions in the temperance societies. Some priests lent their support, however. Ó Súileabháin noted in his diary in 1830 that owing to the sermons of a local priest no one got drunk on St. Patrick's Day, whereas on the previous St. Patrick's Day the diarist had been with the parish priest and 'had sherry and port wine, whiskey and punch enough'. While Bishop Doyle, in reply to an invitation by Carr to join a temperance society, wrote that he had been opposed to intemperance for 20 years, he was not sure what good temperance societies might achieve, although he conceded that they deserved support. He felt that if malting and brewing were exempt from tax and the duty on spirits raised, drunkenness would shortly disappear. This disappearance would be further hastened by reducing the number of outlets for selling spirits and by more strict policing. One Catholic clergyman was active from the early days of the movement in Dublin. This was Father Spratt, a Carmelite priest, who, even after he ceased to be formally involved with the Hibernian Temperance Society continued active in the campaign against drunkenness. Other priests engaged in temperance work in Dublin, in the early eighteen thirties were Father Blake of St. Michael and St. John's, until he was appointed Bishop of Dromore in 1833, and Father O'Connell, who suceeded him. Despite the unfavourable response from Doyle, Carr was able to write, towards the end of 1830, that Catholic clergymen were speaking highly of his intentions and were wishing his temperance society success.[34]

By the middle of the decade the temperance societies had distributed about 200,000 tracts throughout the country. Writing in 1838, Morewood claimed there were 300,000 temperance advocates in Ireland, which seems rather a lot when put beside the comment of another contemporary, John Barclay Shiel, who said that while a few Protestants joined the Hibernian Temperance Society, 'the great body of the Irish never took the slightest interest in the matter' in the period before Father Mathew. The influence of the movement had certainly spread, in the course of the decade, well beyond the main cities and towns, even as far as Connemara, where Barrow, to his surprise, found Big Jack Joyce, who had flourished a double-sized bottle of whiskey when Inglis went to see him the previous year, had in 1835 become a member of a temperance society on a three months' trial period. Temperance tended to flourish best in rural areas when there was support from a local landlord or someone similarly influential like David Malcomson at the Portlaw Cotton Factory in county Waterford. At the end of 1836 A.E. Gayer, one of the secretaries of the Hibernian Temperance Union, said that their standard had been raised in almost every town of considerable size in the country and the annual report of the Union for 1837 claimed that 60 new temperance societies had been established during that year alone.[35]

Much of the credit for the new societies established during 1837 must go to George Carr who began his duties as travelling agent for the Hibernian Temperance Society at the beginning of that year. He also had sufficient energy to maintain the momentum of his New Ross Society. John Finch, an advocate of teetotalism, or abstinence from all alcoholic drinks, visited the New Ross Society in 1836, when it had more than 450 members. Carr himself had not yet committed himself to teetotalism, but there are signs of the influence of English total abstinence campaigners in a report about a man named Leary who was given the title 'King of the Reformed Drunkards' by the New Ross Society in October 1836. But temperance was far from acceptable even in a town where a Society had been established for almost a decade. Keegan used to attend meetings there in 1838 and recorded his impressions in his *Diary*. The very noisy and 'ill-mannered' audience was addressed by Carr and Joshua Martin, a Quaker. 'The few who joined and signed the pledge were hooted and ridiculed by the blackguards who attended more for the purpose of having fun and creating noise than to hear and follow the good advice given by the good tempered lecturers. The Rev. Mr. Carr appears to be very zealous, but not very successful, the people of New Ross being great drinkers.' Many of the new societies did not survive. Noel told of one at Rostrevor, where initial enthusiasm was considerable, but where interest soon faded, and another in Drogheda, which, failing to win the support of the local gentry, was disgraced by the relapses of its members. Remarking on Noel's account of the Drogheda failure, Charlotte Elizabeth attributed such relapses to the priests releasing people from their pledge, but offered no evidence of instances of this.[36]

For early temperance reformers like Edgar abstinence from distilled spirits was recommended because in Ireland such spirits were used in a manner that was harmful to the constitution and 'the great material of drunkenness'. Alcohol in itself was not harmful, as could be observed from the temperate nature of people in wine-producing countries. These earlier societies have been correctly called 'anti-spirit' societies, although some members like Dr. Cheyne and Dr. Urwick personally abstained from all alcoholic drink; neither, however, was in favour of banning wine and beer. The rich, as Crampton put it, were left with their wine and the poor with their porter, adding that they should be moderate in their use. The sole enemy, then, was spirits, 'which inflames the passions, excites and maddens,' whereas beer 'produces little more than a drowsy stupor', as Haliday wrote.[37]

Dissatisfaction with a pledge that renounced spirits but permitted wine, beer and cider was evident in England before the mid-eighteen thirties, especially when it became clear that these last three drinks could be as much a cause of drunkenness as spirits, and in some parts of England actually were. A campaign against drunkenness, to be successful in England, had therefore to oppose all alcoholic drinks. The teetotallers of Preston, Lancashire, who practised total abstinence from all alcohol and preached the new doctrine around the country, were an important development in the progress of temperance, initially in England, but later in Ireland. The Preston teetotallers, too, were mostly tradesmen rather than clergymen, medical men or philanthropists of the earlier 'moderate' temperance societies and held many views and promoted many attitudes that were to give temperance a much wider base than had been the case up to then in England, Ireland or America. These included the teetotallers' belief in the possibility of reclaiming the drunkard to sobriety, the colourful and entertaining nature of the teetotallers' meetings, as well as the opportunities offered to working men both to promote the teetotal cause itself, and in the associations of respectability that went along with being a teetotaller and the opportunities for self-improvement that these offered.[38]

The number of teetotallers in Ireland in the period before Father Mathew was relatively small and not enough is known about them to judge the extent to which these factors, so influential in the spread of the temperance movement in England, might have been applicable to Ireland. It is clear, though, that in Ireland as in England, much of the energy for the promotion of teetotalism came from the ranks of society that the earlier anti-spirits or moderation movement had shown little interest in involving in their campaign. Brian Harrison has written that in England 'when an anti-spirits society adopted the teetotal pledge gentility usually departed in a hurry'. This does not seem to have happened in Ireland. Moderation and teetotalism appear to have co-existed in the Hibernian Temperance Society, and the teetotal pledge does not seem to have frightened off the four Lords among the vice-presidents, and another of the vice-presidents, Sir Francis Le Hunt, was later a prominent advocate of Father Mathew's teetotal work in Wexford. Finally, because spirits were the main drink in the northern part of Ireland temperance campaigners there had always been satisfied with banning spirits alone, while in Dublin there was always some support for total abstinence because it was evident that beer in the city could be as much a cause of drunkenness as spirits, especially among tradesmen and labourers.[39]

The first teetotal society in Ireland was actually in existence more than twelve years before the anti-spirits movement was organised in Belfast, New Ross or Dublin. This was the Skibbereen, county Cork, Society, founded in 1817 by Jeffrey Sedwards, a nailer by trade. Malt, spirituous liquors and 'distilled waters' were forbidden to members, unless prescribed by a doctor or a priest. The Society held parades not only in Skibbereen but in Bantry, Clonakilty, Rosscarbery, Castletownsend and other local towns. The teetotallers were subject to ridicule and abuse, but had a membership of 60 or 70 in 1832. Among the branches established in east Cork was one at Glendore, where James R. Barry's model community discouraged the use of alcohol, and whose presence in the chair at a temperance meeting in Skibbereen when the Temperance Hall was completed in 1841 suggests he remained a loyal supporter into the Mathew era. While geographically a local rather than a national movement, and while no direct connection between it and the work of Edgar and Carr in 1829 has been established, the Skibbereen Society may nevertheless claim significance for several reasons. By appealing directly to all members of society, whether they be sober or drunkards, especially members of the working class, to abandon alcohol entirely, they were prefiguring the teetotallers of Preston, whose ideas in due course were brought to Ireland. As a means of making the impact of this appeal more dramatic, the processions and parades of the Skibbereen teetotallers, too, were to become characteristic of later teetotal movements, especially that of Father Mathew. Weekly contributions were made towards a fund for sick and distressed members of the Society, corresponding to the savings and benefit societies that were to become a feature of temperance societies from 1830 onwards, especially those founded after 1839 on Father Mathew's model. Even the ridicule to which the Skibbereen teetotallers were subjected was something that was endured by members of temperance societies later, borne stoically by a member of the Dublin Temperance Society who wrote that members 'have only shared the fate of the beneficient advocates for the Abolition of the Slave Trade, with whom they are united in principle — contending against a worse slavery'. Finally, as the influence of the Skibbereen Society may have extended as far as Cork city, it is possible that some of the early advocates of teetotalism may have been influenced by its ideas, although what accounts we have of the origins of teetotalism in Cork do not confirm this.[40]

The first teetotal society in Ireland that could be seen as an extension to Ireland of the teetotal movement that was growing in England in the mid-eighteen thirties was that at Strabane, county Tyrone, in 1835. The founder, John Finch, was an Englishman with radical sympathies, who had travelled through Ireland in connection with his business, and was a sympathetic observer of the country's condition. He had been a founder member of the Liverpool Temperance Society in 1830 and was prompted to become a teetotaller by Thomas Swindlehurst, the man who was himself later crowned 'King of the Reformed Drunkards' at Preston. Other missionaries followed, some of them more dramatic and colourful than Finch, but Finch was the most influential in laying the foundations of teetotalism in Ireland. In the course of several visits he established teetotal societies as far apart as Donegal and Waterford, Newry and Galway. His accounts of his teetotal work in Ireland in November and December 1836 were printed in Joseph Livesey's newspaper, the *Preston Temperance Advocate*, during the following summer, and tell us a lot about attitudes towards teetotalism less than two years before Father Mathew joined the movement. The manner of his reception varied from disruption by drunks in Clonmel and Wexford town to the conversion of considerable numbers to teetotalism in Coleraine and Castlebar. He spoke out against the folly of sectarianism in Londonderry and Strabane, where religious differences seem to have been crippling the teetotal societies. In Waterford he rejoiced that a one-legged pensioner had held firm to the teetotal pledge and at the cotton factory at nearby Portlaw, where 'King' Swindlehurst had spoken the previous summer, Finch made 24 new converts to teetotalism, bringing the total number to 87, and, if moderate drinkers were included, 500 altogether were pledged to temperance. The movement remained strong there, and, in an effort to find acceptable alternatives to the public houses, coffee shops were introduced the following year.[41]

Finch was opposed to teetotal societies and moderation societies working together. In Ennis he was pleased to note that the moderation society 'had dwindled to a shadow' and that 'they seem full of zeal in the teetotal cause', while in Sligo, where the two systems were working together he reported that, 'as in other places so in this, it prevents the rapid extension of true temperance principles'. In Belfast, 'this strong hold of moderate drinkers' he challenged all advocates of moderation, including Edgar, to a public debate but his offer was not taken up. Edgar persisted in his hostility to teetotalism, however, and exactly a year later Livesey's paper estimated that there were about 70 ministers throughout Ulster who were teetotallers but 'through the influence of Professor Edgar, some have been induced to withdraw themselves from the public advocacy of teetotalism'. Eventually, disillusioned that the teetotallers did not even consider moderationists like him to have been temperance advocates at all, Edgar withdrew from the movement.[42]

In Dublin a happier state of affairs seems to have prevailed, with the Hibernian Temperance Society including both teetotallers and moderationists among its members, 'standing side by side and pulling together at the strong holds of the common enemy, without jealousy or any sectarian animosity'. Sectarianism, too, according to the biographer of James Haughton, a Unitarian who for many years was to work in close harmony with Father Spratt, was also absent in Dublin. When Finch was there in 1836 he found that 'a good feeling exists in Dublin towards the teetotal cause'. He left copies of his teetotal tracts with Daniel O'Connell, Earl Mulgrave (who had become Lord Lieutenant of Ireland the previous year) and R.G. White, who had founded the first teetotal society in Dublin the previous year.[43]

Finch said his audiences in Ireland had 'consisted principally of the working classes, many of them the greatest drunkards . . .'. The working class would have been well represented at the meeting of the Port of Dublin Temperance Society addressed by Robert McCurdy at the end of 1836. He said he had been attending similar meetings in towns in the north of Ireland and from what he had seen he was sure the cause of temperance was making progress. He was, he said, returning to Ireland after 24 years absence. He came again the following year during which, according to Dawson Burns, he received 372 total abstinence pledges in the course of a fortnight. McCurdy later made the unlikely claim that he had the honour of having introduced the total abstinence principle to Ireland. With an increasing number of working people adopting teetotalism, temperance societies besides that at Portlaw were anxious to provide alternatives to the public houses where their members and sympathisers could meet. In Parsonstown, for example, coffee houses were opened in 1838. 'Mothers and wives induced their husbands and sons to avoid the whiskey shop, saying that for the future there will be no necessity to watch those . . .' wrote the *Irish Temperance and Literary Gazette*, although the newspaper itself remained for some years in favour of the moderation movement.[44]

In his study of the early days of the Irish temperance movement Bretherton, referring to Dublin in 1836, remarked that 'temperance appears to have been a Protestant monopoly'. That the movement was associated with Protestantism is clear from a remark by Noel, who, when he met a Catholic in Drogheda in 1836 'so zealous for the sobriety of the place' he immediately assumed he must have been a Protestant. The association of temperance with Protestantism may have deterred Catholics from active involvement in the movement. When an Irish shoemaker named Thomas Claney, who had been 'reclaimed from drunkenness' in Huddersfield, tried to introduce teetotalism to Sligo in 1836 he met several priests who approved of what he was doing but expressed no wish to help him. Nearly ten years after the first fears of proselytising were expressed by Catholics, McCurdy found Catholics who still believed the temperance movement intended to convert them to Protestantism.[45]

'The main body of the clergy, of all denominations', Judge Crampton remarked in 1836, 'have either hung back from the good cause, or have thrown impediments in our way.' Everyone was not so pessimistic. On his return from Ireland at the end of 1836 Finch believed that there were more Catholic priests than Protestant ministers friendly to the teetotal cause and, provided teetotallers could convince the priests by their actions that their aim was not conversion to Protestantism but to temperance 'we shall very soon have the warm assistance of a great number of them'. Events over the next couple of years suggest he was justified in his optimism about priests. Besides Spratt in Dublin, Father Yore of St. Paul's was to take up the cause, as well as Father O'Connell, who had succeeded Father Blake at St. Michael and St. John's. Over the next eighteen months the *Irish Temperance and Literary Gazette* often referred to the involvement of Catholic clergymen in temperance societies, and, while that newspaper continued to favour the principle of moderation over that of teetotalism, later events showed almost all of those named to have favoured teetotalism. These included Fathers Eager and Coppinger of Middleton, county Cork, Father Scannell of Blackrock, county Cork and Father O'Sullivan of Bantry in the same county. At a meeting in Ennis in 1837 Father Kenyon, then a curate there, went out of his way to emphasise that, far from being hostile to the movement, Catholic priests were actually in favour of the order and sobriety temperance societies were trying to inculcate. Bishop Browne became patron of the Galway Temperance Society in the middle of 1837 and Bishop Kennedy of Killaloe became vice-president of the Parsonstown Temperance Society early the following year. On the evening of his enrolment Lord Oxmantown presided at the meeting and 150 people took the pledge. In a tribute to him four years later Father Power of Nenagh said that because of Kennedy's encouragement 'temperance was more generally diffused in the diocese of Killaloe' at the time Father Mathew began his campaign 'than perhaps in any other in Ireland'.[46]

On his return from a tour of Ireland a correspondent informed the *Temperance Penny Magazine* in November 1838 that temperance was making rapid progress among the lower classes there, especially in the southern counties. 'This happy change', he continued, 'is being brought about by the increasing establishment of Temperance Societies, by the exertions of the priests, who are almost universally great advocates of temperance; and lastly, by the operation of Sir M. O'Loughlin's admirable bill, which inflicts a penalty of 5s., or 48 hours imprisonment, on each convicted drunkard.' Several aspects of his report are of interest. He attributed the change in the first instance to the temperance societies rather than, as might have been expected, to the missions to Ireland of several temperance advocates from England during 1837 and 1838, the most colourful of whom was John Hockings, who spent a large part of 1838 in the same parts of the country as the traveller quoted. His reference to a fine or imprisonment for drunkenness reminds us that other factors besides changes in the rate of duty and the exhortations of temperance campaigners may influence the amount of drunkenness. Finally, his conviction that almost all priests were advocates of temperance suggests that in the year and a half or so since Finch expressed his high hopes of priests the conditions for their involvement had been to some extent met, in that fears of proselytism were not hindering their involvement in promoting temperance. The extent of the commitment of Catholic priests to promote teetotalism, when it was harnessed by Father Mathew over the next couple of years, however, must have surpassed the expectations even of Englishmen so generous in their opinions of Ireland and the Irish as Finch and the anonymous traveller of the *Temperance Penny Magazine*.[47]

CHAPTER 2

Father Mathew

b. 1790

Theobald Mathew was born in 1790 at Thomastown castle in Tipperary, then the residence of Francis Mathew, Baron Llandaff, a family whose title derived from its Welsh origin, but whose association with Tipperary went back to the 17th century when one of the family married the widow of Viscount Thurles. The castle dates from the seventeenth century but was renovated and enlarged in the following century by 'Grand George' Mathew, the first of the family to adopt the Protestant faith. The castle was famous for its hospitality at that period, with forty rooms for guests, who were given the freedom of the house and grounds. Dean Swift once stayed there for several months and Morewood, writing in the eighteen thirties, recalled the generous traditions of Thomastown as illustrative of Irish hospitality, where 'the midnight orgies of Bacchus were often celebrated, with the same noisy mirth as is customary in his city temples'. Prince Puckler-Muskau visited Thomastown in 1828. The house, which had been painted a light blue, he found hideous, but he was impressed to see the noble proprietor was a resident landlord, who was actually directing his labourers' work when the prince arrived. Though resident, the family were 'by no means model landlords'.[1]

On Lord Llandaff's death in 1833 his sister Lady Elizabeth Mathew succeeded him to the property, and when she died in 1842 she left it to her cousin Vicomte de Chabot. 'Her devotion was lavished upon Theobald', wrote Father David Mathew, later Archbishop of Apamea, great grandson of Father Mathew's youngest brother. This

37

devotion did not extend to willing him the estate, or making any financial provision for him which would have been invaluable to him at a time
when his debts were beginning to mount. Archbishop Mathew thought
that she did not leave Thomastown House to Father Mathew because,
as a Capuchin, he could not accept it, but it is as likely that she felt
that, had she left it to him, it would eventually have become the property of the Capuchins. Had she done so, however, as Gwynn observed in
1928, it might have survived as a monastery or school rather than the
abandoned ruin it is today.[2]

Theobald Mathew was born into a branch of the family that had remained Catholic. His father James Mathew had been orphaned as a child
and was taken into the Thomastown household. He remained there for
some time as an adult, becoming a steward on the family estate. He married Anne Whyte and brought up a family of 11 children, a twelfth having died in childhood. When Theobald, who was the fourth son, was
four or five years old, his father took a farm in nearby Rathcloheen, where
the remainder of Theobald's early childhood was spent. The family's
relationship with the Mathews of Thomastown house continued to be
friendly and Theobald spent at least some of his time there. Baron Llandaff, meanwhile, had become a Viscount and finally, in 1797 he was made
the first Earl Llandaff.[3]

Theobald's childhood appears to have been a happy one, despite
chiding from his older brothers, whose boisterous pursuits he found less
interesting than his love of nature or the company of his mother. She,
anxious that one of her sons should become a priest, was delighted when
Theobald expressed an early wish to be one. His godmother, Lady
Elizabeth Mathew, who later inherited the estate, took an interest in his
education. He attended a school run by a Mr. Flynn in Thurles. Though
a few years younger than Theobald, it was probably here that Michael
Quin, who later became editor of the *Dublin Review*, first got to know
him. Quin later wrote that in his childhood Theobald was 'averse from
the boisterous amusements to which boys in general are prone'. He had
enough courage, though, to intervene to save the young Charles Bianconi
from getting bullied while in Thurles, thus beginning a life-long friend-
ship with the future baron of Irish road passenger transport. When he
was twelve or thirteen Elizabeth arranged for him to attend an academy
in Kilkenny, one of the Catholic schools set up immediately after the
1782 Act permitted them. He remained there until 1806, having been
highly thought of by the president of the academy, and having received

the medal for good conduct in his final year.[4]

Quin also wrote that Theobald liked sharing what he had with others, and it was probably a too finely developed sense of this virtue that caused him to leave Maynooth, where, on completion of his studies at Kilkenny, he went at around 17 years of age to train for the priesthood. He was caught entertaining some friends in his room, which was a breach of college rules. As the punishment for this seemingly trivial offence was likely to have been expulsion, he left Maynooth before sentence could formally be passed upon him. He returned to Kilkenny, this time to join the Capuchins, one of the branches of the Franciscan order that had been in Ireland since the early seventeenth century. In 1814 he was ordained a priest by Dr. Daniel Murray, who was later, as Archbishop of Dublin, to become a warm supporter of Father Mathew's temperance work. Returning again to Kilkenny, he became a hard-working assistant in a poor parish and a very popular confessor. His permission to hear confession was withdrawn by the acting head of the diocese who had been wrongly informed that Father Mathew had been in breach of the diocesan regulation that forbade regular clergy like him from administering Paschal Communion. The Provincial of his Order decided to move him to Cork, thinking that 'a change would best ease the unpleasant situation, and soothe the wounded feelings of his injured subject'.[5]

In Cork, Father Mathew was assigned as an assistant to the 'South Friary' or 'Little Friary' in Blackamoor Lane near Sullivan's Quay. The building had once been known as 'Father O'Leary's Chapel' from the name of its founder, who had served in Cork towards the end of the previous century before going to St. Patrick's, Soho, where a bust still commemorates him. The chapel was one of the 'small insignificant dwellings, tucked away mostly in some inconspicuous street or lane', that a historian of the Capuchins saw as typical of the order's places of worship in Ireland in the seventeenth and eighteenth centuries. By the time Father Mathew arrived there as an assistant to Fr. O'Donovan some time in 1814 the Catholics to whom he was to minister were more burdened by poverty than religious persecution. Little is known about his early work in Cork except that, as in Kilkenny, he gained a reputation as a sympathetic confessor to rich and poor alike, a reputation that spread beyond the confines of the immediate neighbourhood of Blackamoor Lane.[6]

He followed the work of one of his relatives, Nano Nagle, founder of the Presentation order of nuns, by setting up a girls' school with local

Catholic ladies acting as governesses in turn. Later he started a boys'
school. He followed the Christian Brothers, who were then providing
education for poor boys in the northern part of the city, by opening a
school in the south, and when the Christian Brothers afterwards opened their school in Sullivan's Quay he was a constant supporter of their
work. He was successful in involving a large number of young people
in his charitable work among the poor and the Josephian Society, a voluntary organisation for visiting the sick, which he founded shortly after
he went to Cork, was still in existence when the Poor Commissioners
reported on it in the 'thirties: they found that it had visited 392 people
in 1834. At a time when many industries in the city were in decline and
large numbers of workers, like woollen and cotton weavers, were
unemployed, he helped soften the blow of destitution by forming benefit
societies. His energy in this direction, and in the forcefulness of his warn-
ings to employer and employee alike about their duties was 'expressed
in a language so earnest, that he was regarded in some quarters as a
visionary socialist'.[7]

The Poor Inquiry noted that most of the funds received by the
Josephian Society came from a burial ground established by Father
Mathew some years before. The funeral service of a Catholic had been
interrupted in St. Finn Barr's cemetery in Cork because the appropriate
permission for clergymen to pray there had not been obtained from the
Protestant Dean. Father Mathew was one of the priests in attendance
and he resolved to provide a new cemetery for Catholics by purchasing
the Botanic Gardens from the Royal Cork Institution. Though formally
opened as St. Joseph's Cemetery, it became known as 'Father Mathew's
burial ground'. While the poor were interred free or for a nominal charge,
fees derived from the interment of Cork's prosperous Catholic middle
class were channelled into charities like the Josephian Society. Such was
the quality of the monuments set among the shrubs that a London
newspaper in 1839 was able to refer to it as 'the handsomest cemetery
in the British empire'.[8]

When Archbishop Ullathorne was in Dublin in the eighteen thirties
he found there was a charity sermon for some institution every Sunday.
They were equally popular in Cork, and Father Mathew was often asked
to deliver one. Though he seems not to have been a particularly gifted
speaker, orator or actor, his earnestness and fervour, according to one
who heard him preaching, enabled his listeners to accept in their hearts
'the words of reproach and correction, the words of encouragement and

hope, the words of peace and comfort that flow from his lips . . .' It is
not surprising that his sermons were successful in raising funds for
charitable purposes, as Maguire, who probably often listened to them,
wrote how 'he shamed the niggard alms-giving of the wealthy by nar-
rating instances of the sublime generosity of the poor to the poor'. He
was also known to practise in his daily life what he preached in the pulpit:
the clerk to the chapel said of him that if the streets of Cork were paved
with gold, and Father Mathew had control of them, there would not have
been a paving stone left in the city by the end of the year.[9]

He had a reputation for non-sectarianism and Thackeray was later to
write of him that he was almost the only man he met in Ireland who
'did not talk like a partisan'. Maguire's book tells us that during the
campaign for Catholic emancipation in the eighteen twenties he was
respected by both Protestants and Dissenters in Cork. He was a member
of the Catholic Association, but it would be interesting to know if he
took any active part in the campaign which was supported by priests
around the country.[10]

Daniel Owen Madden tried to summarize his attitudes to rich and
poor, and their response to him:

To the higher classes, he was exceedingly respectful, and was always considered
by them as one of their order — to the poor he was so gentle in his bearing,
and so patient of their little requests and petitions — so earnest in pleading
their cause, and what was better than kind words or noble speeches, so prac-
tically useful and humane, that they also (the more Christian compliment) regarded him as one of themselves.[11]

Granted that he was 'indefatigable' to use Birmingham's word, in his
efforts on behalf of the needy, and granted his patience and earnestness,
it is still difficult to understand the extraordinary popularity he obviously
had. That he was non-sectarian and nonpolitical was, in the Ireland of
the time, as likely to alienate him from some as to endear him to others.
Coming from the gentry, or close to it, he was, as Gwynn has written,
'a rare figure' for an Irish priest of the period. It is clear, though, that
while this enabled him to move at ease in circles that might have been
difficult for other priests, he was far from snobbish. Asenath Nicholson,
some years later, found him 'as unostentatious of pedigree as the shepherd
boy, who claims no decent beyond the thatched cabin that gave him birth'.
John O'Neill Daunt attributed his popularity to 'his beautiful piety and
holiness'. Maguire acknowledged his piety, humility and modesty, but

saw further to what he called 'a kind of unconscious dignity and even nobleness' which enabled him to achieve that most difficult of all tasks, then or in any age, namely, to treat everyone with 'the same genial courtesy, the same consideration, the same kindly interest and cordial politeness'.[12]

To these attempts by contemporaries to identify the aspects of his character that made him so successful in his religious and social work as much as in his later endeavours for temperance there needs to be added something on his courage. For working among the poor in Cork in the eighteen twenties was a hazardous occupation indeed as may be witnessed by the risks taken by one of his contemporaries, Dr. Dowling, resident apothecary at the Cork Fever Hospital. During 1826 more than 4,000 fever victims were treated there, among them Dr. Dowling himself, who was cured, relapsed and cured again in the course of the year. He lived on, like Father Mathew, to take part in the fight against the cholera outbreak in 1832. Father Mathew immediately offered his services to the part of the city that most needed it, and his zeal in helping the afflicted without regard for his own safety was later remarked upon by religious and civil authorities.[13]

The city that acknowledged Father Mathew as one of its own recovered, like other stricken cities, from the cholera epidemic, and by the late eighteen thirties could be referred to by one of her native chroniclers, with only slight exaggeration, as the 'first commercial city in Ireland'. The harbour, in the three year period 1833-5, was the third busiest in the country, behind Belfast and Dublin. The provisioning of ships for the navy and the export of salted and pickled food employed large numbers, from unskilled workers in the large provision stores to the highly unionised coopers who made the butter firkins to hold the 200,000 barrels of butter a year that passed through the port, the produce of the rich dairylands of Cork and Kerry. An analysis of the occupations in the 1841 census showed that more than 40 per cent of employed men and 30 per cent of employed women were engaged in manufacturing goods. There were several iron foundries in the city, a coach works and several distilleries and breweries, one of which, Beamish and Crawford, was producing as much porter as Guinness's in Dublin during the early years of the decade. When Inglis was in Cork in 1834 he found that though labourers' wages had been reduced 'the fall in the price of provisions had been still greater, and the housing and clothing of these classes had in the same period been improving'. This has been broadly confirmed by a recent study of

food prices and the cost of living in Cork at this time: a labourer spending half of his wages on food would certainly have been able to avoid
starvation. The problem was that so many labourers, here as elsewhere
in Ireland, were unable to find work. Those inhabiting the overcrowded
houses in the centre or the mud cabins in the suburbs, further overcrowded by regular arrivals of more unemployed from the countryside,
while often in receipt of relief from charitable organisations financed
by their more prosperous fellow citizens, were in fact more interested
in finding employment than in obtaining relief. The Poor Commissions
had to concede that, despite improvements, one quarter of the city's
population lived from hand to mouth, eating mostly potatoes, with as
many as 6,000 people destitute, dependent on begging and living 'in
crowded hovels with merely their day rags for covering'.[14]

The House of Industry was an uninviting alternative to begging for
the destitute, although it had nearly a thousand occupants at the beginning of 1834. This number included not only the families of the
unemployed but some of the families of the badly paid labourers who
'often send their families to be supported in the house of industry for
a season'. It was one of several institutions in the city designed to offer
a minimal standard of social welfare and medical care, funded from a
combination of county presentments (money raised from a levy of oc-
cupiers of land), donations, subscriptions and treasury grants. There were
several infirmaries and dispensaries as well as a fever hospital and a
lunatic asylum. More than 7,500 patients attended the main dispensaries
in 1835, with a further 5,000 receiving treatment in their homes. There
was the Fever Hospital, already noted, and there was also the Foundling
Hospital, which had 456 children in the house, and 856 'at nurse in the
country' in the middle of the decade and, though 'much mismanaged'
was, in the opinion of the Poor Commissioners, offering sufficient provision for the City's needs. The Lunatic Asylum, while exhibiting many
of the horrors of institutions of this kind in most countries at the time,
was in fact attempting to implement several improvements, the most important of which indicated 'a real awareness of something very much
to the fore in modern mental treatment, namely the value of occupational therapy and the incentment to rehabilitation offered by work and
personal savings'.[15]

Besides a school in the Foundling Hospital there were 26 other day
schools in the city, providing free schooling for more than 5,000 children
by 1835, a number which the Poor Commissioners thought 'must

embrace a very large proportion of the children of an instructable age'. There was only one school under the National Education Board in 1834, when Protestants were opposed to the system. Provision of Catholic elementary education in the city dated back to the previous century and by the eighteen thirties a school system was in operation run mainly by the Presentation Sisters and the Christian Brothers. The Poor Commissioners found that parents almost invariably sent their children to schools of their own faith, although many of the smaller schools, patronised mostly by the middle class, had Catholic and Protestant pupils being educated together. There were no ghettoes for the poor on sectarian lines — poor Catholics lived alongside poor Protestants. There were some attempts to convert Catholics to Protestantism: the Cork Reformation Society there was committed to 'disseminating the religious principles of the Reformation among Catholics' but 'hold forth no secular inducement to proselytism'. There was an active auxiliary branch of the Church Missionary Society in operation in the city since 1817. There was some recruitment of staff on sectarian lines, especially among the smaller firms, but less in the case of the larger enterprises, where Protestant owners often employed a manual workforce that was 90 per cent Catholic.[16]

While trade unionism was strong among tradesmen in Cork, Chartism gained no significant following there. The Poor Commissioners found combinations strong among shoemakers, sawyers and coopers, with the latter, generally only on half-work, understandably militant in preventing coopers from the countryside getting employment in the city. Hat workers were said to have destroyed the hat trade, but the Commissioners conceded that 'masters and men are represented to have been equally to blame'. The failure of Chartism has been attributed by a modern historian of the city to the general depression among workers such as the weavers, combined with the close relationship between employer and employee in the small workshops, which 'tended to prevent the feeling and articulation of class tensions which fostered Chartism among outworkers and factory operatives'.[17]

John O'Brien has explained how in Cork city at this time there were two elites, one consisting of a prosperous Catholic merchant class and the other, which had control of political power in the city, being largely Protestant. Though there were five times as many Catholics as Protestants, the city's municipal affairs were largely under the control of the Friendly Club, a Protestant and conservative organisation of freeholders who had a hold on corporate appointments and were thus able to run city affairs in the interests of families that belonged to the club. While on the surface relations between Catholics and Protestants were cordial, the campaign for Catholic Emancipation and the passing of the Reform Act inevitably raised the expectation of Catholics and Cork became one of O'Connell's strongholds. In the parliamentary election following the Reform Act the city returned two candidates pledged to the cause of Repeal. The nationalists' success in holding the parliamentary seats was not immediately repeated in the field of local government because of the unjust nature of the municipal corporations. Even before the Government report of 1835 condemned the corporations as 'corrupt and irresponsible' and introduced an act to reform them, the Catholic middle class had organised itself around the Trades Association, and, when the first election for the reformed corporation was held in 1841, the Liberal (mostly Catholic) party had an overwhelming victory over the Protestant Tories who had been running the city's affairs for so long. D'Alton has explained in detail how the Protestant population in Cork responded to the self-confident emancipated Catholicism that, developing alongside the national assertiveness that was embodied in O'Connell, struggled for an increased share in national and local political power.[18]

Cork's Catholic merchants were particularly prominent in the butter trade, in tanning and in distilling. They combined with Protestants in many public matters that were in their mutual interest, like the promotion of a railway from Dublin to Cork or resistance to a suggested raising of the poor rate in 1839 to pay for a new workhouse. They often joined together, too, for charitable or philanthropic purposes, and the Poor Commissioners were satisfied that in Cork they had 'rarely found a sectarian spirit to prevail in relieving pauperism'.[19]

Cork had a rich cultural life. Fraser's *Guide* in 1838 noted the 'Cork Institution, where lectures on various branches of science are regularly delivered by qualified professors. There is also the Mechanics Institute and Library Society. Attached to the Institution is an extensive library, and a museum of natural history'. During the 1837-8 season, members of the Cork Scientific and Literacy Society were addressed on a variety of subjects that included the Natural History of Man, Innate Ideas, Warming Buildings, Music, Drama, the Influence of Literature on Society and the Physical Sciences as a necessary part of a Liberal Education. In the text accompanying the portrait of William Maginn in *The Maclise Portrait Gallery* mention is made of the great number of artists and literary figures Cork city could boast of. Besides Maclise, the painter, and Maginn, the founder of *Fraser's Magazine*, the list included Richard Sainthill the antiquarian, John Hogan, the sculptor, Sheriden Knowles the dramatist, James Barry the painter who like Maclise was a Royal Academician, Crofton Croker and another writer, Father Francis Mahony, better known as 'Father Prout'.[20]

*   *   *

Dunscombe, Martin and Dowden were the three names traditionally associated with the early temperance movement in Cork, although it is not known where the idea to form a temperance society came from or who founded the first one. Rev. Nicholas Dunscombe was curate of St. Peter's, Cork, but had to resign in 1839 because of poor health. At a meeting of parishioners to pay tribute to his pastoral work in Cork Dunscombe took the opportunity, in his reply, of tracing the first discussions of temperance in Cork to 1830, although the movement was not openly organised and advocated until the following year, when he was the first speaker at a public meeting. He left for England shortly after that and did not return to Cork until 1833 when he was appointed curate at St. Peter's. Regrettably, he did not say where he got the idea from, so the suggestion in an article in the *Southern Reporter* in 1841 that the ideas of Skibbereen may have reached Cork city via Rosscarbery and Clonakilty cannot be confirmed or denied. As the Skibbereen society was a teetotal one, however, and as ideas of total abstinence did not get any hearing in Cork until the mid-thirties, it is more likely that Dunscombe derived his ideas on temperance from the moderation societies of New Ross, Belfast or Dublin. According to the temperance historian William Logan, the Cork Quaker William Martin had been to Holyhead in 1830 and, hearing about the movement there, set up a temperance society in Cork on his return, with the help of other Quakers. The third 'father' of temperance in Cork, Richard Dowden (Richard), had established a society by 1833, as an invitation card to one of its functions in that year survives among his papers.[21]

The Poor Commissioners referred to the affairs of one temperance society in the city in their report of 1836. This society had 100 to 120 members, who, obtaining a ticket from the secretary, found it easier to obtain work because of their known sobriety. This led to hundreds of others joining 'merely for that object; it then got into disrepute and was given up'. There were in fact several temperance societies in Cork by 1836, and the Commissioners may have been referring to one founded by Dunscombe before his departure for England. If so, it differs considerably from an account given in 1840 by Thomas Dunscombe, a relation. The society, he recalled, had very few members, and these 'were teased with hypocrisy, with proselytism, with a desire to rob the working man of his enjoyment; they were subject to personal insult, sometimes approaching to personal violence'. William Martin and his followers were subjected to similar treatment, on one occasion having the seats and furniture broken up in a theatre where they were having a meeting.[22]

Given the nature of industry in the city at the time it is perhaps not surprising that members of temperance societies were welcomed by some while being seen as a threat by others. While more efficient production in some industries would have been facilitated by a sober workforce, a widespread renunciation of drink would adversely effect the fortunes of some of Cork's biggest firms. In 1832 Cork distillers paid more than 15 per cent of the total duty paid on spirits in Ireland. Of several large distilleries in the city, that of Daniel Callaghan was the most substantial, producing more than 200,000 gallons in 1834, the year in which the duty on spirits was reduced from 3/4d. to 2/4d. per gallon. According to the Poor Commissioners, only a small amount of spirits was exported from Cork. The same was true of the large quantities of beer brewed there. More than 65,000 gallons were brewed at Beamish and Crawford's in 1833, as well as smaller amounts in other city breweries. Most of this was for a local market in the south of Ireland, partly distributed to customers, in the case of Beamish and Crawford, through a network of tied houses. The number of licensed premises in the city was around 500 in 1836, but seems to have increased by nearly 50 per cent later in the decade. While drinking was widespread among all classes, mechanics were singled out by the Poor Commissioners as the worst offenders. They blamed their clubs and meeting places for promoting drinking and reported the view that, because of their over-indulgence, many mechanics earning between 15/- and £1 a week were living less comfortably than labourers on one third of these wages.[23]

The sectarian bitterness that Lowery saw as pervading all aspects of Irish life in the eighteen thirties was noted in the last chapter, as well as the suspicions entertained by many Catholics that the temperance advocates intended to convert them to Protestantism. There were Protestant missionaries in Cork city and 80 miles to the west a mission had been established at Dingle which was later to epitomise the aggressive Evangelical movement among the rural Catholic population. It is not surprising, therefore, that accusations of proselytism against the temperance society should have surfaced during the early days of the movement in Cork. It must be doubted, however, whether Dunscombe himself could have had any intentions to proselytise. In their address to him in 1839 his parishioners paid particular attention to his charitable work 'among those of a different persuasion', and the *Freeholder*, on the occasion of Dunscombe recovering from the fever, noted that in his work among the poor in St. Peter's parish 'their religion was never a question to him'. The *Dublin Evening Post*, nevertheless, stated clearly, but without giving any evidence to support it, that 'he combined an effort to proselytise the Catholics with his exertions to reclaim the drunkards'. [24]

When Finch was in Cork in 1836 he found that in all the temperance societies in the city except Martin's there were teetotallers and moderationists. Though Martin is credited with being the founder of teetotalism in the city, one of the founders of the temperance society in the village of Blackrock, a few miles from Cork, claimed that at the beginning of 1835 some of those who joined opted for the total abstinence pledge. Of the several societies in the city, Dunscombe's was later claimed by McKenna to have been the largest, with 456 members in 1834. Some of the others had several hundred members on their books, but it is clear that, whether the pledge was teetotal or moderationist, not many tradesmen or labourers joined. A report on a temperance festival at Lloyds' Hotel, Old George Street, in 1838, attended by Dunscombe, McKenna and Dowden, drew attention to the fact that 'the greater portion of the meeting consisted of the middling class and of shopkeepers'.[25]

In Dublin many temperance campaigners had seen that beer was as much a cause of drunkenness as spirits and the same may have become apparent in Cork, as, in the later years of the decade, most of the leading temperance workers had become teetotallers. One consequence of this was that some members of temperance societies who were employed by brewers withdrew their support altogether when total abstinence principles were adopted by a society. Among the teetotallers active in the Cove Lane society, a branch of William Martin's society, were McKenna, Roger Olden and John O'Connell. Martin and Father Mathew were both governors of the Cork House of Industry, later the Workhouse. Martin had often tried to persuade Father Mathew to join the campaign, hoping this might be influential in attracting the Catholic population, most of whom still seem to have been suspicious of what seemed to them a

Protestant and Dissenter movement. Olden had also encouraged Father Mathew to join, as the latter told Birmingham in 1840 and Harriet Edgeworth the following year. Though he added that it was seeing so many crimes caused by drink that led him to consider promoting teetotalism, Father Mathew does not seem to have told anyone the actual circumstances that led him to become directly involved. This is particularly surprising in view of the fact that McKenna, soon to become his secretary, was familiar with these circumstances. Fortunately, an interview conducted with the 87 year old John O'Connell by a correspondent of the *Cork Examiner* in 1890 provided the material for historians of the movement after that date to complete the picture.[26]

Writers before 1890, influenced by Maguire, who wrote the first substantial biography of Father Mathew, believed that he made up his mind to form a teetotal society and went to Martin for assistance. What happened, according to O'Connell, was that sometime, probably in 1836 or 1837, he and two other committee members of the branch of the teetotal society in Cove Lane met Father Mathew on the street, had a discussion with him about temperance, but found that, while he gave his approval to what their society was doing, he did not want to become personally involved at that time. Father Mathew later admitted that he was deterred from joining the temperance movement earlier because of the ridicule to which members were subjected. Meanwhile, a small boost was given to the cause of teetotalism in Cork by 'Father Prout' the writer, who gave a benefit lecture to a large audience in Warren's Place, making the cause, in O'Connell's words 'fashionable as well as popular' in Cork. The next occasion O'Connell went to see Father Mathew was in March 1838, following an incident at a meeting of the Cove Lane branch of the teetotal society. At the meeting some remark was made by a Protestent clergyman named Lombard to which the Catholics present took exception. O'Connell approached Father Mathew with a view to getting an introduction to another Catholic clergyman for advice, but Father Mathew detained him to ask for more information about the incident, the details of which have not been recorded, except that for O'Connell it represented 'the thin edge of the wedge of proselytism'. Having listened, Father Mathew asked O'Connell to arrange a meeting of all the teetotallers he could get together in the Josephian Society rooms in Blackamoor Lane. O'Connell reported this to McKenna, another of the Catholics who was unhappy about Lombard's remarks, and a meeting was arranged to comply with Father Mathew's request.[27]

Nothing was resolved at this meeting, Father Mathew having told the large numbers present that he would announce his decision about renouncing intoxicating drinks at a further meeting in a month's time. This was the famous meeting of 10 April 1838, when Father Mathew addressed another large audience at Blackamoor Lane and told them that while he had always tried to discourage drunkenness, though with limited success, he was now prepared to answer the call of his friends to join the movement. Nobody in health needed intoxicating drinks, he said, and asked people to follow him in signing the book of the Cork Total Abstinence Society, supposedly using the words 'Here goes, in the name of God' as he did so. He was elected president of the new society and McKenna, who had signed the book immediately after him, was appointed secretary.[28]

A story was carried in the *Bristol Temperance Herald* a few years later, in which William Martin, finding Father Mathew sitting between himself and an unnamed Presbyterian minister at the 10 April meeting, remarked that it was pleasant that there was one place they could meet without distinction of creed and unite in doing good, to which Father Mathew is supposed to have replied that it was indeed, 'and there is another place too, where I hope we shall all unite in a like manner'. Whether apocryphal or true, the story indicates the non-sectarian nature of the Cork Total Abstinence Society at its inception. Around 60, probably less, are supposed to have joined at the initial meeting, followed by several hundred at succeeding meetings. It was soon necessary to find a larger venue, and Father Mathew secured the use of the Horse Bazaar on Sullivan's Quay, owned by a convert to the cause, and capable of holding 4,000 people, where he held regular Sunday meetings. McKenna gave an exaggerated figure of 25,000 for the numbers who joined the Cork T.A. Society during 1838, and these were repeated by Maguire. Fr. Augustine has shown that the correct figure was more likely to have been the 6,000 that Quin saw on the register when he was in Cork towards the end of 1838.[29]

McKenna, as secretary, should have known better, as should Maguire, and both should also have been in a position to know that all of those who did join may not have done so through the influence of Father Mathew. For Maguire and McKenna were both on the platform when John Hockings, 'the Birmingham Blacksmith' was in Cork in June 1838, advocating the teetotal pledge. The teetotal society, he told his audience, 'would undertake to cure all the drunkards if the moderation society

would agree to make no more', a reference to the view, often put forward
by teetotal campaigners that the moderationists, by countenancing drinking of alcoholic drinks like wine and beer, were in fact contributing to
the conditions which created drunkenness. There is no record of Father
Mathew attending Hockings's meetings in any capacity. Hockings had
a reputation for making money out of teetotalism, although proceeds
from the Cork meetings went to the House of Industry. Had Father
Mathew met him he might have benefited from Hockings's experience
of making temperance profitable, or at least self-supporting, something
that would have saved him considerable embarrassment later. It is possible
of course, that he was deterred by the very fact that Hockings was charging
an entry fee or that the reputation Hockings had earned as a showman
did not appeal to him.[30]

For his approach was indeed far removed from the boisterous entertainment of the Hockings meetings, as can be seen from a *Cork Standard* report, a few weeks later, on the effect of one of his speeches. His

solemn impressive manner and the substance of all he seeks to impress, are
received with reverential silence only now and again broken by a burst of expressed horror at what he recites: which allows that all who hear him regard
his lecture in the light of a sermon. Then, the pledge they reiterate from his
lips is taken under the deep seal of ecclesiastical authority while the promise
is regarded as a compact with the representative of their Creator.

What the pledge actually meant was to remain a subject of controversy
for some time, and will be considered in a later chapter. It may be said
here, however, that as the Cork Total Abstinence Society was non-sectarian
in origin there was no question of ecclesiastical authority involved. The
Bishop of Cork, Dr. Murphy, had little interest in the movement. Archbishop Ullathorne, in fact, when he visited Bishop Murphy accompanied
by Father Mathew a few years later, was shocked to hear the Bishop tease
the temperance leader's work and concluded that 'the want of hearty
co-operation from his Bishop was obviously an element amidst the good
Father's trials'. The *Standard* identified an important innovation of Father
Mathew's in its reference to aspiring teetotallers repeating the pledge
after him. Despite the fact that previous teetotal societies required written pledges, and that Father Mathew and the others signed the book
at the inaugural meeting of the Cork Total Abstinence Society, this for-
mality was dropped by Father Mathew, who was satisfied with a verbal
pledge. This was to become particularly important when, later,

prospective teetotallers began to appear before him in numbers so great
that a written pledge would have been unmanageable.[31]

While Hockings was no doubt responsible for converting some people in Cork to teetotalism, and while Father Mathew's principal assistants
at the Horse Bazaar, Martin, McKenna and Frank Walsh, a local bar-
rister, all made a contribution to the spread of the movement in the city,
it is clear that the main momentum behind the movement among the
Catholics was Father Mathew himself. While continuing to perform his
duties as a priest he devoted a great amount of time to temperance work,
bringing to it that enormous amount of patience, energy and commitment that had enabled him to achieve so much in his earlier pastoral
and charitable work, and inspiring the same confidence in those he was
persuading to abandon drink as he was previously able to inspire in those
to whom he was confessor or friend. Because he had a record of being
involved in very practical schemes on behalf of the poor, many of them
were prepared to come to a meeting to hear what he had to say. Some
stayed to take the pledge. That he was well suited to the trials involved
in dealing with what we now know as alcoholism is borne out by Justin
McCarthy, who knew him at that time, and wrote of his 'never failing
patience and pity for the drunkard. No matter how often an unhappy
man might have broken his pledge and gone back to his evil habits, Father
Mathew was ever ready with forgiveness and renewed hope, never despairing of the weakling's possible redemption.' His sympathy and patience
with the drunkard may have had their source in his belief that many
of them were driven to drink by their circumstances. While agreeing
with Carr in 1839 that drunkards were 'a foul blot upon our countrymen',
it must be acknowledged, he added 'that there are many extenuating
circumstances regarding them, and principally the misery, the want, to
which they have been exposed, and which (of course with exceptions)
drove multitudes to seek in drink "the antidote" to the recollection of
their sufferings . . .'[32]

Definite signs of improvements attributable to temperance were noted
at a tea party in the city in April 1839 attended by Martin as well as
George Cox and George Gibbs, two other Quakers active in the movement in Cork. 'Easter Monday had always been disgraced by the working men of Cork', said the chairman, James Hyde. 'Fighting, drunkenness
and other excesses, thanks to total abstinence, was extinct.' The extinc-
tion of drunkenness in the city and county of Cork was never to be
achieved, with the figures for the numbers appearing before magistrates

for this offence remaining high throughout the year with the exception of the month of June, but the optimism of the Quakers was understandable. According to the economic historian George Smith, who was writing his exhaustive survey of Ireland while Father Mathew's movement was in progress, Father Mathew was hoping to gain about 500 adherents by the end of 1838, by which time more than ten times that number had actually joined. Locals continued to join during 1839 but the movement in the city that year was characterised more by the great numbers of people travelling from different parts of the country to pledge themselves directly to Father Mathew. The evidence from the Temperance Reports indicates that people began going to Cork in the early part of the summer, although the reply from Thurles suggests it could have been earlier in a few areas. Many of those who went got drunk on the way as 'a farewell to whiskey' and arrived penniless in Cork. Having taken the pledge from him, Father Mathew often had to provide them with sustenance for their journey home. Where did they come from and how did they know about what Father Mathew was doing in Cork?[33]

John O'Connell, in his *Cork Examiner* interview, remembered that shortly after establishing the Cork Total Abstinence Society Father Mathew decided to organise branches in other parts of the city and in towns in east Cork. O'Connell himself was engaged in visiting towns like Passage, Cobh, Aghada, Whitegate, Blarney, Cloyne, Midleton, Carrigtwohill, Glanmire, Fermoy, Rathcormack, Riverstown, Ladysbridge and Carrigaline. Several of these were places where temperance societies had already been established earlier, some of them, like Midleton and Youghal, having been noted as particularly active centres. In some cases, therefore, O'Connell's work in these towns would have been to set up new societies while in others it would have been, perhaps, to convince the moderation societies of the advantages of teetotalism, now that the system, thanks largely to Father Mathew's involvement with the cause, could be portrayed as the only system capable of meeting the challenge of Irish drunkenness. There was also missionary work to the west of the city. William Martin was reported to have demonstrated the absurdity of drinking alcoholic beverages by means of his 'rectifying apparatus' which, having extracted the alcohol from beer, showed it to be no more than dirty water. A man in Ballyvourney was so convinced by this that he planned to go to Cork to take the teetotal pledge from Father Mathew![34]

Besides missionaries from Cork, the message was spread by word of mouth and by newspapers which, while not having a circulation in any way comparable to modern times, were capable of relaying information to key people like parish priests who could then spread news further afield at weekly mass or through private conversations. The *Cork Standard* had carried news of 'three Roman Catholic clergymen' who had made up their minds to promote the temperance cause in Cork on the day following the Blackamoor Lane meeting and continued to give publicity to Father Mathew's meetings. Other newspapers like the *Southern Reporter* and the *Cork Constitution* followed. While the *Constitution* was critical of some aspects of the movement as promoted by Father Mathew it was, in the early days, generally supportive, something Father Mathew acknowledged himself to Father Birmingham in 1840. Maguire's *Cork Total Abstainer* was founded to promote the cause but Maguire, perhaps seeing, as Bretherton has suggested, that the movement might not sustain its original enthusiasm to a degree likely to support a newspaper devoted entirely to its concerns, decided to change it to a newspaper of wider interest. Refounded as the *Cork Examiner*, it still gave the temperance movement substantial coverage. Among newspapers outside Cork that gave publicity to the movement were the *Galway Patriot*, until it closed down in 1839, the *Connaught Journal*, the *Limerick Reporter* from its foundation in the summer of 1839, the *Kilkenny Journal* whose editor Cornelius Maxwell, was a supporter of the movement and the *Dublin Evening Post* whose editor, Frederick Conway, himself took the pledge in 1839. Among Protestant papers, besides the *Constitution*, the *Nenagh Guardian* and *Dublin Evening Mail* were acknowledged by Father Mathew in 1840 to have been helpful, although the *Mail* had become increasingly critical even before the end of 1839. *The Irish Temperance and Literary Gazette* had become the *Dublin Weekly Herald*, and though it remained committed to the moderate pledge, it did, in 1839, acknowledge the good work Father Mathew was doing. It would have preferred, though, that people should give up drinking from a conviction of the harm that it did rather than on impulse, as it feared that taking the pledge on impulse might not have lasting effects.[35]

Until the autumn of 1839 the *Cork Standard* was the only newspaper to draw attention to the numbers coming to Cork to take the pledge, so it has to be assumed that up until that time news of his temperance work there was spread to the rest of the country by word of mouth. This makes the size of the number who came all the more amazing. Malcolm's suggestion that the failure of the potato crop in that year could have influenced people to go to Cork in the hope that they might please their landlords or prevent future disasters with Father Mathew's blessings or medals would seem to lack evidence to substantiate it. None of the newspapers seem to have referred to these as possible motives, nor do any of the Temperance Reports, which often go into considerable detail about the superstitious aspects of the movement, make any mention of prospective teetotallers having gone to Cork to please their landlords or in search of a talisman against economic disaster. There is evidence, though, that employers in cities and towns were anxious for their employees to make the journey to Cork in the hope that they would become — and remain — sober. Workers from Russell's provision curers in Limerick seem to have gone there *en masse*, and cotton workers from Portlaw were sent by the factory manager to Cork in October 1839 as a last resort, the local temperance society having failed to influence them. Other Waterford workers prepared to take the pledge went to Cork to do so because, on their return, they could show their temperance medals to their employers as visible evidence that they had reformed. They could have made the much shorter journey to take the pledge from Father Foley, who was making many converts to teetotalism in east Cork and west Waterford at the time, but Father Foley did not approve of the distribution of medals.[36]

In view of the missionaries that Father Mathew had sent out to various towns and villages in county Cork it is likely that the first travellers arriving to take the pledge were from that county. Distance was clearly important. The Temperance Report from Rathkeale, county Limerick, noted that the first people to take the pledge in that district were those who lived nearest to Cork. Whether influenced by those who had already made the journey to Cork or by newspapers which were reporting almost daily on the movement of people to and from Cork, the crowds continued to arrive through the autumn months. In October the *Cork Constitution* regretted what they considered the superstitious importance of taking the pledge directly from Father Mathew, and wondered if they wouldn't have been better off staying at home and joining teetotal societies in their places of origin. By this time there were in fact branches of the Cork Temperance Society in many cities and towns outside Cork. In some of these branches the pledge was administered by local priests, but most intending teetotallers felt they should travel to Cork to take the pledge from Father Mathew. He, for his part, advised them to join their local temperance society on their return home. The crowds continued to arrive in Cork into the winter. In a letter to the Belfast Total Abstinence Society in November Father Mathew regretted he could not accept their invitation to go there because of the large numbers arriving daily in Cork to take the pledge — 500 on the day he wrote and as many as 4,000 a week.[37]

Birmingham noted that the men of Kilrush were the first outside Cork to make the journey to take the pledge from Father Mathew. Finch held a meeting at Kilrush in 1836, accompanied by the parish priest, Fr. John Kenny, who regretted the great amount spent on drink in the town. People were reluctant to commit themselves publicly, however, until there was 'a sufficient number of signatures to make a respectable appearance before the public'. An attempt was made by the Hibernian Temperance Society, supported by several local gentlemen, to establish a society there a year later. Two priests in the parish were named by Birmingham as being early supporters of Father Mathew. They must have worked hard on the foundations laid by Finch and the Hibernian Temperance Union, for Father Mathew told a meeting in Dublin in March 1840 that there were 1,500 teetotallers in Kilrush 'and they had all walked to Cork, a distance of 112 miles' to take the pledge. The number may seem great, but the *Clare Journal* reported that in one day alone in July 1839, 200 had travelled up the Shannon from Kilrush, Kilkee and other parts of south west Clare on their way to Cork via Limerick. The beneficial change in the condition of the people of Kilrush was noted by their landlord, Mr. Vandeleur, on the occasion of laying the foundation stone for a new Catholic church in the town at the end of 1839, when between 600 and 700 teetotallers joined in the procession. By the beginning of the following year the teetotallers of Kilrush were reported to have organised a benefit system for members, which 'renders most essential service in this particularly inclement season'. By the autumn of 1842, when Father Mathew made a visit to the town that was reported in detail by Kohl, the amount of money spent on spirits there had been reduced from the £30,000 per year at the time of Finch's visit in 1836 to a mere £1,200.[38]

CHAPTER 3

The Temperance Crusade

In Limerick and Waterford, the first two cities outside Cork where Father Mathew administered the pledge, the temperance movement had been established for several years, pledges had become almost exclusively teetotal and large numbers from both cities had been travelling to Cork to take the pledge for some months. The original temperance society in Limerick, as in Cork, had to contend with accusations of Protestant proselytism, although its membership, as well as that of the City of Limerick Temperance Society which succeeded it, consisted mostly of Catholics. A draft copy of the rules of St. Mary's Temperance and Mortality Society, Limerick, has survived among the Temperance Reports. Founded in July 1839, the first rule stipulated that membership was restricted to those 'who can produce Testimonials of their Pledge from the Very Rev. Theobald Mathew of Cork'.[1]

There was a regular trail of prospective teetotallers from Limerick to Cork during the summer and autumn of 1839 and by September the beneficial effects of the movement in the city were being publicly acknowledged by the acting Mayor. In a public letter to Father Mathew he claimed that in a city where inquests had been accustomed to finding alcohol a cause of death, a 'moral revolution had taken place among the people', with police reports lessened and business in the petty courts considerably reduced. In the course of two reports during October the *Dublin Evening Post* told the stories of shebeen owners in Limerick converting their premises to coffee houses, of a distiller having his weekly sale of whiskey there more than halved and of the number of temperance

57

pilgrims from Limerick to Cork having reached the extraordinary number of 10,000. By mid-November the same newspaper was claiming that through the influence of temperance, 'Limerick has become morally a new city'.[2]

He had been invited to Limerick by his friend Bishop Ryan, with whom he had been a student at Maynooth for a short period and to whom, in his distaste for sectarianism and politics, he bore a considerable resemblance. The invitation was to preach a charity sermon in aid of the Presentation nuns' school for poor girls and Father Mathew expressed a wish not to be invited to temperance functions. The sight of the large crowds who lined the streets to greet him on his arrival by the mail coach from Cork must have persuaded him to change his mind. As many as 40,000 strangers had arrived in the city by the week-end, and with lodging houses full, 'two shillings were in numerous instances paid for the privilege of standing in cellars through the Irishtown'. While most came from the neighbouring counties of Limerick, Clare, Kerry and Tipperary, some were identified as coming from Waterford, Galway and Mayo.[3]

On the Sunday he was taken by coach straight from the charity sermon to the Court House where he began to receive prospective teetotallers, followed later in the day by a session administering the pledge at the house of his brother-in-law in Upper Mallow Street where he was staying. He began again in the same place as early as 5 a.m. the following morning when, according to one paper, a pregnant woman died from injuries received in the crush around the house, and, according to another, missiles were thrown at the police sent there to keep order. He returned to the Court House where, by the afternoon, the crowds were so great that Father Ralegh from St. Michael's Church and Mr. Dunbar, Father Mathew's brother-in-law, concerned for his safety, went to the Mayor. The Mayor arranged for an escort of Scots Guards who proceeded to 'liberate' Father Mathew from his followers, who had occupied the space between the New Bridge (later renamed Mathew Bridge) and the Court House. The crowds here 'were so anxious to catch a glimpse of the great apostle that they braved the hoofs of horses and the swords of dragoons to touch the hem of his garment'.[4]

He was 'liberated' by the dragoons who guided him to a green space near Dunbar's house where he administered the pledge to a crowd estimated at 10,000, presumably in batches. On Tuesday he was giving the pledge in batches of several hundred at a time, people entering one door of Mr. Dunbar's house and leaving by another. By the time the

Limerick Reporter went to press that evening they had noticed he was hoarse from having repeated the pledge so often. Clergymen helped him out, saying the words after him, repeated in turn by the teetotallers on bended knees. He left for Cork on the 5 o'clock coach, but not before thanking the Mayor and civic authorities as well as the military for their assistance. Attempts to keep an account of the numbers taking the pledge were abandoned at an early stage and instead of entering the converts on a list they were asked to give their names to their parish priests, who would later be sent medals and cards for them from Cork. Estimates of the numbers who took the pledge over the three days vary from 120,000 to 250,000. There were similar discrepancies surrounding the number killed or injured: *The Limerick Standard* examined the hospital's casualty list and, while three deaths were recorded of people who had come to Limerick to see Father Mathew, none of the deaths arose from incidents at or near his meetings.[5]

The extent of the reported casualties was one reason why the Dublin *Evening Packet* disapproved so strongly of events in Limerick: other grounds for its disapproval were given as the large numbers of people on the streets, the public disorder and assaults on police, as well as the drunkenness of those having their 'farewell to whiskey'. It claimed that 'a greater amount of evil, moral as well as physical, has been produced by his visit to Limerick in a single day than could have been caused — humanly calculating — by ordinary intemperance in six months'. The *Waterford Mail* expressed concern at the same aspects of the visit as the *Packet*, adding a feeling of particular horror at the spectacle of Father Mathew having been 'hailed as a deity, before whom thousands fell prostrate in adoration'. It favoured a 'rational reformation founded on conviction and not arising from intemperate enthusiasm' and doubted if many of those who flocked to take the pledge in Limerick would keep it. The *Dublin Evening Mail* went even further, arguing that not only would no permanent moral good come from the rash and fanatical avowal of temperance, but, lacking moral training and a conviction of the reasonableness of temperance, there was a danger that deprivation from drink would merely sharpen the appetite and, in the long run, create more rather than less drunkenness. The *Kilkenny Moderator* reserved its particular scorn for the temperance medals and their popular association with miracles, despite the fact that there seem to have been no medals distributed during the three days. Under the heading 'Father Mathew's Miracles in Limerick' it argued that those who were now abandoning drunkenness only to embrace superstition, will go back to their 'lawless and viscious pursuits' when the spell is broken and they find the medals do not work any miracles.[6]

Shortly after it became known that Father Mathew had accepted an invitation from Bishop Foran to visit Waterford in order to save drunkards there the expense of travelling to Cork to take the pledge, a committee was formed to try to prevent the kind of accidents that happened in Limerick. But in order to avoid 'public applause' Father Mathew arrived a day early, to the discomfort of the planning committee. Order in fact broke down while he was administering the pledge at Ballybricken on Wednesday 11 December 1839, and he had to withdraw to the Court House, which, fortunately, had been booked in case of rain. There, batches of around 200 were permitted to enter at a time to take the pledge. The following day a company of dragoons from Cahir helped keep order while priests ushered in the batches to the Court House. While some of those taking the pledge were recognised by the local press as people of good character, others were identified as having been the most drunken and brutalised members of the local population. At a meeting after his departure employers in the city were thanked 'for affording their men the necessary opportunity to go forward'.[7]

The *Waterford Mirror*, in trying to arrive at the total number who took the pledge in the city wrote that a figure of 80,000 was calculated by 'those who were constant spectators of the operations of the two days', but added that others estimated the numbers at 60,000. As the latter were less likely to know than those who had been present all the time, the higher figure may be thought the more likely, especially as it was the one later quoted by Bishop Foran. As the population of Waterford was about 23,000 and as an estimated 6,000 of them were teetotallers when the Sub Inspector of Police for the city was writing his report a few months later, it would seem that more than 70,000 people came from outside the city for the occasion. Newspapers noted that most of the crowds came from county Waterford, but many were also identified from Wexford, Carlow, Wicklow, Kildare, King's and Queen's counties.[8]

When Father Mathew was passing through Clonmel on his way back to Cork from Waterford on 12 December 1839 he expressed his intention of returning there to give the pledge five days later, and this information was made public from the altars of Catholic churches in the town on the Sunday, two days before his arrival. He arrived late at night, appropriately in a Bianconi carriage. Appropriate, in that Clonmel was the headquarters of the Bianconi transport system, and Charles Bianconi, a future mayor of the town, was to put his carriages at the disposal of Father Mathew, free of charge. As early as November 1839 attention was drawn to the profits made by proprietors of vehicles in conveying passengers to Cork to take the pledge: not prepared to walk like the men of Kilrush, they hired 'vehicles of every description from the post-chaise to the jarvey' as well as 'extras' of Bianconi. The astute businessman had chosen a prosperous town to settle in. When Inglis was there in 1834 he saw no signs of the poverty he had witnessed in Limerick and Waterford, and large amounts of grain, on which the prosperity of the town was based, continued to be milled there and sent down to Waterford for export. Though Finch's temperance meeting in the town in 1836 had been disrupted by three drunks, he was confident enough about his efforts there to hope 'that the fruits will be seen on a future occasion'. Arriving at 2.00 a.m. Father Mathew was administering the pledge at the Court House at 9.00 a.m. A reported 30,000 took the pledge, followed by at least as many the next day. In the early days of his travels around the country no county received more concentrated attention from Father Mathew than his native Tipperary, beginning with his giving the pledge to an unspecified number during a visit home to Rathcloheen in September 1839. In one day in January 1840, 10,000 took the pledge from him in Thurles and twice that number took it during a visit to Nenagh in March the same year. Father Scanlan, the parish priest of Nenagh, was a zealous advocate of teetotalism, as was Father Birmingham of Borrisokane, who invited Father Mathew to that town on his way back from Galway. In Cahir, where Father Mathew stopped to administer the pledge on several occasions in 1840 while passing through, Lord Glengall was an enthusiastic supporter. Cashel was one of the many towns in Tipperary where a temperance society based on the principles of the Cork Total Abstinence Society was flourishing before his visit. Despite the local Dean refusing to allow the Cashel Temperance Society to use the famous Rock for Father Mathew's visit (he considered the movement to have been 'the work of the Devil'), Cashel seems to have been one of the places where Protestants took the pledge in significant numbers. In Roscrea, which Father Mathew visited twice in the early months of 1840, there had been a temperance society for some time, with a membership of 200 in 1836.[9]

Father Mathew's first visit to Connaught was in February 1840, when the *Dublin Evening Post* reported that 60,000 took the pledge in Gort over three days, although the Sub Inspector of Constabulary for the district put the number at exactly half of that. A temperance society had been active in Gort since at least October 1839 and in Galway town, the scene of Father Mathew's next great mission in Connaught, there were three flourishing temperance societies, one of them dating back to 1836. By 1840 this society had become known as the Parent Temperance Society, no doubt to indicate that it was older in origin than the Galway branch of the Cork Total Abstinence Society, which was founded in 1839, and the Galway Trades' Mechanics Institute, Total Abstinence and Mortality Society, a re-founding of the original Galway Mechanics Institute which had folded up some years before. In the last two weeks of 1839 the Parent Temperance Society distributed 600 of Father Mathew's temperance medals from its Middle Street premises, but it is not clear if all who received them had been to Cork, or perhaps Limerick, to take the pledge directly from Father Mathew. Some priests in the town did give the pledge, as one of the rules of the Mechanics Institute Temperance Society stated that no one could be admitted unless he had taken the pledge from Father Mathew 'or any one of the Catholic clergymen in the town who are appointed to distribute the medals'.[10]

His invitation to Galway, as to Limerick, was to preach a charity sermon in aid of a school run by the Presentation nuns. He must have been expected to stay on after the sermon to give pledges, as on the same day as the sermon was announced the *Connaught Journal* drew attention to the necessity of making arrangements to avoid accidents. Clarke's Yard, Merchant Road, was acquired, and here, over three days, large numbers, reported variously as having totalled 60,000, 80,000 and 100,000, were divided up into batches of between 200 and 300 to repeat the words of the total abstinence pledge. To natives of the town were added crowds 'from the remotest parts of Connemara, and from the counties of Mayo and Roscommon'. Most people in the Claddagh took the pledge as well, but, in their case it must have been re-taking it, as it had been reported two months earlier that everyone in the Claddagh was already a teetotaller. He left Galway on St. Patrick's Day, and having stopped several times along the way to give the pledge, arrived in Loughrea late at night. At nine o'clock the following morning he began to administer the pledge from the window of a house in Artillery Barrack Square. The movement was already strong in Loughrea, many having gone to Cork to take the pledge, partly through the influence and support of some of the employers of the town and partly through the advocacy of Dr. Coen, Bishop of

Clonfert. There was agreement that large numbers came into the town from the countryside, but there was the usual disagreement about the number who took the pledge. At Loughrea, unlike Galway, some people approached Father Mathew to take the pledge in a state of obvious drunkenness, but it was noted that he refused to accept their pledge in that state. He concluded his mission to Galway with two days in Portumna. Birmingham, who accompanied him during his stay in Galway, estimated that between Galway town, Loughrea and Portumna, as well as the many villages he stopped at on the roads between the three towns, between 180,000 and 200,000 took the pledge.[11]

In Dublin, as in the rest of Ireland, the transition from the 'moderation' to the 'teetotal' principle in temperance societies in the mid-eighteen thirties was characterised by an increasing involvement of the working classes in the movement. When Hockings was there in 1838 a large part of his audiences consisted of workers. He was a particularly gifted speaker and kept his audiences' attention for a whole two hours. He dwelt on the state of the working classes in the north of England, where teetotal societies had been able to counteract the harmful effects of using malt liquors. His skilful use of 'anecdote and happy illustrations' made a deep impression on his audience, and he concluded his speech by an appeal to the working class, which, added the Dublin paper reporting it, 'we hope will be attended with good effects'. A *Dublin Evening Post* report on a procession by the Dublin Catholic Temperance Society in 1839 noted that those in it 'were of the lower order'. No doubt influenced by reports in the *Dublin Evening Post* of Father Mathew's successful crusade, interest in teetotalism among Catholics in Dublin increased greatly towards the end of 1839, so that Father O'Connell's Metropolitan Total Abstinence Society could claim 6,000 members, and this and other teetotal societies combined to form an impressive procession through the city on St. Patrick's Day, 1840.[12]

Father Mathew travelled to Dublin by coach from Cork on 28 March 1840 and preached a charity sermon at the Church of the Conception in Marlborough Street before undertaking a series of six consecutive daily meetings at Beresford Place. There, on an open space behind the Custom House, he gave the pledge to crowds that the *Dublin Evening Post* reported as totalling 50,000, a figure that was almost identical to that compiled by the Police Superintendent on duty throughout the week. In drizzling rain, Dubliners were joined by men and women from counties Meath, Kildare, Longford, Wicklow, Wexford and Carlow. Father

Mathew returned to preach a charity sermon in September. He was back in Dublin for another charity sermon in November, and a platform was again raised for him at the back of the Custom House. Lord Morpeth and Dr. Spratt were among those who took the pledge. In the course of his speech Father Mathew referred to some Dublin teetotallers who wanted to hand back the pledge to him as their employers would not retain them as teetotallers. He had no very helpful advice to offer, saying only that it would be immoral for employers to make any man do what was against his will. Despite some poor weather 33,000 took the pledge over three days.[13]

From the account given so far of Father Mathew's early travels to parts of the country where his work was most influential some patterns begin to emerge. Temperance societies had already been established in most of the towns he went to, usually founded by Protestants and dating back to the mid-thirties or earlier. More recently, control of these societies had passed to Catholics or new Catholic temperance societies had been formed, with priests in prominent positions. Temperance had become almost synonymous with teetotalism and teetotalism had become almost synonymous with Father Mathew. He was the acknowledged leader of the movement in the towns he went to: his visit merely reinforced this. Many of the teetotallers had been to Cork to take the pledge but some local priests had given it. There was a distinct impression, though, that it was somehow more beneficial to receive it directly from Father Mathew. Father O'Connell, for example, recommended that members of his Metropolitan Total Abstinence Society 'should be confirmed in their good resolves by the solemnity of pledging themselves again in the presence of the great Apostle of Teetotalism'.[14]

Father Mathew himself seems to have done nothing to prevent people believing that taking the pledge from him was more effective than taking it from a local clergyman. However big the crowds assembled to take the pledge from him, the only role given to other priests present was to organise the crowds into batches of several hundred or, on some occasions, to help relay the words of the pledge to all corners of the assembly. He was aware of his own particular power and influence. The success of the temperance movement in Ireland, he wrote to S.C. Hall, 'depends on the continuance of my exertions . . . no other individual possesses the same influence'. He was strongly opposed to charity sermons where an entry fee was charged, so the fact that he accepted an invitation to preach one in Limerick under those conditions suggests that, despite his protests, he was eager to go there to set the national crusade in motion, with himself the sole missionary. But that his awareness of having particular influence should not be dismissed as vanity is evident from the lengths he went to to avoid personal acclaim, as when he arrived a day early in Waterford.[15]

The words of the pledge were as follows: 'I promise, with the Divine assistance, as long as I will continue a member of the Teetotal Temperance Society, to abstain from all intoxicating drinks, except for medicinal or sacramental purposes; and to prevent, as much as possible, by advice and example, drunkenness in others.' Birmingham, who witnessed him give the pledge on many occasions, wrote that on the batch repeating the words of the pledge, Father Mathew extended his hand and prayed, 'May God bless you, and grant you strength and grace to keep your promise!' Birmingham added that Father Mathew pronounced the word 'drunkenness' 'as if he were loathing and execrating something'. By abandoning the earlier practice of temperance reformers, who asked for a written pledge from those about to renounce alcohol, Father Mathew was able to pledge such large numbers in a relatively small time. Once pledged, teetotallers were asked to give their names to their priests, who would then arrange for certificates and medals to be sent from Cork.[16]

The Circular from the Inspector General of Constabulary asked questions about the religious affiliation, social class and sex of those who had taken the pledge within particular police districts. The Temperance Reports, in reply, indicated that while the vast majority of those who took the pledge were Catholics, some Protestants had done so in nearly all districts and substantial numbers had done so in a few. The Sub Inspector for the City of Limerick reported that between 250 and 300 Protestants had taken the pledge there, though only two were known to have done so in Waterford. In county Tipperary, 'a few' were reported from Thurles, 30 from Nenagh, 20 from Clonmel and none from Roscrea. Bearing in mind that Father Mathew was a Catholic priest, as were most of the local officers of teetotal societies, and that some Protestant newspapers were hotile to the crusade, these figures suggest that many Protestants felt the movement to have been as anti-sectarian as Father Mathew wanted it to be.[17]

Major Volkes, a Resident Magistrate in Limerick, reported that in the city the pledge had been 'taken by all classes of artisans, by some shopkeepers and others of those ranks and generally by the ranks below them . . .' In Waterford 'respectable men above the working class' took the pledge at Bishop Foran's house in the evening when Father Mathew was in Waterford, not wishing, presumably, to join the thousands assembled to do so in front of the Court House during the day. A 'Great many' above the working class were reported to have become teetotallers in Cahir, possibly influenced by Lord Glengall, but at Thurles it was, with the exception of one or two gentlemen, 'confined to the lower classes of the peasantry and to tradesmen'. From county Galway it was reported that few above the working class had taken the pledge in Loughrea, the wives of some respectable farmers had done so in Portumna and in Gort between 16 and 20 gentlemen had enrolled, three of them Roman Catholic clergymen.[18]

Question 4 of the Circular asked 'Whether any, and what number of Women, or of Men above the working class have taken the pledge.' Some replies took this to mean that a return of all women who had taken the pledge in a district was required, while others took it to refer only to women 'above the Working Class'. The reports from Limerick and Waterford seem to have taken the former interpretation, listing 500 and 1,000 respectively. When Father Mathew was in Dublin in 1840 he heard that many ladies would join the movement if, like the gentlemen in Waterford, they could be spared having to approach the public platform. He arranged a meeting for them at the Stock Exchange and 500 joined. The Dublin correspondent of the *Nenagh Guardian* reported that afterwards

he dismissed the women with a recommendation to keep their pledges for the sake of example to others, and with much gallantry assured them that he did not administer the pledge to them because it was necessary by their habits of life, but because it would induce their husbands, brothers and friends to become teetotallers.

Almost exactly four years later in a speech in Cork he made it clear that he did not consider drunkenness a vice only of men or of the poor. 'The gentleman or lady get drunk in their parlour', he said, 'and are taken by their servant and put to bed. The poor get drunk in a public house and are turned out by the publican, they are then taken up by the police.'[19]

Children also took the pledge: Justin McCarthy did so when he was 'little more than a child', John Denvir took it three times as a nine year old when Father Mathew came to Liverpool and Susan Dowden, Richard Dowden's daughter, took it as a girl when she brought a letter from her father to Father Mathew. Some otherwise sympathetic contemporaries like John Keegan found the pledging of children 'extreme' and the hostile *Galway Advertiser* described as 'monstrous' the implicit supposition that all Irish children would become drunkards if they did not take the pledge. Father Mathew, though, placed great importance on pledging 'the rising hope of Ireland' as he called them. Seeking financial assistance to continue his crusade in 1844 he wrote that 'it is absolutely necessary that I should proceed from parish to parish through the Kingdom and in particular that I should induce all the children to take the pledge'.[20]

In commenting upon the benefits derived from Father Mathew's work, many of the Temperance Reports noted that some of the improvements had been evident even before his visit, usually dating from the time the first pilgrims went to Cork, and some saw other influences at work besides temperance. The Resident Magistrate in Thurles was Joseph Tabuteau, who knew the area well, having been there for eight years at the time. He drew attention to improvements at fairs, markets, races and on holidays, but added that rioting had been declining for some years before that and in fact had almost ceased. A similar point was made by the Sub Inspector at Newport, who, remarking that while taking the pledge had made people's conduct better, wished a share of the credit to be attributed to the 'vigilance and interposition of the Constabulary'. Tabuteau's Diary offers evidence of improvements at the five-day race meeting at Thurles. The 1839 meeting was accompanied by disorder, fighting and affrays, which were broken up by the police who arrested the ringleaders, while the event for 1840 was peaceful, with people returning soberly to their homes after the races. In Cashel people were 'becoming more orderly', with only four cases of intoxication at a fair attended by 25,000. In Nenagh people were 'becoming frugal, industrious and attentive to their families'. Major Volkes, the Resident Magistrate in Limerick, reported in March 1840 that, despite a rise in the cost of provisions (turf alone had trebled in price) the poor were less destitute than they had been because they no longer spent their money on drink.[21]

The increased industry of workers in various occupations continued to feature in accounts of the crusade for some years. The Dungarvan fishermen had been catching more fish since they became temperate, reported the *Dublin Evening Post* and went on to hope that those of Galway, 'a very drunken and obstinate generation' who ignored improved methods of fishing, might follow their example. An anonymous visitor to the Claddagh a few months after Father Mathew's visit to Galway noticed that the effects of sobriety were showing themselves in improvements to the fishermen's cottages, but the hoped-for changes in attitudes to fishing methods were not to come for many years, by which time the suburb had suffered severely from famine and emigration. The Halls drew attention to a report of the Mining Company of Ireland that attributed the improvement in the company's affairs in part to the sobriety of the miners. The 1841 report of the Waterford Temperance Society noted that 800 of the 1,000 miners in the Knockmahon mines had taken the pledge and that, from being quarrelsome and idle, they had become peaceful and industrious. The Temperance Report from Limerick city reported builders and other employers there saying that as a result of Father Mathew's work, men were worth half as much again as they had been before they took the pledge and that 'none of their work is spoiled as it used to be'. A merchant in Waterford paid teetotal seamen 5/- a month extra simply because it was in his interest to do so. Kohl had heard that many of the upper classes had taken the pledge to set an example to their inferiors, hoping that sober tenants might be able to pay the rent more regularly than drunkards. The year before Kohl was in Ireland Father Mathew had said that many of the landlords in the north of Ireland were in favour of temperance, as 'where temperance prevailed, the land was best cultured and worked, and the rents were best paid'. A number of the gentry in different parts of the country did in fact take an active interest in his work, including the Duke of Leinster, the Marquis of Landsdowne, the Earl and Countess of Kenmare, Lords Cloncurry, Glengall, Listowel and Wallscourt. Richard Allen, however, regretted that so few of the middle and upper classes supported the movement, something that was also lamented by John Cadbury after his visit to Ireland in 1842.[22]

The drink industry suffered. In Clonmel 16 pubs closed and most of the sheebeen houses had been 'obliged to give up altogether' in the five months between Father Mathew visiting the town and the Sub Inspector writing his report. A dozen closed in Nenagh while at Roscrea and Cahir, though the pubs stayed open, most of them were selling nothing but coffee. But even the life-line of coffee was cut off for the hapless publicans of Waterford, 60 of whom had to close their premises by April 1840:

some Publicans have added coffee to their business, but the Clergy have directed the Temperance Society not to partake of coffee in any house where spirits are sold — this has been scrupulously obeyed by the Society, consequently a further number of spirit retailers are expected to discontinue. The applications for Spirit Licenses heretofore averaged about twenty each quarter — at last January Sessions there was but *one*, for this coming Sessions, there are but two.

Some of them, according to a report by the Waterford Temperance Society a few years later, went in to the grocery and provisions business, and the Sub Inspector for Loughrea reported that the owner of a brewery in the town 'has discontinued his business and is talking of converting his premises into a slaughtering yard for hogs and commencing the Bacon trade'.[23]

At the beginning of 1841 it was reported that only one of Galway's three distilleries — that of the Persse family — was working, those of Lynch and Joyce having closed down. It was not unusual for a distillery to be closed for part of the year — when Dutton was working on his statistical survey in 1820 none of the Galway distilleries was in operation. The Census for 1841 records only one distiller in the town and a government return on distilleries in 1851 confirms there was only one distillery in Galway from 1841 to 1844. When Robert Charlton visited the Limerick distillery of Stein, Brown and Co. in 1842 he was happy to have found it 'now silently going into decay', having been at a standstill for some time. John Cadbury, another English Quaker, visited the distillery shortly afterwards and confirmed that it presented 'the aspect of a deserted village'. He added that he had also heard that the copper and metal cauldrons were on their way to England for melting down, which was unlikely, as the distillery was shortly to come into operation again. In the same year Kohl met a distiller who was prepared to 'extend his speculations to other fields, and to manufacture whiskey for exportation to foreign markets' to compensate for his losses. George Roe, the Dublin distiller, saw the improvements Father Mathew's work had brought about as sufficient compensation for the financial loss his business had sustained. Many of Father Mathew's immediate relations were distillers. One of his brothers had appointed him guardian of his young family, with a distillery the main asset remaining at his death. 'I could not consistently let it for the purpose of distillation, though I was offered a rent of five hundred pounds a year', he wrote later, '. . . though my poor brother never uttered a complaint, I have the sorrowful conviction that his death at the early age of 47 was occasioned by the failure of his trade.'[24]

That members of his own family incurred financial loss through his temperance crusade was often referred to by Father Mathew and to some extent disarmed his critics, as did his encouragement to publicans to take up selling provisions where the profits made would be on items more conducive to the public good. It seems highly unlikely, however, that all publicans put out of business were able to find alternative products to sell, or that all distillers were as fortunate as Kohl's informant in finding an outlet overseas or as magnanimous or patriotic as George Roe. A drunken riot that occurred when he was in Ardmore in 1842 was attributed by Father Mathew to publicans, who, he thought, had probably bribed the rioters, adding that 'he had known them to give drink for nothing on similar occasions'. In the course of following his progress around the country through contemporary newspapers and temperance periodicals I have not seen any reference to riots similar to those at Ardmore or to the distribution of free beer anywhere except in England, where, in Bermondsey in south London, a group of anti-teetotallers interrupted his meeting. The amount of beer they were carrying, the *Times* correspondent suggested, could never have been purchased by 'so low-lived and ragged a set of ruffians'. There were suggestions in the early part of 1842 that 'races and steeple-chases' were got up by publicans with a view to getting people to break the pledge and in a letter to James Haughton some time later Father Mathew expressed his concern at the extent of the opposition to his work:

The antagonists of temperance are more energetick [*sic*] than ever, and their machinations must be counteracted. Distillers and Brewers establishing anew at their own expense and risk, public houses all over the country. Getting up races and reviving the horrid amusement of cockfights, which latter, have already been attended by the most deplorable consequences.

It is possible that he exaggerated the opposition, bearing in mind that the extract quoted formed part of an appeal for money to enable him to continue his crusade, and there was certainly no opposition to his work in Ireland comparable to the riots fuelled by drink sellers in Germany in opposition to the temperance movement there around the same time.[25]

The distiller who spoke to Kohl told him that whereas he once employed 90 men in his distillery he now employed only 50, but as these were all teetotallers they could do more work than the 90 used to do. One wonders what happened to the 40 who became unemployed. It was this aspect of the movement that was later deplored by Walter Meyler, one of those arrested in the excitement of 1848 and whose uncle had an interest in George Roe's distillery. He blamed Father Mathew's work for the ruin of countless distillers, brewers, grocers and country shopkeepers, forcing most of their employees to emigrate and the elderly among them into the workhouse. Apart from its harsh consequences for many people employed in the production and sale of drink, the overall effect of the temperance movement on brewers, distillers, farmers and publicans has been seen by a modern economist as 'another twist in the deflationary spiral' of the pre-Famine Irish economy, weakening its capacity to meet the crisis of the Famine.[26]

As so many of the traditional amusements of people were bound up with drinking it is not surprising that from the earliest days of the movement an interest was taken in how these might have been affected by the widespread decrease in drinking. William Nash, the Resident Magistrate in Clonmel, wrote in 1840 that while 'Fairs or Patrons' that had been held almost exclusively for the sale of whiskey were deserted, people in his district 'still preferred Dances, hurlings, and Public houses, the only difference being that they drink Lemonade and Ginger beer instead of Malt Liquors'. In Nenagh, the 'customary amusements of hurling, ball playing etc. are conducted without quarrelling or disturbance of any kind'. From Carrick-on-Suir, where 'broils, scuffles and affrays' had ceased, it was reported that people there had no amusements at all![27]

There had been moves to abolish Dublin's notorious Donnybrook Fair before the advent of Father Mathew, but they were given new impetus by his movement. A nostalgic participant in the 'whiskey brook' of former days was disgusted to learn of 'a timperance tay party at Donneybrook' in 1841, and in order to maintain peace and order at the fair the following year 'a force of 200 police, together with the entire of the mounted force of that body' were on duty. There were 87 arrests for drunkenness, which prompted the *Dublin Evening Mail* to question the supposed benefits of Father Mathew's work. Grant attended the fair during his visit to Ireland in 1843 and noticed nobody among the 50,000 assembled to have been 'under the influence of spirituous liquors'. For the following year's fair Dr. Spratt was assured that the regulations forbidding the sale of drink between certain hours were going to be enforced, and in a field next to the Fairgreen James Webb warned teetotallers against entering the tents where drink was sold. Despite the combined efforts of the temperance movement and the Dublin

Metropolitan Police the fair and its attendant amusements continued for some years. When a committee was formed to raise funds to buy out the rights of the family that owned the site of the fair in 1855 prominent advocates of temperance in Dublin were actively involved. These included Dr. Spratt, James Haughton, Dr. Yore and the Earl of Carlisle (formerly Lord Morpeth), then Lord Lieutenant, and Father Mathew wrote a letter to the *Freeman's Journal* congratulating the people of Dublin on the abolition of the fair.[28]

The resistance of Dubliners to the abolition of Donnybrook Fair indicates a continued need for public displays and entertainments in mid-nineteenth-century Ireland and Kohl noticed how the temperance movement in 1842 was 'kept in motion' by public demonstrations, processions, meetings, festive parties, band parades, speeches, dances and noise. Malcolm has seen this aspect of Father Mathew's work as providing a substitute for the country's traditional pastimes that had been associated with drink and from which the teetotaller was necessarily excluded. For while teetotallers may have returned home sober from the races at Thurles in 1840 when the great wave of enthusiasm for temperance was at its height, Fr. Mathew was aware that to maintain them in their constancy to their pledges alternative entertainments were essential, although he personally may have had no more appetite for them than he had for the 'boastful, diffuse and exaggerated language' that characterised the handbills, tracts and newspaper copy that promoted his movement. The local temperance societies played a central role in this attempt to get teetotallers involved in alternative amusements, or, as Harrison has put it in the context of teetotalism in England, 'to enable teetotallers to survive in a drink-ridden society'.[29]

From the Temperance Reports we learn that these local temperance societies met monthly, weekly, or in some cases nightly. That for Portumna met monthly and placed great emphasis on regular attendance, with a fine of 2/6d. for missing a meeting. The society for Pallas Green, county Limerick, met weekly and, like so many others, contributed to a newspaper for the use of members. Those at Carlow and Dingle met every night, which prompted the father of a member of the Dingle Society to complain to the Head Constable of the district that his son's earnings were decreasing since he became a teetotaller as he was spending all his time at meetings! The report from Kilydysart noted that 'a kind of Brotherhood' was thought to exist between members and that from Gort explained that at meetings there members related to each other in turn the good effects temperance was having on their lives. Newspapers often referred to the proceedings at temperance meetings as 'entertainment' when, as in Cork in April 1839, all that went on was that temperance advocates made impassioned speeches. Sometimes the speeches were followed by dancing and singing, as at Charleville towards the end of 1839, when the participants retired 'highly delighted with the night's entertainment'. A report from Clifden in 1840 referred to teetotallers challenging (and defeating) non-teetotallers in a 'leaping match'. [30]

While most local societies had meeting rooms of some kind from their earliest days, with sufficient accommodation at least for members to practise their instruments and read the newspapers, a concern for the cultural content of what went on in the rooms and halls became apparent in 1842. At the beginning of that year James McKenna, at that time Father Mathew's secretary, recommended the establishment of newsrooms and libraries 'for the use of the working classes'. At the end of the year writers in the *Nation* were advocating reading rooms, museums, lectures and musical performances to replace the pastimes associated with drink that the temperance movement had taken away. Richard Allen reported that in Dublin a group of scientific lecturers, in response to a 'thirsting for mental improvement' had begun their work before large audiences at a temperance hall, which was not identified. In praising the Parent Temperance Society's band in 1844 the *Galway Vindicator* wondered 'What can be more benevolent than to confirm them in their Temperance habits, by accustoming them to the love of these innocent delights, rather than the gross sensualities of the pot house or tap room?' The Cork Temperance Institute's programme for 1845-6 included lectures on temperance and astrology, as well as one on hydropathy, the law of fluids and the steam engine, the city of Cork, and 'On the Progress of the Drama'. The last lecture was by Justin McCarthy, who later in life wrote an interesting account of the Institute, from which we learn, among other things, that many non-Catholics were members and that it 'was supported by a large number of citizens who held a certain position in Cork'. More modest temperance societies in poorer quarters of the city might not, therefore, have issued a formal invitation card like that received by Richard Dowden for a soirée there in 1845, enclosing two tickets for friends and concluding with the request, 'You will please to wear your collar.'[31]

The local temperance societies also had a role in exerting the social pressure that was so important in ensuring that members kept the pledge. Apart from the positive influence of the feelings of 'Brotherhood' noted

in Kilydysart, where belonging to a closely knit group might have deterred a waverer from abandoning his pledge, there were, it was reported
from Mountmellick, 'persons nominally appointed to watch the public
houses and report any of the members who frequent them'. The Resident Magistrate from Carrick-on-Suir emphasised the importance of public
opinion as a factor in keeping teetotallers from breaking the pledge, and
the small number who violated it in Waterford city were 'reported to
the clergy by the members of the Society, and the fear of this had a
wholesome effect upon its members'. That social pressure was a factor
in maintaining the movement is evident from newspapers. There was a
report in 1840 that no one could enter a public house in Ballinasloe
without attracting attention, and in the same year a traveller through
Tipperary who asked for a glass of whiskey in a shop was told not to
speak of such a drink locally 'or you'll be kil't'. At the end of 1839 a
Bunmahon miner reported with pride how a drunk was ducked in the
sea by teetotaller miners and at Callan in March 1840, Father Mathew
himself told, with apparent approval, how a drunken man was sprinkled
with cold water. In a speech at the end of the same year he told the
story of a woman seen drunk in Clonmel. The indignant onlookers, though
they did her no physical harm 'expressed their contempt so strongly that
she was obliged to go into a house to avoid them'. The speech was greeted
by cheers from his Cork city listeners and Father Mathew added, in what
appears to be terms of regret, that the sight of similar drunkenness in
Cork would have been treated as a joke. There were reports of actual
violence against teetotallers who broke their pledge in Nenagh and
Carrick-on-Suir, and in Ballina a woman was pelted with missiles and
dragged along the ground by teetotallers who thought she was drunk,
although the correspondent of the *Mayo Constitution*, who reported the
event, thought she was perfectly sober.[32]

Sometimes social pressure took a lighthearted form, as when a young
gentleman, according to Father Mathew, refused to marry any lady unless
she was a teetotaller. It could also take the form of competition between
temperance societies in different towns, as McCarthy explained, 'a village
would have felt ashamed of itself if it could not establish a temperance
hall and marshal a temperance band'. The movement was strongest in
the towns, Lord Landsdowne told the House of Lords in 1843, because
there 'the people were placed under the influence of public opinion'.
In some places social pressure was aided by traditions of abstinence in
local folklore, as in the parish of Killaloe, county Clare, where it was

believed that the Dalcashians abstained from drink at times of war with the Danes.[33]

Kohl acknowledged that temperance compaigners in Ireland made use 'of the services of those great declamatory organs, the daily and weekly journals in which eulogistic and frequently exaggerated reports of their proceedings are inserted'. The *Dublin Weekly Herald*, the Temperance newspaper that had succeeded the *Irish Temperance and Literary Gazette* in November 1838 complained a year later that while publicans may well patronise many newspapers, such newspapers were doing their patrons no service by not reporting the progress of temperance. The *Herald* itself had been slow in recognising the significance of Father Mathew's work, and when it did, expressed reservations about taking the pledge on impulse rather than through conviction. It was the provincial newspapers that took the lead in publicising the work of Father Mathew in its early stages. As noted in Chapter 2 the *Cork Standard* reported his earliest meetings, followed by the *Southern Reporter*, described by Wendele in 1839 as 'a whig-radical journal', and the conservative *Cork Constitution*. These were followed by, among others, the Conservative *Limerick Chronicle*, the liberal *Limerick Reporter*, the *Waterford Chronicle*, the *Galway Patriot*, the *Connaught Journal*, the *Kilkenny Journal* and *Wexford Independent*. Newspapers supporting the cause in Tipperary included the *Nenagh Guardian*, followed by the *Nenagh Gazette* when it was founded in 1841, the *Tipperary Free Press*, a newspaper that 'voiced popular feeling in burning language', and the *Tipperary Vindicator* from 1844. The *Dublin Evening Post* carried reports of the temperance work of both Father Mathew and Father Foley from the autumn of 1839, but the reports were mostly taken from provincial newspapers. The *Post*, *Freeman's Journal* and *Dublin Evening Mail* gave reports of his visits to Dublin in 1840. As the movement grew and suspicions were aroused in some quarters that temperance was somehow associated with Repeal, Conservative newspapers like the *Mail* (described by Grant as 'ultra-Tory' in its views) and *Constitution* withdrew their support, although some, like the *Limerick Chronicle* and *Nenagh Guardian* did not. It needs perhaps to be remembered, though, that a newspaper like the *Connaught Journal*, which gave excellent coverage to Father Mathew's work in Galway, had a circulation of only 2,500 in the middle of 1840.[34]

Father Mathew acknowledged the help his movement received from the press on his first visit to Dublin in March 1840. At Loughrea at the beginning of 1842 he thanked the press of Connaught and the *Clare*

Journal and paid a tribute to Mr. Meany, a reporter on that paper, who was a teetotaller. Efforts were clearly made at a local level to cultivate the interest of newspapers. Among the guests at the large Temperance Tea Party at O'Reilly's Great Room, Athlone, on 30 October 1840 were the proprietors of the *Roscommon Journal* and the *Athlone Sentinel*. Mr. Campbell of the *Galway Vindicator*, was called upon at the Mechanics Institute's Temperance Festival in Galway in 1841 and was 'most kindly received'. The *Connaught Journal* was sufficiently interested in the movement to print a pamphlet on its progress by John O'Neill of Bunowen Castle. The issue of the *Wexford Independent* for 15 April 1840, the week after Father Mathew had visited Enniscorthy and Wexford town, had half of its four pages devoted to temperance news and events, including a biography of Father Mathew. Despite this, Father Mathew gave the impression at Leeds in 1843 that the support his movement got from Irish newspapers was less than the teetotal movement got in England. This can hardly have been true. Although there were ten newspaper proprietors among Harrison's occupational analysis of prominent teetotallers in England between 1833 and 1872 there was no equivalent there of the detailed reports Father Mathew's meetings and missions received in the national and provincial newspapers in Ireland. This continued up to, during and after the Famine, though with progressively less space given to the coverage of meetings and with the Dublin newspapers more interested in Father Spratt's temperance work from 1845 onwards.[35]

While temperance societies could provide alternative entertainments to drink-related pastimes and could, aided by civil and religious authorities and a generally sympathetic press, exert social pressure on waverers to prevent them breaking the pledge, they could also provide tangible evidence that it was better to be a teetotaller than not to be one. Though he was careful to steer clear of party politics, as will be seen in Chapter 5, Father Mathew was nevertheless a believer in that social mobility which Harrison has seen as characteristic of early teetotal meetings in England. By investing their money in their children's education rather than by spending it on drink, he told the meeting at Beresford Place during his first trip to Dublin in 1840, teetotallers might see some of their offspring

brought up as counsellers; some as doctors; and perhaps it might be that a member of this society, however originally humble, by persevering, would live to see his son raised to the exalted station of a judge of the land. But to this, the drunkard could never raise his prospects. In fact, he had no prospects whatever.

At Enniscorthy a week later he told the story of a 'miserable object' from Kilrush who took the pledge from him in Cork. Meeting him a year later Father Mathew found his appearance to have improved so much that he thought he was talking to his son. The Resident Magistrate at Pallas Green, county Limerick, noted that people were not only better dressed but improved in their looks.[36]

Those who had raised themselves up by their own exertions were the sober, he said in Cork at the end of 1840 and at Toomyvara the following year he promised his audience that the temperance pledge would be a means of advancing them in the world. And during the Famine he told a meeting at Ballintemple that temperance was the basis of worldly prosperity. Even beggars were convinced, as Kohl observed, that wearing a temperance medal would lead to an increase in the alms they received, as donors felt the money would go towards improving the beggars' condition rather than on drink. One of Father Mathew's Dublin supporters, Father John Miley of the Metropolitan Church, believed that the temporal advantages of sobriety would have been sufficient to ensure that teetotallers would persevere, and newspapers friendly to the movement often pointed to similar benefits. Marriage had decreased in the areas where the movement was strongest, reported the *Morning Register* in 1840, taking for granted the benefits that might accrue from slowing down the population growth. An editorial in the *Freeman's Journal* the following year drew attention to the improvements temperance brought to the health of the poor, 'and to them health is money'. Both the manager and physician of Malcomson's cotton factory at Portlaw, county Waterford, confirmed that the health of the workforce there improved since they had become teetotallers.[37]

Visible evidence of the increased prosperity of teetotallers might have been found in increased deposits entered in savings bank paying-in books but many police districts in Tipperary, for example, were unable to furnish any information under this heading on the Chief Constable's Circular because there were no savings banks in most rural areas. The Sub Inspector for Nenagh reported that the local temperance society, a particularly active one, had £60 on deposit at a savings bank and an increase in small deposits was noted in Clonmel, where it was also noted in connection with loans from the bank, that many people 'who hitherto could not get security, do not find difficulty at present procuring it, owing to their improved habits of life'. There were substantial increases in deposits in the cities. The Sub Inspector for Limerick wrote that between five and six hundred new deposits had been opened in the savings bank in the weeks immediately after Father Mathew's visit there. All three Dublin branches of the Meath Street Savings Bank Association showed increases in the number of depositors each year from 1839 to 1841. The Sub Inspector for Waterford reported that there had been no increase in deposits at savings banks in the city, but by the end of the year an increase of £275 was in fact shown, followed by an increase of a further £400 in 1841. As a final note on the reputation for thrift with which teetotallers were becoming associated, mention may be made of a remark by Brother Murphy in the Waterford Temperance Society's annual report for 1841. He estimated that the property of the labouring class in the city had increased by more than £100,000 in the past two years in the form of clothes, furniture and other domestic comforts, a figure that was repeated by James Silk Buckingham at a meeting in Exeter Hall, nearly a year later. Buckingham had spent some time in Waterford during 1842 and had attended a temperance meeting addressed by Father Mathew at Ardmore. Neither he nor Murphy explained how their figure of 100,000 was arrived at.[38]

The family of a teetotaller who died or fell on hard times was protected from the lowest levels of destitution by the teetotal societies' welfare schemes. In Waterford city at the beginning of 1840 there were plans

to create a Fund by a weekly collection of one penny for the maintenance of their sick, the burial of the dead, and for affording a small gratuity to the widow of a deceased member, to enable him to provide for herself and family.

The St. Mary's Temperance Society in Limerick covered relief of the sick and burial of the dead for a premium of 2d. per week. As well as providing for deceased members' families, the Ennis Temperance Society subscribed 'so much a month for medicine and advice for the sick poor'. Bishop Foran of Waterford drew attention to the usefulness of the benefit societies in 1842 and recommended that more teetotallers should join them. He had recently had to renew the pledge for several hundred people, he said, mostly from outside the city, and none of them had belonged to the benefit societies. As a reason for belonging to them he drew attention to the regulation which forbade anyone who broke the pledge from drawing on the funds of the benefit societies, thus offering the incentive of self-interest to supplement more idealistic motives. The

annual report of the Waterford Temperance Society for 1843 drew attention to six of these benefit societies in the city and suburbs 'under the
superintendence of their respective parochial clergymen', with a total
membership of 1,373.[39]

*   *   *

Before turning to look in detail at particular aspects of Father Mathew's
work two items remain to be considered in the present overview of his
crusade in the years leading up to the Famine. The first concerns the
extent to which his debts may have impeded the progress of the movement and the second deals with the actual number of those who took
the pledge.

In response to suggestions that he was making money from the sale
of medals and cards, Father Mathew told a meeting at Beresford Square
in 1840 that he had given away thousands of medals and cards free of
charge and that he had only begun to ask payment for the medals when
he found he was in debt. He referred to other expenses he had to meet,
like finding shelter for the thousands who came to Cork to take the pledge,
as well as providing food for them on their way home. Other calls on
his resources were noted by Bishop Ullathorne when he saw him in Cork
the following year: he was employing three secretaries, incurring charges
for postage and printing and had up to then paid £1,600 towards setting
up and maintaining temperance bands. His ex-secretary claimed that
money collected for medals often never reached Father Mathew, although
he was nevertheless obliged to pay the medal manufacturers' bills. 'He
was too liberal in his donations for charitable and other purposes connected with the temperance movement', McKenna added, 'I often
remonstrated with him but in vain. He used to reply that the cause could
not progress without this mode of action, that he was better pleased to
lose all he had in the world, than to make money by the movement.' Father
Mathew himself wrote, shortly after he was summonsed for non-payment
of a medal manufacturer's bill, that 'I'm better pleased to be in debt,
than to be open to the accusation of being influenced by mercenary
motives.' He had been expecting to become financially secure on the
death of his cousin Lady Elizabeth Mathew, but when she died at the
end of 1841 she left him nothing. This does not appear to have made
him any more provident, for he continued to order medals from manufacturers and gave many of them away free. His visit to England in 1843
was a particular drain on his resources, for, he later wrote, he was 'obliged to give cards and medals gratis to the children of all the schools, to

the poor, in a word to every one that wished to have them without payment'.[40]

He wrote to Joseph Sturge in 1845 that his family, despite having capital invested in distilleries, helped him pay off money owing to medal manufacturers. His visit to England was partly funded by £450 from the Mathew Testimonial Fund. This had raised money to set up an 'enduring monument' to his work but it was agreed instead to put the money at his disposal. The Committee in Dublin were anxious that there should first be some enquiry into his chaotic financial affairs as 'it is not only necessary to pay his debts, but to set Father Mathew on his legs so that he can go on independently and unencumbered'. He was touchy about any interference in his financial affairs, but the amount raised, once expenses had been met, was in any case inadequate to clear his debts. When he received his summons for debt the aged Maria Edgeworth regretted that his power for doing good in the future might be impaired. And she was right. 'The agents in great public movements cannot proceed without money', Father Mathew wrote to James Haughton in a letter in which he drew attention to the importance of revisiting those areas where he had established the movement. For, while local temperance societies could offer their members mutual support, they tended to operate in isolation without any administrative structure to connect them to each other or to any system of regulation or control other than a visit from Father Mathew. When these visits had to be curtailed the movement inevitably suffered, depending so much as it did on the charisma of one individual. A public appeal in Cork, several meetings in Dublin and an efficiently organised subscription in England were together sufficient to put him back on his feet for the time being, but financial difficulties were to continue to impede the progress of the crusade.[41]

An accurate assessment of how many took the pledge would be impossible but by March 1840, Father Mathew himself was able to claim that more than 700,000 had done so. Bearing in mind that 150,000 may have taken it in Limerick alone the previous December, the figure of 700,000 may be accepted as fairly reliable, and may, indeed, be considered the *last* reliable figure. Conflicting numbers given by different newspapers have been noted already, and while the figures were not always as diverse as in the reports from Galway, there was some discrepancy in reports from most places and little information on how the figures were arrived at. An exception was in London, where a Rev. R.G. Smith, together with some assistants, attended all of Father Mathew's meetings and counted everyone who took the pledge at each meeting. In Dublin the numbers recorded by the Metropolitan Police corresponded almost exactly with those of the *Dublin Evening Post* but there was no indication in the Police Superintendent's report as to how his daily returns were arrived at, and it is possible that they were given to him by the organisers or even taken from the newspapers. Returns of numbers taking the pledge at meetings, in any case, while a barometer of enthusiasm for the movement at different times in different places, can offer little help in determining the total number who became teetotallers. In the first place the numbers taking the pledge were not always reported, and even when they were, there was usually no distinction made between those who were taking it for the first time, those who were taking it because they had previously taken it but had broken it, and those who were taking it for the second time so that they might be 'confirmed in their good resolves' by taking it direct from Father Mathew, as Father O'Connell's teetotallers did in Dublin. In March 1840 the *Nenagh Guardian* referred to men who, taking the pledge while drunk in Parsonstown on one day, travelled the following day to take it while sober from Father Mathew at Nenagh. Were they recorded twice in the register of teetotallers kept in Cork?[42]

If they were they would have been contributing to part of what Malcolm has called Father Mathew's 'phantom army' which consisted of those for whom certificates were requested from Cork but who never actually received them. But certificates for them would not have been requested from both Parsonstown and Nenagh temperance societies, so they would probably have appeared once only on the register. On the more general point of a 'phantom army' it may be questioned whether those for whom certificates were requested but who never received them were necessarily 'phantoms'. The register, as we know from those who saw it, was a list of the names of those who had taken the pledge. Cyrus Clark, for example, saw his servant's name entered as number 600,001 in February 1840. Either he took the pledge from Father Mathew in Cork and had his name entered by Father Mathew or McKenna, or he took it at one of the meetings outside Cork, when his name would have appeared on a list from his local priest or temperance society secretary requesting temperance certificates or medals. On receipt of the list, McKenna would have entered his name in the register. Whether or not he ever received the certificate hardly matters. The only circumstances under which the dispatch of numbered certificates could have distorted the total number who became teetotallers were when such certificates were ordered for people who never took the pledge or when they were ordered for the same person more than once. That many people broke the pledge and took it again is certain. Whether or not their names appeared more than once in the register is something we may never know as it has not survived.[43]

A year after Cyrus Clark examined the register McKenna, in the presence of Father Mathew, told a meeting in Cork that there were at that time 4,647,000 teetotallers in Ireland. Such a figure would have entailed an average of more than 10,000 a day taking the pledge in the course of the year. As seen earlier in this chapter there were indeed particular days on which more than 10,000 took the pledge during the year under consideration, in, for example, Galway, Nenagh and Dublin. In September 1840 as many as 90,000 were reported to have taken it in Boyle, county Roscommon, over two days. But even such large numbers on particular days would not have been sufficient to raise the daily average for the year above 10,000, taking into account pauses in the campaign and the fact that even during some of his most intensive campaigns, as on his first visit to Dublin in 1840, there were days on which the total number who took the pledge from him was well below 10,000. Following his visit to Kilkenny the local paper reported that 'since his departure the Rev. J.P. O'Reilly has been engaged from morning to night in the same holy work'. If this means, as it seems to, that local priests sometimes administered the pledge after Father Mathew's departure from their parish, and that those so pledged were added to the list of those requiring certificates from Cork, then the figure of 4 million converts to teetotallism in one year was not a totally unrealistic one, always bearing in mind that it may have included some who were taking the pledge for the second or third time.[44]

Late in 1842 Kohl quoted Father Mathew as saying there were 5 million members of the Irish Total Abstinence Society at that time. A year later Grant, seeing only five and a half million names on the registers, believed that Father Mathew's rapid movements prevented another one and a half million appearing on the lists. Speaking at Dunkerrin at the beginning of 1846, Father Mathew said that there were six million teetotallers in Ireland. The relatively small increase in the numbers who took the pledge after the spring of 1841, has led Malcolm to write of 'stagnation' having set in after that date, and as causes for this suggests the rise of agitation for Repeal and an improvement in economic conditions which 'removed some of the material motivation from pledge-taking'. Thrift as one of the motives for taking the pledge has already been considered and in Chapter 5 the relationship between temperance and Repeal is examined. Here it may be noted that by February 1841, if 4½ million people had indeed become teetotallers, nearly everyone likely to take the pledge in the country had been reached by one of his missions, with the exception of Ulster, so that gaining new recruits became progressively more difficult, with membership numbers consequently increasing at a much slower rate. Newspapers showed a declining interest in giving full details of his visits, but this may be because such visits simply became less newsworthy as time went on rather than a reflection of a lack of enthusiasm on the part of teetotallers. The reports from Magistrates and County Police Inspectors in 1843 make no reference to a decline in enthusiasm for teetotalism, and the impression gained is that throughout the country temperance societies were vibrant institutions, with predictable exceptions. These included Tuam and Longford, which were located in dioceses where Father Mathew was not allowed to carry on his crusade.[45]

From 1843 onwards the movement undoubtedly suffered from Father Mathew's inability to revisit regularly those areas where the movement had taken root but where regular personal appearances by the acknowledged leader of the movement were needed to maintain enthusiasm. Journalists noticed this and remarked on it. In April 1844 the *Galway Vindicator* noticed drunken incidents in the vicinity of Galway town and suggested there was need for another visit from Father Mathew, though it added that teetotalism 'is well sustained among the members of the three temperance societies of the town'. Two of the incidents were fatal: a pledge-breaker from Bohermore fell into the Dock Basin running away from the Coast Guard Watch and a young man was killed, reputedly by pledge-breakers, in an incident arising out of a hurling match. The claim that teetotalism was still strong in the town is substantiated by the attendance of 500 at the soirée celebrating the seventh anniversary of the Parent Temperance Society. The Society's band was present at a soirée organised by the Cork Temperance Society at their Middle Street premises in March 1845, and they were also in attendance when O'Connell visited the town four months later. Speeches at the soirée are instructive as to the state of the temperance movement in the town as the Famine approached. The president, Father B.J. Roche, in proposing a toast to Father Mathew, expressed the hope that he might soon be free from his financial embarrassments and able to come to Galway again, when he would find the teetotallers resolved to persevere in the system of temperance which had done so much good for themselves, their families and the community at large. The determination of the people of Galway to keep the pledge was stressed also by Rev. A. Killeen of the Parent Temperance Society, and the vice-president of the Galway branch of the Cork Temperance Society said that nowhere in Ireland could men be found more devoted to the cause of temperance than in Galway. And while hopes of a unified temperance movement in the town had not been realised in that there were still three separate societies, Father Roche in his speech drew attention to the 'active co-operation' of the other two temperance societies in the town in promoting the cause of temperance. Shortly before Father Mathew returned to the town in January 1846 after a long absence the *Vindicator* drew attention to the many pledge-breakers in Galway and encouraged them to avail of Father Mathew's visit there 'to redeem yourselves from infamy'. At the evening entertainment in his honour he referred to the reports of lapses but declared that this was not the case: people were more ardent than ever and converts were every day increasing, and on his return to Cork went so far as to say at the Corn Exchange there that his impression on the way back from Galway to Cork was that drunkenness had been banished from Ireland.[46]

When Father Mathew was in Dublin in 1844, large numbers took the pledge at Kinsealy and Finglas including, according to James Haughton, many who had not done so before. This suggests that at this and similar meetings many of those who took the pledge had taken it before. When he was in Kingstown in October 1845, half of the 10,000 who took the pledge were reported to have been doing so for the first time. There may be evidence here, perhaps, that the movement was still an active one and that so many had already taken the pledge that those doing so for the first time were worthy of special mention.[47]

Father Scanlan's energies in Nenagh continued until he was promoted in 1844, by which time the number of public houses in the town had been reduced from 113 to 18. In reply to a testimonial delivered to him on his departure from Nenagh he made the observation that as more converts were made to teetotalism, the sacraments were more frequented, so that 'religion had a new conquest in every convert to teetotalism'. Enthusiasm continued into the following year, when 15,000 were reported to have taken the pledge on the first Sunday in April, when Father Mathew came to preach a sermon in aid of Nenagh chapel. A temperance procession, which Father Mathew was unable to attend, was held there the

following month, and the list of participants reveals that the movement had
retained something of its strength among the tradesmen of the town, whose
conversion from 'continual drunkenness' had been reported by the Resident Magistrate five years earlier. Marching under their respective flags were
weavers, masons, smiths, carpenters, painters, bakers, tailors, butchers, brogue-
makers, nailors and of course labourers. Later in the day 'pledge breakers
and habitual drunkards' got up a fight in the town and some were taken
into custody. When the police patrolling the town were attacked later in
the evening, their drunken assailants were described as coming from the
countryside, while their rescuers were the teetotal townspeople. More details
of the incident, and an indication of similar attitutes elsewhere would be
needed before suggesting this as evidence that the movement was better
supported in the towns than in the countryside.[48]

No doubt there were relapses in other parts of Tipperary, although Father
Mathew was reluctant to believe that they could have been on anything
but a very small scale. Speaking at the Corn Exchange in Cork on New
Year's Day 1845 he said that he had recently returned from a large
temperance meeting in south Tipperary and he had heard nothing of any
pledge-breakers there. At a meeting at Dunkerrin early in 1846 he felt
confident enough to claim from documents in his possession that not one
teetotaller in 500 violated the pledge. This was a particularly surprising
claim at that place and at that time as, at nearby Roscrea a few months
previously, the parish priest and curates had reported evidence of attempts
at 'swearing the people not to pledge'. While the number of lapses were
certainly greater than the optimistic proportion conceded by Father
Mathew, there are indications that enthusiasm for teetotalism was maintained in many areas at a level comparable to the early days. At Thurles,
for example, drinking premises had been reduced by more than half between 1838 and 1845. Drinking must have been fairly moderate in the
32 public houses remaining, as the Resident Magistrate for the area, who
had replaced Tabuteau, was able to write the following about a period
that included Christmas 1844 and New Year 1845:

17 persons only have been brought before the magistrate, *twelve* of whom were
itinerants. When it is considered that the population of this town exceeds *seven
thousand inhabitants*, and that *two markets* are held *weekly*, at which a *vast
concourse* of the adjoining tenantry attend, and also a monthly fair, I think
I could not adduce a more convincing proof of the fixed fidelity with which
the temperance pledge is observed. I do not know nor have I heard of a *single
instance* of its violation in this locality.[49]

CHAPTER 4

Drinking and Crime

In the last chapter it was noted that, in response to the Chief Constable's circular, many of the Temperance Reports drew attention to the reduction in drinking and drunkenness in police districts in the southern counties. Many also referred to improvements in public behaviour at fairs and markets, although some were careful to add that other factors, like better policing, had also played a part in bringing about these improvements. As regards crimes arising out of drunkenness, several reports, like those from Kilkenny and Lismore, were emphatic that these had been reduced 'since the introduction of the Temperance Society' and the sub officer from Skibbereen was even prepared to quantify the improvement, reporting that in his district such crimes had been reduced by half. Other officers were more cautious. The report from Ballickmoyler, for example, felt it was too early to comment on the subject, that from Kanturk believed it made no difference, while the Sub Inspector for Bruff drew attention to the difficulty of assessing the number of crimes arising out of drunkenness because, he wrote, drunkenness 'was often made the excuse for having committed violence where the individual was in reality not under the influence of intoxication at the time'.[1]

Even before the advent of Father Mathew there were claims from temperance advocates that most crime was caused by excessive drinking. John Edgar told the Select Committee on Drunkenness in 1834 that the propensity to drink among the Irish was 'very extensively connected with crime' and Father John Kenyon, the future nationalist, told a meeting

86

of the Ennis Temperance Society in 1837 that three quarters of Irish crime could be attributed to alcohol. Father Mathew himself believed that nobody had a better nature than the Irish people and that the atrocious crimes they committed all originated in 'the use of intoxicating drinks'. He told his audience at Maynooth in 1840 that taking the pledge would free them 'from the commission of crime, for it is drunkenness that leads to crime'. He liked to cite the view of judges that drunkenness was the cause of most crimes, and was proud of the fact that by the end of the summer of 1840 'there was not a single teetotaller prosecuted before a jury for any crime throughout the entire kingdom'.[2]

When teetotalism was adopted by an increasingly large number of people for the first time, as it was at the end of 1839 and in the early months of 1840, and when many of those who became teetotallers had previously had a reputation for drunkenness, it is to be expected that there would have been a reduction in those crimes directly related to drinking. There were, for example, 23,227 convictions for drunkenness in Ireland in 1840 compared with 38,678 in 1839. In Limerick, the scene of Father Mathew's first mission outside Cork in December 1839, the reduction is more dramatic. From an average of 165 for the first eleven months of 1839 the number convicted for intoxication fell to 31 in December, and continued at the low level of an average of 63 per month for the first six months of 1840. Few would dispute the claim that Father Mathew's work was the main cause of the decrease. But the claim that his work may have caused a reduction in serious crime is more controversial. There was a very large decrease in the amount of alcohol consumed in Ireland in the years between 1839 and 1845 while at the same time there was a reduction in the incidence of serious crimes. The present chapter is primarily concerned with the extent to which it may reasonably be said that Father Mathew's temperance movement may have been responsible for this reduction in crime. First, however, it is necessary to make a few observations on the reduction of spirits consumption, both in the country as a whole in the years 1839-45 and in two areas to which Father Mathew himself paid particular attention between 1840 and 1842.[3]

The decrease in the amount of spirits consumed in Ireland from the late eighteen thirties onwards (Table 4.1) took place despite an increase in population, thus increasing the real percentage decrease. It should be noted, however, that in the year of the biggest decrease — 1840 — there was a reduction in the rate of duty on spirits. There was a further reduction in 1842 but this only lasted until the following year when there

TABLE 4.1

GALLONS OF LEGALLY DISTILLED SPIRITS CONSUMED
IN IRELAND 1832-1845

		% movement
1832	8,657,756	
1833	8,168,696	5.6 decrease
1834	9,708,416	18.9 increase
1835	11,381,223	17.2 increase
1836	12,248,772	7.6 increase
1837	11,235,635	8.3 decrease
1838	12,296,342	9.4 increase
1839	10,815,709	12.0 decrease
1840	7,401,051	31.6 decrease
1841	6,485,445	12.4 decrease
1842	5,290,650	14.4 decrease
1843	5,546,483	4.6 increase
1844	6,451,137	16.3 increase
1845	7,605,192	17.9 increase

Source: *Return of the Total Number of Gallons of Spirits distilled and charged with duty . . .
1800-1845.* P.P. 1846 (361) xliv, p. 427.

was a return to the 1840 rate. Annual detections for illicit distillation
increased from 1,004 in 1840 to 3,456 in 1843, the highest of any year
since 1835, and began to decrease again after 1843, the year the duty
was reduced. Within the overall context of a substantial reduction in spirit
consumption in the seven years from 1839, rises in the rate of duty were
accompanied by reductions in the amount of legal spirits consumed and
increases in the number of illicit still detections, while reductions in the
rate of duty coincided with increases in the amount of spirits drunk and
decreases in the number of detections. The effects of changes in the
rate of duty clearly had some influence on the reduction of spirits consumed, although evidence from the Temperance Reports, newspapers
and travellers confirm that the main cause of the decrease was the work
of Father Mathew.[4]

Given the unique influence of Father Mathew himself on the move-ment at the time it may be useful to consider briefly the variations in spirit consumption in Dublin and Galway, two areas he visited often be-tween 1840 and 1842, with a view to exploring any possible relationship between a mission from Father Mathew and drink consumption in par-ticular areas. Table 4.2 shows that a large decrease in spirit drinking took place in the city and county of Dublin during the six and a half week period, known as the 'Round', following Father Mathew's first visit to Dublin at the end of March and the beginning of April 1840. The decrease was in fact more than two and a half times the decrease nation-ally during the same period — 38.5 per cent compared to 15.2 per cent for the country as a whole. The only area in the country that showed a larger decrease in spirit consumption during the same Round was Wex-ford, and Father Mathew was actually in county Wexford during that period. The extent of the decrease may have been influenced to some limited extent by an increase of 4d. per gallon in the rate of duty towards the end of the Round in question, but this would have affected all areas

TABLE 4.2
LEGAL SPIRITS CONSUMED IN THE DUBLIN EXCISE AREA 1840-42

6½ week periods	gallons	6½ week periods	gallons
5 Jan-19 Feb 1840	249,934	5 July-22 Aug 1841	179,787
19 Feb-5 Apr 1840	218,323	22 Aug-10 Oct 1841	172,014
5 Apr-20 May 1840	134,251	10 Oct-20 Nov 1841	168,649
20 May-5 July 1840	148,271	20 Nov-5 Jan 1842	192,209
5 July-22 Aug 1840	173,799	5 Jan-19 Feb 1842	192,793
22 Aug-10 Oct 1840	176,701	19 Feb-5 Apr 1842	146,804
10 Oct-20 Nov 1840	142,328	5 Apr-20 May 1842	126,779
20 Nov-5 Jan 1841	193,094	20 May-5 July 1842	125,910
5 Jan-19 Feb 1841	157,699	5 July-22 Aug 1842	146,937
19 Feb-5 Apr 1841	142,759	22 Aug-10 Oct 1842	140,471
5 Apr-20 May 1841	144,032	10 Oct-20 Nov 1842	150,450
20 May-5 July 1841	141,035	20 Nov-5 Jan 1843	176,875

Source: *Spirits (Ireland)* P.P. 1843 (75) Ll, pp. 347-8.

of the country equally. That this decrease in consumption was not an annual event for the time of year is suggested by the figures for 1841, when there was an *increase* in consumption during the equivalent Round, and those for 1842, when there was a decrease of less than half that for the country as a whole. Over the whole two years there was a decrease in consumption, punctuated by increased figures for the Rounds that covered the Christmas period and influenced from March 1842 onwards by the large increase in duty that was introduced in that month.[5]

From Table 4.3 it would seem that there was a significant decrease in the consumption of legal spirits in the excise area of Galway, which included most of the county, in the period following Father Mathew's visits to Gort, Galway, Loughrea, Portumna and surrounding areas in the early part of 1840, helped to some extent by a 4d. rise in the rate of duty on spirits in May 1840. No noticeable decrease in spirits consumption seems to have followed his visit to Galway in October 1840, nor that of January 1842 when the amount consumed was the highest in any period since early 1840. The large decrease shown in the figures from April 1842 are as likely to have been caused by a further one shilling increase in the rate of duty imposed in March 1842 as by Father Mathew's influence. His visit in September 1842 seems also to have had little influence on the spirits consumed. Spirits on which no duty was paid continued to be produced, especially in the western part of the county. In April 1842 there were seven people in Galway gaol for this offence, and a year later there were twelve.[6]

Perhaps the most striking thing about both tables is that in two areas where the temperance movement was strong, where Father Mathew was nurturing it with personal visits and where large numbers were coming forward on each occasion to take or retake the pledge, a large amount of spirits was still being consumed. In Dublin this came to as much as $3\frac{1}{2}$ gallons per head of population per year, considerably more if children and teetotallers are excluded. To this must be added illegally distilled spirits (less in Dublin than Galway) and other alcoholic drinks like wine and porter. Guinness's brewery alone sold 4 million pints in the Dublin area in 1841. The only pattern about Father Mathew's influence to emerge from the two areas is that while an appreciable decrease in spirits consumption followed an initial crusade in an area, subsequent visits were less effective.[7]

*   *   *

Geoffrey Pearson has written that crime statistics 'are notoriously unreliable as measures of the actual extent of criminal activity'. An

TABLE 4.3
AMOUNT OF LEGALLY DISTILLED SPIRITS CONSUMED IN GALWAY EXCISE AREA 1840-42

6½ week periods	gallons	6½ week periods	gallons
5 Jan-19 Feb 1840	22,028	5 July-22 Aug 1841	14,852
19 Feb-5 Apr 1840	15,381	22 Aug-10 Oct 1841	16,471
5 Apr-20 May 1840	14,555	10 Oct-20 Nov 1841	18,837
20 May-5 July 1840	10,357	20 Nov-5 Jan 1842	20,800
5 July-22 Aug 1840	11,900	5 Jan-19 Feb 1842	21,718
22 Aug-10 Oct 1840	11,817	19 Feb-5 Apr 1842	16,331
10 Oct-20 Nov 1840	16,784	5 Apr-20 May 1842	12,785
20 Nov-5 Jan 1841	16,397	20 May-5 July 1842	10,426
5 Jan-19 Feb 1841	17,252	5 July-22 Aug 1842	11,799
19 Feb-5 Apr 1841	19,928	22 Aug-10 Oct 1842	14,918
5 Apr-20 May 1841	14,437	10 Oct-20 Nov 1842	16,168
20 May-5 July 1841	11,858	20 Nov-5 Jan 1843	18,428

Source: *Spirits (Ireland)* P.P. 1843 (75) Ll, p. 347.

extreme response to this unreliability is to dismiss them altogether, taking the view that 'the criminal statistics have little to tell us about crime and criminals in the nineteenth century'. A more positive approach is to accept that these figures do in fact exist, that they are not totally reliable, and from there try to identify in what respects they are weak and 'to discuss the difficulties and dangers in utilising them, showing how they may be circumvented'. These difficulties include public attitudes to crime at different times, the efficiency of the courts in the administration of justice, the effectiveness and consistency with which the police enforce the law, as well as the consistency and uniformity of their reports on the crimes committed in their various police districts. In the case of Ireland it is reasonable to suppose greater reliability in the figures on the last two counts, relating as they do to the police. An efficient national police force was in operation in Ireland throughout the period under discussion, whereas in England and Wales no comparable unified system existed and many areas had no police force at all. While variations in

TABLE 4.4

SELECTED OFFENCES REPORTED TO THE POLICE JULY 1836 - DECEMBER 1839

	Homicide	Firing at the person	Assaults on police	Incendiary fires	Robberies	Killing, cutting or maiming cattle	Demand or robbery of arms	Riot & faction fights	Rescuing prisoners & resistance to legal process	Appearing armed
1836										
July-Dec	105	36	57	158	318	187	54	141	77	38
1837										
Jan-June	126	29	45	169	430	220	119	80	70	81
July-Dec	102	62	40	285	297	173	127	95	61	29
1838										
Jan-June	113	19	49	233	237	139	75	64	42	18
July-Dec	128	28	35	222	155	159	101	61	28	27
1839										
Jan-June	111	28	49	245	198	191	75	58	26	35
July-Dec	70	28	46	164	173	238	76	45	31	26

Source: 'Return of all Outrages and Offences of which special report has been made to the Constabulary Office from the 1st day of July 1836 to the last day of March 1840.' P.R.O. (L), H.0. 100 262.

(92)

the vigour and efficiency with which the law was enforced may still have persisted, and while there was no doubt some variation in the degree of accuracy with which crimes were reported from the police districts throughout Ireland, a nationally organised force must have made the variations much less likely than in England and Wales.[8]

On the question of which kind of crime statistic is likely to tell us most about the amount of crime that occurred at any particular time, a useful guide to the degrees of accuracy of the various forms of criminal statistics has been developed by Gatrell and Hadden, along the lines that the further removed from the actual crime the statistics are, the less reliable they will be. 'Thus the number of offenders imprisoned will constitute less precise indices of the actual number of offences committed than the number of indictable committals; and the number of committals will in turn be a less precise index than the number of offences recorded as known to the police. The number of offences known, in short, are for most purposes the best statistics available.'[9]

The first set of criminal statistics to be examined here records the number of crimes reported to the police and as such constitutes the most reliable form of criminal statistics according to Gatrell and Hadden's guide. The crimes listed were chosen by an early biographer of Father Mathew to substantiate the claim that the temperance movement was responsible for a reduction in crime 'among those classes of the community most liable to be tempted to acts of violence or dishonesty'. He took 1837, 1838 or 1839 as the year to be compared to 1841, the year when Father Mathew's crusade perhaps reached its height.

The number of homicides, which was 247 in 1838, was only 105 in 1841. There were 91 cases of 'firing at the person' reported in 1837, and 66 in 1841. The 'assaults on police' were 91 in 1837, and 58 in 1841. Incendiary fires, which were as many as 459 in 1838, were 390 in 1841. Robberies, thus specially reported, diminished wonderfully — from 725 in 1837 to 257 in 1841. The offence of 'killing, cutting or maiming cattle' was also seriously lessened: the cases reported in 1839 being 433, and 213 in 1841. The decrease in cases of 'robbery of arms' was most significant; from being 246 in 1837, they were but 111 in 1841. The offence of 'appearing in arms' showed a favourable diminution, falling from 110 in 1837, to 66 in 1841. The effect of sobriety on 'faction-fights' was equally remarkable. There were 20 of such cases in 1839, and 8 in 1841. The dangerous offence of 'rescuing prisoners', which was represented by 34 in 1837, had no return in 1841![10]

Table 4.4 shows the number of cases reported to the police in Ireland for each of the ten offences referred to by Maguire in six-monthly periods,

TABLE 4.5

DECREASE OR INCREASE IN SELECTED OFFENCES REPORTED TO THE POLICE BETWEEN 1837 AND 1839 AND BETWEEN 1839 AND 1841

	Homicide	Firing at person	Assaults on police	Incendiary fires	Robberies	Killing, cutting & maiming cattle	Demand or robbery of arms	Faction fights	Rescue of prisoners & resistance to legal process	Appearing armed
1837	228	91	95	454	727	393	246	34	131	110
1839	181	56	95	409	371	429	151	20	57	62
1841	105	66	58	390	257	231	111	8	0	66
% decrease 1837-1839	20.8	38.5 (Increase)	0.0	9.9	49.0	9.2 (Increase)	38.6	41.2	56.5	43.6
% decrease 1839-1841	41.9	17.9 (Increase)	39.9	4.6	30.7	46.2	26.5	60.0	100.0	6.5 (Increase)

Source: As for Table 4.4 and Maguire, *Father Mathew*, pp. 200-201.

(94)

from July 1836 to December 1839. It is clear from the Table that there was a decrease in most of the offences over the period (the agrarian offence of killing, cutting or maiming cattle being the only one to show a substantial increase). A decrease in the occurrence of these crimes was already in motion by 1839, then, before Father Mathew's work could be expected to have had any significant influence on the country as a whole. Table 4.5 illustrates the extent of this decrease, by calculating the percentage reduction in the numbers for each offence between 1837 and 1839, and between 1839 and 1841. For half of the offences the decrease for the earlier period was greater than for the later. While making no claims to conclusive proof, there is at least a very strong suggestion here that the improvements attributed to the beneficial effects of temperance, insofar as they relate to a reduction in crime, were already well under way before Father Mathew's movement took hold of the country.

That there were improvements in Ireland under the Whig administration, at least up to 1839, is clear from evidence before the Select Committee on crime, set up in that year by Lord Roden, who was hoping to show that there had been an increase in crime while his party, that of the Tories, had been out of office. Thomas Drummond, the Under Secretary, who, under the Chief Secretary Lord Morpeth was responsible for law and order in Ireland, was able to successfully demonstrate to the Committee that, contrary to Tory expectations, the state of Ireland as regards crime during the Whig Administration was, compared with ten years previously, very satisfactory. He was able to do this by showing that, while there had been an increase in convictions for less serious forms of crime like disturbing the peace, this could be accounted for by the increased vigilance of the 'New Police' after 1836; at the same time there had been a reduction in the number of 'aggravated crimes' like murder and robbery.[11]

Perhaps because it was seen to be uniquely Irish, there is one particular type of offence, that of faction fighting, on which there is a considerable amount of contemporary evidence to supplement the criminal statistics. The returns for this form of crime do not appear on the chart signed by Inspector General of Police Duncan McGregor, on which Tables 4.4 and 4.5 are based. Instead, they are recorded under the heading 'Riots and Faction Fights', probably because while there was unlikely to be any confusion among the participants as to which were riots and which were faction fights, the authorities may not have always been able to distinguish them. In Table 4.5 I have calculated a figure for faction fights for 1837,

taking the number for that year to have represented the same proportion of 'Riots and Faction Fights' as it did in 1839, that is, just under
twenty per cent. Even if this estimated figure for 1837 casts doubt on
the reliability of the reduction between 1837 and 1839, the 60 per cent
reduction between 1839 and 1841 is unaffected. What weight should be
given to this reduction, and how much had the temperance movement
to do with it?[12]

There were certainly claims by supporters of the movement that it was
responsible for bringing an end to faction fights. A few days after Father
Mathew's visit to Limerick at the end of 1839 a speaker at a temperance
soirée in the city said that 'men who have been in faction fights for a
quarter of a century . . . now meet and shake hands in brotherly love,
which never crossed before in peace', and that this was due to Father
Mathew. Seven years later the submission of the Irish Temperance Union
to the World's Temperance Convention in London reported that riots,
faction fights and other forms of public disorder that were so common
in Ireland before the temperance movement were by that date seldom
seen. While some might attribute this to the efficient police system, the
report continued, the Union had no doubt that teetotalism should be
given the credit.[13]

In the early eighteen twenties Crofton Croker recorded the terrifying
array of weapons he saw as a group gathered for a faction fight, 'about
twenty men were armed with muskets and fowling-pieces, and others with
scythes and bayonets stuck on poles'; Le Fanu recalled that around the
same period men were actually killed in faction fights in county Limerick.
However, Mathew Barrington, Crown Solicitor for the Munster Circuit,
in his evidence before the Select Committee on Crime, saw faction fights
as having been in decline since 1829, the year of Catholic Emancipation.
George Cornwall Lewis' colourful accounts of faction fights, which first
appeared in 1836, described events from the previous decade or earlier.
Monsignor Kinsella told de Tocqueville in 1835 that village and family
vendettas were then less frequent than formerly, but still occurred. 'The
Government', he added, 'has long noted these differences without distress,
for it feared our union against itself.' With the arrival of Drummond
as Under Secretary, the police were ordered 'to intervene at the slightest
sign of a disturbance, to disperse the factions and arrest all disorderly
people'. He banned many fairs and markets where fights were likely to
occur, and by 1840, when he died, 'the factions were on the wane'.[14]

There were few more enthusiastic supporters of the temperance cause in Ireland than the Halls, and few more willing to attribute the maximum beneficial effects to the work of Father Mathew. Yet even they admitted that the police were mainly responsible for stamping out faction fighting, adding, perhaps rather confusingly, that it was temperance that enabled people to see how revolting such behaviour was. Yet if faction fights were in decline throughout the 'thirties, the most that could be argued for Father Mathew's work as a factor in reducing them is that it was instrumental in accelerating a reduction that was already well under way.[15]

*   *   *

One way of testing the claim that Father Mathew's temperance crusade was an important factor in the decrease in criminal convictions would be to see if there was a greater reduction in convictions in those areas in which his movement was strongest. The circular from the Inspector General of Police referred to earlier was sent to police districts in twelve counties, all in the southern part of the country. (These are the counties designated with the letter 'T' in column two of Table 4.6.) While Father Mathew's campaign took him to most parts of the country for one visit at least, it was in these southern counties that his main energies seem to have been concentrated. Apart from his visits to Dublin, nearly all his early itinerary was in these counties, as noted in Chapter 3. The accounts of contemporary travellers seem to confirm that the strength of the movement was in the southern part of the country. The Halls, themselves advocates of temperance, remarked on the movement's progress on many occasions in their three-volume report of their tour of Ireland. Apart from their tribute to Dr. Edgar in the account of Antrim, all their attention to the spread of temperance was confined to southern counties: Carlow, Kerry, Waterford and of course Cork, where Father Mathew's work was described in detail. Six of Kohl's eight substantial references to the temperance movement are in the 'T' counties, including a lengthy description of Father Mathew's visit to Kilrush. Like the Halls an advocate of temperance and like Kohl an admirer of the effects of Father Mathew's work in Ireland, Asenath Nicholson recorded the movement's success in Tipperary and Kilkenny. In his detailed study of the origins of the Irish temperance movement Bretherton has concluded that, in considering the spread of temperance, it was not Dublin or Belfast that led the way. Rather, 'One thinks of Waterford, of Limerick and especially of Cork, beacons that burned bright throughout their restless hinterlands.' But Dublin did have a well-organised and popular

TABLE 4.6

COUNTIES, IN ORDER OF PERCENTAGE DECREASE IN CONVICTIONS, BETWEEN 1839 AND 1845, AND THE PROPORTION OF THE POPULATION OF EACH COUNTY CONVICTED IN 1839

			Percentage movement 1839−45	Convictions in 1839: 1 in every
1	Dublin		66.8 −	150
2	Roscommon		64.8 −	632
3	King's County	T	59.8 −	391
4	Cavan		58.3 −	805
5	Clare	T	57.0 −	1,174
6	Galway	T	54.2 −	1,380
7	Antrim		50.4 −	613
8	Westmeath		49.1 −	667
9	Queen's County	T	47.1 −	462
10	Monaghan		43.5 −	1,078
11	Meath		38.8 −	839
12	Cork	T	35.9 −	698
13	Sligo		35.8 −	1,198
14	Tipperary	T	35.4 −	460
15	Longford		35.3 −	692
16	Fermanagh		34.8 −	964
17	Louth		34.1 −	705
18	Armagh		33.0 −	824
19	Leitrim		31.6 −	1,168
20	Wicklow		28.3 −	660
21	Carlow	T	28.1 −	440
22	Kilkenny	T	26.4 −	1,112
23	Donegal		25.3 −	1,976
24	Limerick	T	24.7 −	726
25	Waterford	T	18.7 −	667
26	Londonderry		14.9 −	1,033
27	Wexford	T	14.5 −	1,086
28	Mayo		10.6 −	1,954
29	Tyrone		3.5 −	1,379

30	Kerry	T	0.9 −	662
31	Down		0.7 +	1,319
32	Kildare		7.9 +	1,004
Average T counties			34.1 −	698
Average non T counties			34.7 −	958

(The averages for T and non T counties both exclude Dublin)

Source: *Comparative Table . . . results of proceedings.* P.P. 1846 (696) xxxv, p. 180; *Census for Ireland 1841.* P.P. 1843 (514) xxiv, p. 544.

temperance movement throughout the period under discussion. As the only large urban centre in the country at the time, however, it had a great many features that made it untypical of the country as a whole. While it is listed in Table 4.6 it is not included in the averages at the foot of the Table.[16]

It can be seen from Table 4.6 that all but two of the 32 counties had a decrease in criminal convictions in 1845 when compared with 1839. The *per capita* conviction rate for 1839 shown in the right hand column (arrived at by dividing the population of each county by the number of convictions) indicates that, on average, the counties in the top half of the table had a higher conviction rate in 1839 than those in the bottom half. In other words, the counties with the worst crime rate to begin with had, on average, the greatest decrease in crime. On this basis alone the counties where the work of Father Mathew was concentrated, having had a much higher *per capita* conviction rate in 1839 than the others, might be expected to show a greater percentage decrease than the other 19. (Dublin is not included in these calculations.) In fact the decrease was slightly less.

If these figures provide little evidence that crime decreased any more in the 12 counties taken together than in the rest of the country, the picture from the ranking order of counties is no better. While King's County, Clare and Galway show substantial percentage decreases, there was a bigger decrease in Roscommon than in any of the counties where the movement was strongest. Six of the 12 counties where temperance was strongest appear in the bottom half of the Table. Kerry shows almost no decrease and Wexford, where Kohl found great enthusiasm for Father Mathew's work in 1842, had only a slight improvement.[17]

*   *   *

'I cannot help saying', said Judge Crampton at the Spring Assizes at Clonmel in 1839, 'that the Mass of Violence and Blood appears to give your county a fearful Pre-eminence in Crime, a Disregard of human Life, not alone beyond every other County in Ireland, but over every other part of the civilized World.' While Tipperary's reputation for crime may literally have produced a shake in the hand of some contemporaries who recorded it, as Hoppen has noticed, when the population of the county is taken into account, it was not particularly disturbed, as Hurst has shown. It was one particular form of crime prevalent in Tipperary that earned it a reputation for lawlessness: agrarian outrage. Keegan, who worked with the Ordnance Survey there in 1840, found that apart from 'agrarian offences', Tipperary was as free from crime as any other county, and a local magistrate noted in 1842 that when houses were broken into for fire-arms, money and other valuables were often left untouched.[18]

It was a form of crime with which Father Mathew himself must have been long acquainted. In 1815 William Baker, a magistrate, was murdered while going through the demesne of Lord Llandaff at Thomastown on his way from the Special Sessions in Clonmel. Speaking at Nenagh in 1842 Father Mathew was reported as saying that he felt ashamed of the outrages that had been committed in Tipperary since his last visit. A few months later the human consequences of this form of crime were to be brought home to him further with the assassination of James Scully of Kilfeacle. The Scullys were neighbours of the Thomastown Mathews and when Father Mathew delivered his first sermon in the chapel at Kilfeacle in 1813 at least one of the Scullys was present.[19]

Though often thought of as sectarian or nationalist in origin, agrarian outrages were in most serious cases connected with the occupation of land. James Scully was not only a Catholic but a Repealer and a friend of O'Connell. Although his assassins were never brought to trial, it is most likely that they were Catholics, that the person on whose behalf the crime was committed was a tenant farmer on Scully's estate and that the motive was fear of removal or eviction arising out of the landlord's efforts at improving his property. If most publicity was given to the murder of landlords or magistrates, they were by no means the most numerous victims of agrarian crimes: two outrages that occured on 11 April 1841, indicate the more typical kind of victim. Three armed men with blackened heads fractured Thomas Burke's skull at Kilmore, near Nenagh, because 'he was employed by a man who was about to dispossess some tenants and was suspected of having given information of unregistered arms'.

At Silvermines on the same day there were assaults on the two sons of a man who had been left a farm by another son, who had emigrated to America, having abandoned to destitution his wife, from whom he had received a fortune.[20]

Table 4.6 shows that the decrease in crime in Tipperary between 1839 and 1845 was slightly above average for the country as a whole. A more detailed examination of the crime figures for the county between 1831 and 1845, however, indicates that the reduction in crime over the last seven years of the period was more striking than is suggested by the figures in Table 4.6. When the extent of crime is defined as the number of people committed for trial for every thousand of population, the extent of crime in Tipperary each year from 1839 to 1845 was never as high as double the average for the country as a whole, as it had been in each of the eight preceding years — in 1836, for example, it was more than four times, and in 1837 more than seven times the average for the whole of Ireland.[21]

Table 4.7 shows the number of offenders committed to Nenagh and Clonmel gaols every year from 1839 to 1845 for those categories of crime, usually associated with agrarian outrages. It should be noted, however, that not all such offences were necessarily agrarian in origin. Some murders, like the small number of child murders, obviously were not. Some serious assaults were the result of personal quarrels unconnected with land. When the motive for an assault is given as rape, for example, that assault has been excluded from the figures. Offenders for larceny, minor assault and riot were lodged in the County Gaol and, while some of their offences were agrarian in origin, they have been excluded so as to confine the figures to serious crimes only. [22]

The figures show that while serious outrages continued in Tipperary throughout the seven-year period, there was a reduction of considerable magnitude in the offences listed as 'Murder and manslaughter, conspiracy to murder and shooting at persons'. There was, in other words, a substantial reduction in the most serious category of crime. While there was an increase in these offences in 1845, the figure is still only just over half that for 1839, and if actual murders and manslaughters alone are extracted from the figures, that for 1845 is in fact less than half that for 1839.[23]

Agrarian crimes, wrote Father John Kenyon to a newspaper in 1842, 'spring from poverty and vary with the distress of the agricultural population'. His view was shared by another supporter of Father Mathew's

work, Father Cornelius O'Brien, parish priest of Lorrha, in his evidence
before the Devon Commission. Asked if outrages were connected with
the want of con-acre he answered that it was from the misery the people
suffer that so many outrages were committed, 'they are reduced to a
state of poverty, and are reckless'. Agrarian crimes, on this basis, ought
to have been high in 1842, a particularly harsh economic year, whereas
in fact they were particularly low, and in the case of actual murders and
manslaughters, the lowest for the seven years. As this was also the year
when the smallest amount of legal spirits was consumed in Ireland for
several decades, at least partly attributable to Father Mathew's movement, there would seem to be grounds for suggesting that there may

TABLE 4.7

**COMMITTALS TO NENAGH AND CLONMEL GAOLS FOR
SELECTED OFFENCES, 1839-45**

	1839	1840	1841	1842	1843	1844	1845
Serious assaults	31	97	32	28	31	71	41
Murder and manslaughter, conspiracy to murder and shooting at persons	183	114	63	52	55	53	104
Unlawful assembly, riotous assembly, demanding arms, appearing armed, attacking houses (compelling people to quit, etc.)	67	79	53	69	59	59	81
Arson and attempted arson, houghing and maiming cattle, threatening language and letters, unlawful notices and oaths, taking and holding forcible possession	25	33	38	21	17	18	22

Source: *Committals (Ireland)* P.P. 1840 (453) xxxviii, pp. 518, 520; 1841 (101) xviii, pp. 612, 614;
1842 (91) xxx, pp. 498, 500; 1843 (105) xlii, pp. 244, 246; 1844 (138) xxxix, pp. 246, 248;
1845 (44) xxxvii, pp. 251, 253; 1846 (696) xxxv, pp. 66, 68.

have been a connection between the reduction in serious outrages and the temperance movement in that year and indeed throughout the period under examination.[24]

One argument in favour of the view that Father Mathew's work may have had an influence on reducing the number of agrarian outrages in Tipperary is that he often spoke out against them and the secret societies who were responsible for them. As early as March 1840, the *Dublin Evening Post*, in response to the *Dublin Evening Mail*'s accusations of political purposes in the temperance movement, insisted 'that the principle on which the Temperance Societies are established is, a *total abstinence* from secret and political societies. This has been repeatedly impressed by FATHER MATHEW.' His hostility to secret societies was indeed unambiguous. If someone asks you to join one, he said eight months later in Dublin, you should denounce him to the authorities, and when he gave the same advice at Lucan in 1842 he was greeted with loud cries of 'We will.'[25]

His claim that teetotallers never took part in agrarian outrages was questioned in 1841 when it was suggested that secret societies in fact had a preference for teetotallers among their recruits because their known sobriety would make them less likely to betray secrets. Speaking at Ballyshannon, county Donegal, he said he had made enquiries to the secretaries of temperance societies and was told by them that 'not a single teetotaller had become a member of any of these illegal societies'. The information supplied to him must surely have been inconclusive, as members of secret societies who committed outrages punishable by death, transportation or prison if they were caught, were unlikely to disclose the fact of their membership of such societies to the secretary of a temperance society or to anyone else. More convincing, perhaps, was the claim contained in a resolution to obtain a life annuity for Father Mathew in 1846: no prosecution for outrage, it asserted, had ever been instituted against any member of a temperance society.[26]

A second argument in favour of the view that Father Mathew's work may have had an influence on reducing the number of agrarian outrages in Tipperary is that it was thought to have done so by some influential nationalist politicians. When Tom Steele, O'Connell's 'Head Pacificator' was in Tipperary at the end of 1844 and the beginning of 1845 he was supported and encouraged by Catholic priests throughout the county in his efforts to preserve the peace and prevent disturbances and outrages. At a meeting in Nenagh chapel, at which Steele was present, it was resolved

that however confidently they may rely on the peaceful dispositions of the people, their hopes of continued tranquillity rest mainly on the strict observance
of the Temperance Pledge, for the teetotaller, having the complete mastership
of himself, could not be seduced by the spy or the informer, or excited to the
commission of acts, whose moral enormity he is able to appreciate, and from
which he sees ruin would be brought upon himself and calamity upon [his]
beloved country.[27]

In proposing the motion Father Egan noted that secret societies often
got teetotallers to break their pledge before seducing them into committing outrages. There is in fact some evidence to suggest that, in the
northern part of the county at least, secret societies saw temperance as
a hindrance to their activities. Ribbonmen around Roscrea were found
to have been trying to get teetotallers to renounce their pledge in 1843
and a circular was issued by the Roscrea Temperance Society condemning their actions.[28]

The argument that the temperance movement could not have had the
influence claimed by Father Mathew and nationalist priests was circulated
in a pamphlet written by a Tipperary magistrate in 1842. The movement
was unfavourable to preventing disturbances, the pamphlet declared,
because the temperance societies' committee rooms were offering access to newspapers 'containing foul and seditious harangues'. The *Dublin
Evening Mail* agreed with the pamphleteer, quoting him twice in the
space of a week, and expressing regret that the Lord Lieutenant had not
barred teetotal processions. While conceding that reducing drunkenness
was desirable, the *Mail* felt temperance should be promoted through
parish teaching rather than by popular assemblies. Organisation of such
a peasantry as the Irish, the *Mail* felt, 'invariably leads to disturbance
and outrage'. The London *Morning Herald* expressed disappointment
that the temperance movement had not increased people's sense of moral
responsibility in Tipperary, adding that 'the breach of the pledge to
FATHER MATHEW is in their fanatical estimation a far more serious
offence than murder or theft'.[29]

Though it was, like the *Mail*, a Tory newspaper, the *Nenagh Guardian* disagreed with its Dublin counterpart about the pamphlet, and, having
been closer to the situation than either the *Mail* or the *Herald*, perhaps
more weight ought to be given to its opinions. It made the case for the
temperance movement as a check on immorality and crime, 'and one
that will ultimately tend to bring about the state of social order

so much desired . . .'[30]

If the 'foul and seditious harangues' that the pamphleteer took exception to were a reference to O'Connell's speeches, these could not then, or later, have been shown to encourage agrarian violence. He made a particular point of speaking out against such outrages in Tipperary. At one of his 'monster meetings' at the Hill of Grange near Nenagh in 1843, he warned against the dangers of Ribbon societies and illegal oaths and early in 1844 he warned against Ribbonmen while speaking in Clonmel. Nor would the priests who were prominent in the temperance reading rooms have countenanced violence. In the course of a long speech in the House of Lords in 1842 Lord Glengall referred to 'the youthful agitating Roman Catholic clergy of Ireland' as being unhelpful in gaining convictions against the perpetrators of outrages. He referred to two priests in Tipperary who had denounced outrages and he hoped that more would follow them. The Marquis of Normanby replied that while he had been Lord Lieutenant of Ireland (1835-39) he had received 'the most effective assistance from Catholic priests'. That day's proceedings in the Lords were terminated on their Lordships learning of an assassination attempt on the life of the youthful Queen Victoria, but enough was said to suggest that while priests may indeed have been opposed to agrarian violence, their outspoken condemnation of it and their assistance in opposing it would have been less enthusiastic under a Tory government than under a Whig government working in harmony with O'Connell. The *Dublin Evening Post* saw the Catholic clergy in Tipperary as valuable for producing tranquillity in the county. Those priests who had been assigned as agitators by Lord Glengall, it was argued, had been trying 'to assert for the people their constitutional rights, as well as to point out to them their religious and social duties'. By so doing they had increased rather than reduced security.[31]

While priests may have had some influence in countering agrarian outrages, there is no evidence that they were any more active in doing so in the seven-year period under discussion than in the years preceding it. There was, though, an increase of 100 in the number of police in the county in 1842 and this would certainly have been a factor in the reduction of outrages. The encouragement given by O'Connell and Steele and the role of the 'pacificators' of the Repeal movement to prevent outrages must also be taken into account. Venedey was in Ireland in 1843 and related how Repeal wardens had pre-empted faction fights in Tipperary and how repeal police had arrested 'several agents of the secret societies' that had been agitating among the rural population. How much of the reduction of outrages may be attributed to temperance, therefore, or indeed to any of the other factors named, cannot be determined. The balance of evidence, however, would suggest that it was certainly one of the causes of the decrease. That all the factors were subservient to the social conditions which caused the disturbances is suggested by the increase in serious outrages again in 1845 with the onset of the Famine.[32]

As in 1838 when Drummond reminded Tipperary magistrates that property had its duty as well as its rights, Baron Pennefather's charge at the Grand Jury of Tipperary in 1845 that the peace and tranquillity of the county could best be obtained and secured by the gentry performing their duties, caused a stir of excitement throughout the county. But what did the Baron prove, asked one nationalist newspaper, except that agitation must ever spring up at the beck of injustice? As suspicions of famine proved more likely to be confirmed with every report from the countryside, the *Morning Chronicle* opposed the *Morning Post*'s suggestion that the remedy for crime in Ireland was the abolition of trial by jury. On the contrary, it was argued, the cause of crime is the extreme wretchedness of the population, and their distress drives them to atrocities. In Dublin the *Pilot* was arguing that the coercion laws Ireland needed were not those contained in Peel's bill but 'laws to coerce the landlords into justice'. In this state of disharmony and in the four years of famine that followed, any influence the work of Father Mathew may have had was understandably diminished in the face of more compelling social pressures.[33]

CHAPTER 5

Teetotallers and Repealers

Father Mathew and Daniel O'Connell were sent at the same time to regenerate the nation, claimed a history of Ireland published in Boston in 1846, the one to make the country sober, the other to make it free:

Father Mathew must therefore be ranked with the repealers, though I rather fear I shall offend by the remark: yet, without his agency, O'Connell never could have called millions and half millions around him with such perfect security as he has done and continues to do, to the great terror of the English aristocracy, who see in those peaceful, sober, discontented myriads, the mighty armies which they cannot conquer, and to whom they know they must at last surrender.[1]

That Father Mathew's work would become associated with that of Daniel O'Connell was inevitable, given that both found their support, or most of it, among the Catholic population. For, while both their movements went to great lengths not to exclude Protestants, in practice very few Protestants were actively involved in either, and many were actively hostile to both. Both had considerable support from the influential Catholic priesthood and hierarchy, and, while it is true that the enthusiasm of the latter for Father Mathew's work was somewhat less than that for O'Connell's, it is also true that several bishops did publicly support his temperance crusade and that, as in the case of O'Connell and Repeal, those who did not openly support him did not openly oppose his work.[2]

O'Connell's speech at Bandon at the end of 1839, where he said he would watch the temperance societies' influence before unfurling the banner of Repeal, initiated a discussion on the relationship between the movements. The *Limerick Standard*'s extreme interpretation of the relationship, formulated after Father Mathew's visit to the city at the end of 1839 — that the two movements were joined together in a seditious conspiracy against English rule in Ireland — was taken up in the new year by the *Dublin Evening Mail*. Quoting the Bandon speech, it reminded its readers of the sobriety that preceded the 1798 Rebellion, and that temperance was 'the mask — or the instrument, rather, of some ulterior designs'. The St. Patrick's Day, 1840 procession in Limerick offered the *Standard* further grounds for concern. Led by Father Nolan on his 'charger', 15,000 teetotallers marched through the city with their medals suspended from green ribands and bands playing 'party' tunes. The *Standard*'s fears had been justified, its predictions fulfilled. 'St. Patrick's Day' and 'Garryowen' seem to have constituted the 'party' tunes, although the former seems hardly surprising considering the day and the latter considering the city. The green ribands may have seemed contentious as green had been adopted as a symbol of Irish nationalism in the '98 Rebellion, although the colour had been looked on much earlier as distinctively Irish. Colonel Piper of the 38th Regiment stationed in Limerick refused permission for his band to take part in the procession, a decision that was applauded by the *Dublin Evening Mail*, who went on to arraign the Colonels at Enniskillen and Dublin who had not acted similarly, reminding them of Wellington's opposition to teetotal societies in regiments.[3]

Apart from the 'emblems of popery' on view, the *Dublin Evening Mail* was convinced of the 'political bearing' of the Dublin St. Patrick's Day procession by the party tunes, shamrocks and the absence of crowns on flags. And how was it, it wanted to know, that of the two meetings arranged to follow the procession, the one devoted solely to temperance and addressed by Dr. Urwick was poorly attended, while the other, concerned with the repeal of the corn laws, was crowded? The *Waterford Mail* sympathised with its Dublin namesake. A society which embraces all religions should not carry emblems of a particular one, and a society that is not political should not array itself 'in the characters which the worst and most desperate of political associations have adopted'.[4]

In his St. Patrick's Day address to the Wexford Temperance Society the secretary, Mr. Hurley, refuted allegations of the 'revolutionary motive' of the movement, pointing out that sectarian and political works were forbidden in the fifteen reading rooms Father Mathew had established in Cork, with everyone seeking admission to them compelled to make a declaration that he did not belong to a secret society. He quoted from a recent speech made by Father Mathew at Nenagh where he forbade teetotallers from joining secret societies and confirmed that members of the Wexford society agreed with him.[5]

The reading rooms in Cork, under Father Mathew's direct supervision, may indeed have been able to exclude newspapers advocating political activity of a subversive nature, but not all temperance halls and reading rooms were able or willing to do so. In response to the Circular from the Chief Inspector of Constabulary, the Sub Inspector of Police in Bansha reported that in his district the temperance society newsrooms took in newspapers 'of Violent Politics' although it should be noted that neither the newspapers, nor the temperance rooms that took them, advocated violence. The same officer noted that people who took the pledge 'are bound by certain rules and regulations, exclusively relating to the maintenance of order among members of the society'. This order, together with the parades, bands and banners, flags and medals to which Tory newspapers took such exception, was seen as a threat, especially in rural areas. In Kenmare, the society, while 'ostensibly for the purpose of temperance, is also a sort of organisation of the radical party' and at the close of a temperance meeting there on St. Patrick's Day, 1840, the participants were told that they would have to prepare for the war against their enemies. Protestants in Charleville were reported as seeing the temperance society as 'a deep political, religious engine' and from Macroom came the view that the temperance society could, in the event of a disturbance, be made a very powerful 'working engine', followed by a recommendation that a watchful eye be kept on it. The report from Corofin expressed the fear that the temperance movement could become subservient to religious or political purposes by means of its organisation on a parish basis, with local committees, office holders and lists of members enrolled by parish priests. A similar concern was voiced by a newspaper report in Westmeath a few months later. Having noted that Father Mathew had told those who had taken the pledge at Castletown Delvin to give their names to the parish priests on their return home so that they could be formally enrolled, the newspaper concluded that 'the Teetotallers will turn out a fine rebel Army some bright morning'.[6]

The Sub Inspector for Abbeyleix felt that 'the Roman Catholics are quite as well organised for mischief without the Pledge as with it'. From several districts came reports of hearing references to previous Irish battles lost through drunkenness, with the suggestion that this would not be the case next time. O'Connell's election in Clare, preceded as it was by a period of sobriety, was also cited as an instance of the value of temperance in attaining political ends, a point that was also made a few months later by Father Roche at a Repeal meeting in Galway in the presence of O'Connell himself. Reports which dwelt on political aspects of temperance were in a minority overall; of the 45 replies received to the Circular only ten replied positively that there was a political motive behind the temperance movement, although a further ten replied that they did not know or had been unable to find out.[7]

If most of the police officers on the spot had some hesitancy in attributing political motives to the teetotallers, the London *Times* had not. The display of numbers and watchfulness over their words and actions were two of the expedients of the rebels of 1798, it informed the public after the St. Patrick's Day procession. The display of force on temperance marches and the widespread sobriety throughout Ireland, then, 'may have arisen from motives the reverse of moral'. It may, in other words, have been the prelude to a rebellion. The *Dublin Evening Post* refused to acknowledge any similarity between 1797 and 1840. Ireland in 1840 had a government in which she had confidence, declared the newspaper that had firmly defended O'Connell's alliance with the Whigs in Parliament. The government was committed to justice and landlords were reminded of their duties: furthermore, the nation was loyal to the Queen and had not Father Mathew refused to give the sign of peace to anyone who belonged to a secret society? Ireland's enemies, the *Post* concluded, disappointed that the Irish are not pulling each other's eyes out, must resort to attacking Father Mathew.[8]

In Sligo a few months later a Tory newspaper noted that the 'banners and other insignia' on view at temperance processions were similar to those used by the rebels of 1798 and one of the participants was reported as saying that he had not seen such a sight since the battle of Ballinamuck. When Father Mathew was approaching Galway on his way to Clifden the teetotallers of the town marched out to Oranmore to meet him, with bands and banners, and hats 'decorated with ribbons of every disloyal hue, while on their flags were apparent, in very large characters, the party characters that distinguished the rebels of '98'. In this instance, the reference to the men of 1798 was, or seemed to have been, accidental. The secretary of one of the local temperance societies explained how the Claddagh fishermen, wishing to celebrate the festival of St. John's

Eve, had collected flags from various ships in port. One of these was a Welsh flag with '98' printed above 'A.B.C.'. The letters stood for the 'Ancient Briton Society' and the number represented that of the ship launched by the Society under their mutual assistance scheme. The *Galway Advertiser*, it was argued, had inserted an apostrophe to the left of the number and omitted the three letters beneath. The *Advertiser*, by way of response, merely blamed the printer.[9]

In March 1840, the Duke of Buckingham had asked the spokesman on Irish affairs in the House of Lords if he knew anything about a temperance procession in Carlow, led by two priests. This procession had the special permission of the Lord Lieutenant, and the Duke had a placard with him that indicated as much. Lord Normanby (who as Earl Mulgrave had been Lord Lieutenant of Ireland himself until the previous year) replied that he would enquire into it and in a few days reported to the Lords that the stipendiary magistrates of Ireland had some time ago applied to the Lord Lieutenant for instructions on the proceedings to adopt for St. Patrick's Day processions. The Lord Lieutenant told them that there was nothing in the nature of temperance societies to make their processions illegal and that the magistrates should therefore not interfere, unless, of course, to prevent a disturbance. The placard the Duke had shown him was from an individual teetotaller, not from a temperance society, and the colours used in the processions were red and white, 'not tricoloured, emblematic of party feelings'. Normanby went on to say that the Lord Lieutenant had told him he had seen the Dublin procession on St. Patrick's Day, that he was pleased at the triumph of sobriety and good order it represented and that he had seen nothing in it to suggest party feeling.[10]

Normanby's remarks must have been pleasing to Father Mathew, committed as he was to keeping the movement non-sectarian and non-political. His own liberal theology may be illustrated by a sentence from a letter to a correspondent in England where he looks forward to greater toleration in religious matters: 'Not a toleration founded on indifference to all religion, but a toleration founded on the charity of the Gospel, which leads us to believe that the followers of an erroneous worship may be pleasing to the Deity from the purity of their hearts and the invincibility of their conviction.' With his Anglo-Irish background and Catholics and Protestants among his relations, his views were far from typical of an Irish priest of the time. From a speech at Monaghan in 1842 it is clear that he had tried to put them into practice throughout his life as a priest:

For 27 years I lived in Cork, and if any one says I ever interfered in the slightest degree with his social or religious feelings — if ever I interfered with the landlord or his tenant — if ever I sought to have a servant employed or disbanded on account of his religious feelings — if I refused to clothe the naked, feed the hungry, and harbour the houseless — I will hide my head with shame, and renounce the honour of being a follower of my Saviour.[11]

That he retained his reputation for anti-sectarianism to the end of his life is suggested by a request from the *Cork Examiner* on the occasion of the unveiling of his statue in Cork eight years after his death. The proceedings, it said 'should be of the very character as that of which Father MATHEW himself would have approved, were he still amongst us — that is *unpolitical and unsectarian*.'[12]

You have only to look at his face, a Tory politician was told when he suggested that Father Mathew could call the people of Ireland into battle, to see that there was nothing warlike in it. 'Party feeling lay asleep in his presence', James Haughton wrote of him and Thackeray, when he spoke to him in Cork, found him to have been unique among those he met in Ireland in that he did not talk like a partisan. Given the state of political strife in Ireland, he wrote to S.C. Hall, 'I could not effect much good unless I was untainted by party bias or control.' But it is clear that while a display of political neutrality was most conducive to his work for temperance, he had a personal dislike of party politics that predated his involvement with the movement. Maguire has recorded, presumably on the authority of Father Mathew himself or of members of the Mathew family living at the time he was writing his biography, that as a boy of eight Theobald had heard stories of the 1798 rebellion and retained memories of the revenge that followed its collapse. When to this is added the fact that at least one friend of his family was the victim of an agrarian outrage, it is not surprising that he was opposed to secret societies. Even without these experiences his moderate disposition and conservative views on most subjects except alcohol would have led him to oppose violent politics, though perhaps not with such force and consistency. But why was he so opposed to engaging in non-violent politics? A contemporary view of the reason for his aversion to party politics was given by McGlashan in the *Dublin University Magazine.* Father Mathew, he wrote, had once encouraged some poor voters to vote for a candidate favourable to Catholics, but, when the voters were evicted by their landlords, he was unable to get the candidate, who had been elected, to help them. Insofar as his own political opinions could be inferred, he was a paternalistic conservative, with a belief 'in a well ordered hierarchical society'. High and low were sitting at the same table, he told a meeting of teetotallers in Galway, and while all were 'in conscience bound to move contentedly in their own sphere, to pay respect to every man according to his rank in society, yet, if they continued as they were going on . . . they would be all innocence ennobled'.[13]

It was not possible to occupy such a prominent position in public life in Ireland at the time and to promote a movement that advocated such a radical change in the way people lived without incurring accusations of political engagement. On most occasions he was able to sidestep the issues, at least to the satisfaction of his followers. On St. Patrick's Day, 1840, he was invited to be a fellow guest with O'Connell at a dinner in Kilroy's Hotel, Galway, when they were both in the town, but he left during the day and had Father Roche, active in both temperance and politics in Galway, give his apologies. When he was accused by the *Dublin Evening Mail* of saying that the excise on spirits went to a 'foreign power' he denied that he was 'turning politician' by doing so, but was merely pointing out that of every 6d. spent on drink 5d. went to the exchequer and ld. to the publican. His success among the strongholds of the banned Orange Order in Ulster was a tribute to his ability to avoid political or religious subjects in the course of his crusade and to convince his listeners, for a time at least, that their differences were irrelevant. The Catholic Bishop of Kilmore advised him against going to Cootehill where placards had appeared saying he was not welcome, but he was received enthusiastically by the Protestants in the town and later claimed that the hostile placards had been posted up by a Catholic publican. The Enniskillen correspondent of the *Dublin Evening Post* reported with obvious relief that Father Mathew's visit there in 1843 had gone off without incident: 'Many, very many, were of opinion that there was not a more critical spot in Ireland for Father Mathew to bring the people about him than Enniskillen; it has been tried, and the trial has, thank God, been most successful — virtue has triumphed.' He was well able to adapt to changing circumstances: at the beginning of his crusade he was careful not to administer the pledge in Catholic churches for fear the movement might be seen as sectarian, but felt no longer obliged to exercise such caution, he told his audience at Nenagh in 1845, now that 'our object and end is as clear as the sun'.[14]

While Father Mathew himself was always careful to say nothing that would give grounds for a political or sectarian interpretation of his work and in his frequent condemnation of secret societies showed a respect for constitutional processes that should have satisfied the most apprehensive Tory, there was little he could do to prevent others from giving a political slant to the movement. When Father Mathew spoke in Galway in March 1840, his address was thought by the *Morning Chronicle* to have given 'as energetic and earnest an assertion of the respect due to their superiors in rank, landlords, magistrates, and all in authority, as the most zealous Conservative could desire'. But Father Roche, President of the Galway branch of the Cork Total Abstinence Society and an active supporter of O'Connell, was reported as saying that as Ireland was lost by intemperance her independence would be regained by sobriety. His remarks were found 'reprehensible indeed' by the *Galway Advertiser* which felt that the advocates of temperance must have 'an ulterior object' in view. The paper would withdraw its support for the movement, now that it had revealed its 'political aspect'. The same paper was even more appalled when, a month later on the occasion of the Queen's birthday, Galway teetotallers burned an effigy of Lord Stanley and carried it on poles through the street, in contempt for his Registration Bill which had been brought before the House of Commons. When the police interfered they were pelted with stones, several receiving injuries, disturbances which Father Roche laid at the door of the Mechanics Institute teetotallers rather than those of his own Society.[15]

There was an attempt around this time to identify the temperance movement with a form of politics more militant than the constitutional changes advocated by O'Connell. That this attempt was unsuccessful is not surprising, given the regularity with which Father Mathew (and O'Connell) condemned secret societies. The *Limerick Standard* published a document found in a house in county Limerick which suggested there was a connection between Ribbonism and Teetotalism. The Limerick city teetotallers asked for an enquiry and the investigating magistrates were satisfied that there was no connection between the document and the temperance societies. As noted in the last chapter, Father Mathew continued to denounce agrarian outrages and the secret societies that planned and executed them and, as seen in Chapter 4, there is evidence that his movement may have had some influence in reducing this form of crime in county Tipperary.[16]

Parades by temperance societies continued through the spring and summer of 1840. Some were careful to ensure that their branch should not become associated with politics, as at Castlebar in April, when the local society carried a banner declaring 'This is not the cause of any sect or party.' However much Tory newspapers may have exaggerated the public disquiet felt about marches, the Whig Lord Lieutenant felt obliged to issue a proclamation in July that, in effect, forbade processions 'if they exhibited any Party Emblem or are accompanied by music playing Party Tunes'. The proclamation acknowledged the benefits of the temperance pledge on Ireland 'in the improved habits of the people and in the diminution of outrage', and it was this that caused the Tory Earl of Westmeath to raise the matter in the House of Lords. Astonished that the representative of the Sovereign had approved of the temperance pledge 'which he considered to be nothing else than a piece of mere slipslop ... a Popish device', he wanted to know if the proclamation was authentic and Lord Normanby, for the Government, told him he had no reason to doubt it. Slipslop the pledge may be, he continued, but he too was convinced of the beneficial changes it had brought about in Ireland. While the Duke of Wellington gave his opinion that he was in favour of banning all assemblies, the Earl of Devon assured the house of Father Mathew's non-political motives, and the Earl of Wicklow, while approving of Father Mathew's work, felt there were parties in Ireland capable of redirecting the honourable motives that guided his work into other purposes.[17]

Father Agnew, Chairman of the Mechanics Institute and Temperance Society in Galway, welcomed the proclamation because, unlike previous proclamations which he felt had been anti-Irish in spirit, this one 'bears testimony to the national improvement resulting from the observance of temperance' and merely requested societies to avoid ostentatious displays. Some attempts were made to enforce the proclamation's restriction on nationalist banners and tunes. When teetotallers from Mullingar, Granard, Oldcastle and other towns marched into Castletown Delvin they had some of their banners and musical instruments removed by the local magistrate. At Newport Father Mathew himself asked that the band greeting his arrival there should stop playing and that the flags should be removed. The *Dublin Evening Mail* was scandalised by the Lord Lieutenant's proclamation being ignored at Newport, although the *Dublin Evening Post* said the processionists had simply acted in ignorance of it. What was on the banners seems to have been harmless enough, one of those charged with carrying a banner saying, 'there was nothing frightful on it but angels and those things'. All charges against the Newport teetotallers were dropped when the Lord Lieutenant was assured that they planned no similar display for the future. At Killala permission had been given to local teetotallers to hold a rally without banners or music but they went ahead and held one with both. The local magistrates let the matter pass without interference.[18]

O'Connell, meanwhile, had launched the Repeal Association and was indeed keeping a close eye on the growth of the temperance movement. Addressing the South London Catholic Temperance Society he denied the temperance movement was political, but added that in the hour of trial the best politicians will be those who have taken the pledge, and so 'in temperance there was patriotism'. By this time he had moved from his position of 'Justice for Ireland' to a demand for the restoration of the Irish Parliament. Intending at first to have provincial Repeal meetings at Newry, Tuam, Thurles or Cashel and Kilkenny, with simultaneous meetings in all parishes to petition for Repeal, he decided instead to concentrate his initial attention on the west of Ireland. A crowd of 50,000 heard him speak at Castlebar, 100,000 in Galway's Eyre Square and the meeting at the Market Place in Tuam attended by Archbishop MacHale of Tuam and Bishop Browne of Galway, showed 'the prominent part which Connacht has taken in the present agitation for Repeal'.[19]

At the end of August Father Mathew warned his audience at Sandyford, Dublin, that political discussion and religious controversy should be avoided in teetotal societies. An address from the Kilkenny teetotallers to O'Connell when he was there for the Repeal meeting in October suggests that while the restriction on political discussion was probably widely adhered to, the political sympathy of teetotallers was not in doubt. As teetotallers we wage war against intemperance, the address began, but outside the temperance rooms 'we cordially join the ranks of our fellow citizens, and consider ourselves then as strangers to nothing that can tend to the amelioration of our country'. Hence they offered their approval of O'Connell's endeavours for the freedom and happiness of Ireland. O'Connell in his turn praised the teetotallers for excluding political discussion from the temperance rooms and declared himself happy with their support outside, for, he added, 'if a man by becoming a teetotaller should cease to be a patriot, their number should be very limited indeed'.[20]

It may be wondered if teetotallers were able to compartmentalise their enthusiasms for temperance and Repeal as neatly as the address from Kilkenny indicates, or if the temperance rooms did not in fact play a significant role in preparing the way for Repeal. For while political discussion was indeed forbidden by temperance societies' rules, the fact that

Father Mathew referred so often to the importance of these rules suggests that in some places at least they may not have been obeyed. In Galway town, for example, it was noted in a local paper that discussions in Father Agnew's Mechanics Institute and Temperance Society were characterised by an 'absence of all political or angry topics'. Father Killeen and Father Roche were the presidents of the other two temperance societies in the town, the Parent Temperance Society and the local branch of the Cork Temperance Society respectively. These two priests were on the Repeal Committee of Galway town, and it would be difficult to imagine them enthusiastic about forbidding discussion of Repeal in their societies' rooms. Additionally, it would have been difficult in any temperance hall or room to prevent informal discussion of topical events. While Father Mathew assured a correspondent that the *Pilot* newspaper, O'Connell's mouthpiece, was never permitted in temperance rooms, other newspapers were allowed, and in the intense political climate of the early eighteen forties, almost every issue of every newspaper carried features which could provoke political discussion. It may have been, then, that O'Connell's praise for the rule excluding political discussion from temperance rooms was influenced by the knowlege that it was rarely enforced. This would perhaps explain a later complaint from Father Mathew about O'Connell, to the effect that it 'required my utmost efforts to exclude his agitation from our halls, and it was in a spirit of opposition he established Repeal Reading Rooms'.[21]

Besides providing a place where people could meet and possibly discuss topical events, there were other ways in which the rooms may have helped prepare the way for Repeal. 'Mathew's emphasis in order, discipline, respect for institutions and, of course, sobriety', writes Oliver MacDonagh in his recent biography of O'Connell, 'was identical with O'Connell's ground-plan for all his agitations.' The Temperance Reports confirm that great attention was paid to the orderly running of the societies, and that committee meetings took place in the rooms, with energy given to benefit societies, the purchase of newspapers, arrangements for public displays as well as keeping an eye on members and reporting those who broke the pledge. The Reports are disappointing, however, in that they reveal almost nothing of the kind of cultural activities, if any, the members may have been engaged in at the rooms, apart from reading the newspapers and band practice. We know from other sources, though, that Father Mathew devoted a lot of energy to promoting a taste for reading among young teetotallers, not only among the middle and upper class youths like those who attended the Cork Temperance Institute, but among the poor as well. In March 1840, the *Connaught Journal* announced the Loughrea Temperance Society's plans to establish a library as 'a source of amusement and mental improvement to the members'. The rooms, finally, by providing opportunities for tradesmen to meet together (the Mechanics Institute and Temperance Society in Galway was confined to tradesmen, their children bound to professions and apprentices in at least their second year of apprenticeship) may have helped them raise their image of themselves. The confidence they gained from marching through the streets in an orderly, sober and dignified manner at temperance processions could have made them more receptive to the call of Repeal. That some 'influential persons' were violently hostile to the establishment of temperance halls and rooms even in areas where almost everyone had taken the pledge, suggests that this particular link between temperance and Repeal was entertained by the authorities.[22]

*   *   *

Towards the end of 1840 O'Connell himself became a teetotaller and regularly referred to the benefits of temperance. About to depart for Scotland after his visit to Belfast at the beginning of 1841 he addressed a crowd from the steamer deck on the necessity and advantages of teetotalism, a manoeuvre, a hostile commentator wrote, which 'brought him a number of parting cheers'. Teetotal bands greeted him when he was in Galway on St. Patrick's Day and in the evening he attended a temperance festival. On the same day at a procession in Sligo one of the banners showed him on his knees receiving the pledge from Father Mathew. At the Rotunda in Dublin the following month he told his audience that he had become a teetotaller because he could not recommend to others what he would not do himself — Judge Crampton, it appears, had taunted him with not practising what he preached.[23]

With the approach of the general election of 1841 the *Southern Reporter* argued that the Irish people were now better able to wrestle with their enemies than ever before. While it was true that Father Mathew's temperance societies eschewed politics, they have nevertheless made the Irish a more thinking and unified people, and by means of the temperance reading rooms 'will be the means of giving a direction and enlightenment to the national mind; and though politics are, and justly, excluded from these Societies, the information obtained, and the moral habits engendered, will silently work well for Ireland. All this will show itself at the approaching elections.' As ever anxious to be seen to be neutral in politics, Father Mathew ordered that temperance bands 'are not to attend any political meeting or play in public until the General Election will have terminated'.[24]

While the City and County of Cork did indeed return candidates in the elections who were committed to Repeal, including O'Connell himself for the county, nationally the election did not further the cause. Partly through poor organisation, the number of Repeal M.P.'s at Westminster was considerably reduced. The Tories were returned with a large majority led by Sir Robert Peel, O'Connell's old enemy. The reform of the closed corporations had now been concluded and in Dublin, where £10 leaseholders had the municipal vote, O'Connell was easily elected as Lord Mayor. His first public compliment in his new office was addressed to the teetotallers of the city. On taking up his office, O'Connell had pledged that in his capacity as Lord Mayor no one would be able to discover from his conduct what his religion or politics were, and to a great extent he kept to this during his year of office, though in his personal capacity he of course continued to be a Repealer. He continued also to wish to be associated with the work of Father Mathew, to whom, according to Maguire, he caused considerable embarrassment when, in his capacity as Lord Mayor of Dublin, he decided to honour the teetotallers of Cork by marching with them in their Easter Monday procession.[25]

The decrease in Repeal agitation during 1842 did not lessen attempts to have temperance parades stopped but the Tory Lord Eliot defended the teetotallers in Parliament with as much enthusiasm as his Whig predecessor had done two years before. Repeal began to gain momentum again at the end of the year, with several large meetings, and early in 1843 it seemed that the prediction made by O'Connell three years before that Repeal would 'soon spread like wildfire' was at last to be realised. By this time the *Nation* newspaper had been founded by Charles Gavin Duffy, Thomas Davis and John Blake Dillon. More influenced than O'Connell by ideas of culture and nationalism outside an Irish context, their newspaper, besides providing news of the progress of agitation for Repeal, also tried to promote aspects of Irish culture which would give the concept of the Repeal more substance than the purely political dimensions that were emphasised repeatedly by O'Connell. It is not surprising, therefore, that they would want to understand the temperance movement in the context of Irish history and culture. Elements of some of their ideas were already present in the Temperance Reports in 1840,

where sobriety was in some districts seen as a step towards national libera-
tion. Two years later the *Dublin Monthly Magazine* wrote that 'A sober
people are eminently entitled to political freedom' and added that liberty
was only dangerous in the hands of a drunken and licentious population.
P.Q. Barron told his audience in Waterford at the end of the same year
that while he did not wish to connect temperance with politics, Irishmen
'should love teetotalism the more because of the infallible certainty that
the death warrant of drunkenness was the forerunner of national
greatness'.[26]

In the *Nation* Thomas Davis went back a step, to see drunkenness
in Irishmen's past as related to their political subjection, and the
temperance movement as

the first fruit of deep-sown hope, the offering of incipient freedom. The moment when political organisation, social action, and the rudiments of education
had set the people thinking, hope came down upon them like the dew, and the
fever of their hearts abated.

As this hope of improvement is gradually realised, as the Irishman's intellect and taste improved and as his self-confidence increased, so will
the need for 'the mad joy of drink' decrease. Father Mathew's achievement was to have got the people to understand this. Perhaps influenced
by these sentiments Venedey felt that the pledge, which he would not
normally approve of for a civilised people, was acceptable for the
Irish.[27]

Commenting on what he saw in 1842, Kohl felt the temperance movement had taken on an anti-English character because O'Connell and
other leading nationalists had 'sanctioned it by their approbation'.
Maguire, a friend of Father Mathew and a supporter of O'Connell, felt
the latter was genuinely sincere in advocating temperance and saw his
period as a teetotaller as evidence of this sincerity. More recent
assessments have been less charitable. Elizabeth Malcolm feels that his
support for Father Mathew was 'motivated by political expediency', arguing that it would have been out of character for him to adopt teetotalism
because of his customary habits and way of life, because of his brewing
interests and because of his advocacy of the Irish spirits industry in Parliament. His concern for the progress of the movement dated from 1839
at least and Guizot in early 1840 found him enthusiastic about the permanence of the revolution that Father Mathew had brought about. That
his enthusiasm extended to his becoming a teetotaller himself suggests

he was more sincere than those of the gentry who applauded the movement without ever considering taking the pledge themselves. He was not the only one who became a teetotaller whose habits and way of life might suggest such a change unlikely. The Temperance Reports recorded that in most parts of the country the greater proportion of those who took the pledge had previously had a reputation for drunkenness. (O'Connell had no such reputation.) He was not the only one who approved of Father Mathew's work whose commercial or professional interests might have been threatened by it. As noted in Chapter 3, George Roe, the Dublin distiller, applauded Father Mathew's work despite the financial loss to his business. That O'Connell returned to drinking after about a year and a half as a teetotaller is undeniable, joining the many who did so on 'medical' grounds. Given his enormous work-load at the time, however, it may have been that in his case the medical advice was based on a genuine concern for his health rather than mere evasion. We have no way of knowing. But when he told a meeting at Roscommon in August that no one who breaks the temperance pledge shall be allowed to become a Repealer he was being something of a hypocrite — Venedey had seen him drinking champagne at a meeting at Athlone two months before.[28]

*　　*　　*

The Dublin Corporation debate on Repeal which began on 28th February 1843 and which ended with the motion in favour being carried by 41 votes to 15, gained international publicity for O'Connell's Repeal agitation. The Easter Monday temperance procession through Dublin a few weeks later was thought impressive by the *Dublin Evening Post* in that it showed large numbers of young people growing up in the habits of temperance, but the *Dublin Evening Mail*, noticing some of the banners to have carried a harp without a crown, thought them 'indicative of the accordance of the brethren, in the cry for Repeal, and symbolically, pointing to the separation of the countries — SEPARATION!'[29]

The 'monster' meetings (so named by the *Times*) at which O'Connell addressed large crowds in or near many of the big towns began in April and continued throughout the summer and autumn. Temperance Bands were usually present. At Waterford at the beginning of 1842 Father Mathew said there were 300 bands set up by temperance societies, with 6,000 musicians. He had himself paid for the instruments for some of the bands and had made contributions to others. They were acceptable recreational

alternatives to the public houses and added a colourful and lively aspect
to the movement. In a letter to an English correspondent Father Mathew
spoke of them as 'humanising' and 'elevating' the Irish people. When
Daniel O'Connell joined in the temperance procession through Cork in
1842 a local paper counted fifty temperance bands marching past. Particular praise was given to the performance of the band from Globe Lane
on that parade, and several of the Tipperary bands, in particular those
from Nenagh and Tipperary town, were often complimented on their
musical abilities, but the impression given by contemporaries is that the
overall standard was poor. There was no lack of enthusiasm — James
Silk Buckingham noticed that some bands marched up to thirty miles
to attend meetings — but the music was poorly arranged and at big
assemblies it was not unknown for a dozen bands to be playing at the
same time without a single air in common! Kohl wrote despairingly of
a temperance band he heard in Cork, playing 'sounds more detestable
than even the caterwarling of cats'.[30]

Some Tory newspapers, as noted earlier, took exception to the 'party
tunes' the bands played at temperance meetings and processions and
there were occasional complaints about them desecrating the Sabbath
but, with one exception, Father Mathew was pleased with the performances of his band up until 'Repeal Year'. The exception was the band
from Castlebar which, accompanied by a mob, played outside a church
while a prominent Protestant missionary was trying to make himself heard
inside. Castlebar teetotallers were severely reprimanded by Father Mathew
for permitting the band to be used for what he called 'sectarian purposes'. 'Your strict adherence to the rules of the society from henceforth
is the only reparation you can make for the past', he told them in an
open letter which was printed in several newspapers.[31]

'A few of them may have violated our neutral Rules', Father Mathew
wrote in the letter mentioned in the last paragraph, and in another letter, undated but written when the monster meetings had got underway,
he claimed that 'out of every three hundred temperance bands, not twelve
have violated our fundamental rule of abstaining from political strife'.
He added that newspapers, for unspecified reasons, were exaggerating
the number of temperance bands at Repeal meetings and that there were,
in any case, many bands made up of teetotallers that were not under
his control. He wrote elsewhere about three temperance bands that had
'suffered much persecution from the Parochial Clergymen, for having
refused to attend' Repeal meetings. Nevertheless, it is clear from

newspaper accounts that temperance bands were prominent at nearly all the monster meetings. The collusion of newspapers throughout Ireland that would have been necessary to give a false impression on the subject, even if there was a motive for it, would have been unthinkable, given political and religious differences among the newspapers of the day. He had to reluctantly accept the attendance of temperance bands at Repeal meetings and parades, as the alternative was to confront them and expressly forbid them to attend, when he would have run the risk of losing what he considered 'powerful auxiliaries' to his work.[32]

The majority of those attending the monster meetings were in any case teetotallers. When O'Connell asked everyone at the Athlone meeting who was a teetotaller to raise his hand, almost all present did so. Reporting this, Venedey added that O'Connell could not have brought so many people together in peaceful agitation 'if Temperance had not first spread its soothing blessings among them'. At a meeting at Caltra, Co. Galway, attended by 70,000 people in May, the *Nation* correspondent didn't see a single individual there who showed signs of drink. Duffy's notes on the Repeal meeting at Tara echoed Venedey's impressions at Athlone: 'Before Father Mathew's mission the experiment of collecting half a million of people at one place, and exciting them with stimulating oratory, would have been perilous, probably disastrous.' He told the story of three men who were forbidden by local teetotallers from going to Tara because they had broken the pledge.[33]

Some who did not agree with O'Connell's aims acknowledged the beneficial influence of Father Mathew's followers on Repeal agitation — Ken Inglis quotes a Protestant writing in 1857 who believed that teetotalism had prevented bloodshed and rebellion at the time of the monster meetings. Other Unionists were suspicious about the order in the temperance movement. Could not the regular military restraint under which they had been brought, asked Rev. Tresham Gregg of the Dublin Protestant Operative Society, echoing sentiments expressed three years earlier in some of the Temperance Reports and in some Tory newspapers, make the teetotallers 'very dangerous enemies of the English power?' Unionists also questioned why Orange parades should be forbidden — the Orange Order was banned at the time — while 'Rabid Repealers and Teetotallers are permitted to march through the land, more especially on Sunday, desecrating the Sabbath?'[34]

In May 1843 the government had circulars sent to County Inspectors of Constabulary and Stipendiary Magistrates in Ireland asking specific questions about the Repeal movement in their counties and districts. Both circulars asked about the connection between the Repeal Association and temperance societies and the replies provide some insights into the relationship between the two movements.[35]

Of the County Inspectors of Constabulary who replied to the question, one third felt there was no connection between Repeal Association and temperance societies in their county, or merely referred to the fact that many people belonged to both. The North and South Ridings of Tipperary are, rather surprisingly, among this group. While in most cases the Inspector noted that there was no connection (Carlow, Kilkenny), or that he was not aware of any (Antrim, East Cork), the report from Mayo was more specific, reporting that the Castlebar temperance band refused to attend Repeal meetings. The reparation Father Mathew had demanded of them the previous October had obviously been made. About one sixth of replies reported a weak connection between the two movements, offering as evidence no more than that teetotal bands played at Repeal meetings, or that Repealers were encouraged by priests to join temperance societies. The replies from Westmeath and Monaghan, for example, noted that temperance bands attended the meetings at Mullingar and Carrickmacross respectively, while that for Longford said that priests there, speaking at Repeal meetings, recommended that Repealers should join temperance societies.[36]

The remaining half of the replies indicate a strong connection between Repeal and Temperance at a local level. From some counties (Limerick, Waterford, Sligo, Roscommon, East Galway, King's and Queen's) we learn little more than that the two movements were seen as one and the same thing or that their aims had become identical, although in the case of Queen's County it was added that the word and will of the priests governed both. From Leitrim it was reported that the temperance movement there 'is now adapted to and perverted to the mischievous intentions of a party'. Despite the original good intentions behind the movement there, the Inspector feared 'that the Roman Catholic members of the Temperance Societies would as individuals, almost to a man, enlist under Mr. O'Connell's banner should his objects absolutely require it.' The teetotallers of county Londonderry were thought to be 'available for any seditious purpose', and there was an accusation that those in Dublin were using their bands and parades to familiarise their members' minds with military organisation. So close were Repeal and temperance associated in Wexford that the County Inspector's report noted that Repeal speakers 'have thrown fixity of tenure, release from poor-rates, tithes and the Temperance system all into the balance with Repeal'. He was of the decided opinion that 'if a breaking out took place, instead of marching to the Temperance halls they would march elsewhere, the bands playing a very different tune from "Father Mathew's March", and white wands and badges would be replaced by arms and the Irish revolutionary cockade'.[37]

Stipendiary magistrates were distributed unevenly throughout the country, with more in the 'disturbed' counties — one seventh of all magistrates' replies to the Circular, for example, came from county Tipperary. For this reason it is not possible to compare the Magistrates' replies in any statistical way with those of the County Police Inspectors, but they are of interest in that they supplement the latter's impressions. The strong connection between the two movements indicated by the County Inspector of Constabulary for King's County is confirmed in the Magistrates' reports from Tullamore and Shinrone, and the Constabulary report from county Waterford is confirmed by the Magistrate at Dungarvan. The eight reports from Magistrates in Tipperary confirmed the report from the County Inspector that nowhere in the county was there a strong connection between Repeal and temperance.[38]

The Magistrates' report from Tullamore suggested that some temperance societies had been converted into secret societies, and from Newtown Hamilton it was reported that 'the Ribbon confederacy is an adjunct of it (i.e. the temperance society), ready to assist in any way to accomplish its designs'. The Magistrate from Omagh had even more serious charges to report, having observed 'a frequent reference to the Temperance Society among the Ribbon pass-words; for instance, "Have you got the medal?" and in many cases I have seen the medal in possession of Ribbonmen'. Had he learned of this, Father Mathew would have had to revise his often stated belief that no teetotallers belonged to secret societies, although it may perhaps be added that just as Ribbonmen found it in their interest to endorse Repeal, they may also have claimed membership of teetotal societies for similar reasons. But even in Cork city itself, Father Mathew had his own problems. He wished to prevent temperance bands taking part in Repeal parades, a magistrate reported, 'but they did not mind him and on they went'.[39]

In some cases the Magistrate's reports do not confirm the picture given by the County Inspectors of Constabulary, but this is hardly surprising as the latter were attempting to give the overall position in their

counties while the magistrates' remarks were generally confined to a particular part of a county. While 'a very intimate connection' was seen
to exist in Castleconnell between the movements, confirming the Constabulary report for Limerick county, the Magistrate from Rathkeale felt
that the majority of teetotallers there were opposed to temperance bands
attending Repeal meetings and the Magistrate from Limerick city believed
that political questions were not entertained in temperance societies. The
two Magistrates who reported from Leitrim actually said the opposite
to the Chief Constable, one saying there was no connection between the
Repeal Association and the temperance society in Mohill and the other
saying that there was not even a Repeal Association branch in Leitrim
town. Of the three reports from Roscommon, two Magistrates confirm
the connection noticed by the County Inspector, while the third, from
Athlone, was emphatic that the movements had 'no connection whatever'
except that all the teetotallers were Repealers.[40]

While it was clear from the reports from Inspectors and Magistrates
that there was a connection between the two movements, there was an
absence of any concrete evidence to suggest that the Cabinet should be
unduly worried about the role of temperance societies. Any harm they
could do by promoting Repeal at a local level and enabling the monster
meetings to take place without the drunkenness that would have
discredited Repeal had to be weighed against the known strictures of
Father Mathew on politics in temperance rooms and his opposition to
secret societies, as well as the potentially stabilising role the temperance
societies might play if and when the government had to take action against
O'Connell. Peel remained suspicious, even after he had made his first
move against O'Connell, a move that met with surprisingly little opposition. In reply to a letter from Eliot, the Chief Secretary, who was seeking employment for Father Mathew's brother Charles, Peel took the
opportunity of asking if Eliot was 'perfectly satisfied as to the purity
of intention and uprightness of the proceedings of Father Mathew'. Eliot
replied that Father Mathew was unable to hinder people becoming
Repealers and that while Earl Glengall had informed him that efforts
were indeed made to associate temperance with Repeal, Father Mathew
himself was opposed to this.[41]

By this time Peel had taken his major decisions about how to deal
with the threat of Repeal and had begun to act on them. Faced with
the conflicting pressures of permitting O'Connell to continue to treat
the Union with contempt, the demand for action against Repeal by Irish

Unionists (supported by the Lord Lieutenant but not the Irish Secretary), demands from some Whigs and Radicals in Parliament not to do so and the widespread sentiments of anti-Popery that still flourished in England (as Father Mathew had experienced in London), Peel eventually resolved on banning the last Repeal meeting of the season planned for Clontarf in October. He took legal action against O'Connell and other leading Repealers and at the same time addressed himself to some of the causes of disaffection among the Catholic population, to whom Repeal had seemed so attractive. In the first he was successful, thanks to a considerable extent to O'Connell agreeing to stop the meeting at short notice and to many Repealers, especially priests, who persuaded people already on their way to Clontarf to return home peacefully. In the second he was partly successful, in that O'Connell was arrested, tried, fined and sentenced to a year in prison without any outbreak of violence. He was released after half his sentence by a decision of the Law Lords. It would seem that the celebrations for his release were nowhere marred by drunkenness. When he went to Kilkenny, St. Mary's Temperance Society, with band and banners, turned out to meet him, and he was reminded by Father Mulligan that temperance had made his monster meetings possible.[42]

Although the implementation of his third decision, conciliation, met with some opposition, he was able to make progress with his Charitable Donations and Bequests Bill and with the increased endowment of Maynooth College. Most opposition was directed against his system of non-denominational higher education. Although the 'mixed' colleges were set up in Galway, Cork and Belfast, their establishment met with the hostility of the majority of the Catholic clergy and were denounced by the hierarchy and the Vatican who feared 'that this neutral system of education would harm religion'.[43]

By the middle of 1845 Father Mathew was able to congratulate Peel on the progress he had made. In the preamble to one of his many petitions to Peel to advance the career of his brother Charles (who had to give up his distillery because of the temperance movement) Father Mathew told him that the result of his conciliatory policies towards Ireland 'will prove you the best and most fortunate Minister, that ever presided over the destinies of this mighty Empire'. While the manner in which it was presented may have been calculated to flatter Peel, we may take it that it represented his true opinion of the Tory leader, as a few months later he had declared himself satisfied with Peel as fulfilling his expectations

in calming and pacifying the country. Within a month he was writing
to Peel again, complaining that the system of police promotion, which
he felt placed too much emphasis on the apprehension of criminals rather
than preventing the crimes. He regretted 'the inflammatory harangues,
addressed to a suffering population, filling the minds of men with false
notions of their strength, and rights' and was even willing to accept a
ban on all public processions, including temperance processions, if it
was thought that this would save lives.[44]

While his last letter sounded like that of a man in low spirits indeed,
he was soon involved again in temperance work and, within a few months,
in Famine relief work also. During 1846, as Famine conditions worsened,
the rift between the Repeal Association and the Young Irelanders, which
had been in evidence during the discussions on the 'wicked' colleges
favoured by the latter, widened. Duffy, Meagher and others followed
William Smith O'Brien out of Conciliation Hall when it was found impossible to reach a compromise on the 'peace resolutions'. A conference
aimed at trying to reconcile 'Old' and 'Young' Ireland the following year
was described by John O'Connell as having 'failed of good results'. An
Irish League containing both parties was actually formed in July 1848,
but was short lived.[45]

*   *   *

In October 1846 John O'Neill Daunt noted in his diary that Father
Mathew, with whom he had just spent the evening, seemed to sympathise
with the Young Irelanders against O'Connell. Everything known about
Father Mathew's political attitudes up to this time inhibits us from believing he could have favoured a policy that might involve force over one
that was committed to peaceful agitation. Such sympathies, also, would
have put him at a distance from the vast majority of the bishops and
priests throughout the country, very few of whom had any time for the
secularist and at times anti-clerical attitudes of the Young Irelanders.
To put O'Neill Daunt's impression of Father Mathew's sympathies in
perspective, however, several factors need to be taken into account. The
first is that at this stage the debate was very much a theoretical one
— no one was actually planning a violent insurrection. The differences
between the two parties in Conciliation Hall was probably exaggerated
and the split possibly engineered by the O'Connell faction so that they
might be rid of those whose vocal opposition to a Whig alliance was
an embarrassment to them. Few, then, would have seen much substance
behind any threat of force the Young Irelanders might allude to. Would

they have been as substantial, even, as the veiled threats that had so
often accompanied the massed ranks that attended the monster meetings
of 1843?[46]

Secondly, some of the Young Irelanders' ideas, especially their anti-
sectarianism and their aspirations for the regeneration of Ireland by means
of a campaign against ignorance, were close to some of Father Mathew's
own. Thomas Davis had died in 1845, but Duffy had a similar interest
in the intellectual and moral aspects of the Young Ireland and temperance
movements. He had plans to 'perfect' teetotal societies to create 'agencies of popular enlightenment' and in his priorities for Confederate Clubs
in 1847, the true enemy was identified as 'neither the armed soldier
nor the partisan judge only IGNORANCE and PREJUDICE'.[47]

Thirdly, and perhaps most significantly, many of those who broke with
Conciliation Hall were either personal friends of Father Mathew or firm
supporters of his work. In Cork the Young Irelanders included Isaac
Varian, M.J. Barry and Denny Lane, the latter surviving long enough
to take part in the Father Mathew centenary celebrations in 1890. Varian,
who spoke at a temperance meeting at the beginning of 1839, was active in the work of the Cork Temperance Institute and chaired the meeting
that prepared an address for Captain Forbes who had sailed the
Jamestown from Boston to Cork with famine relief provisions contributed
by the people of Massachusetts. Barry, though not a teetotaller himself,
accompanied Father Mathew to see the Brown Street Temperance Room
in February 1848, where Father Mathew referred to him as his friend.
With Lane, Barry was an early believer in the ideas of Young Ireland,
but they were at first reluctant to set up a Confederation Club in Cork,
where support for O'Connell was traditionally very strong.[48]

Outside Cork, Lord Wallscourt, who had assisted Father Mathew on
his temperance mission to Connemara in 1840 and who joined the Confederacy in 1847, was probably the most eminent of his connections among
the Young Irelanders. William Smith O'Brien was a consistently active
supporter of his work, although Father Mathew was careful to disassociate
himself from Smith O'Brien's pledge not to drink until the Union was
repealed. When Smith O'Brien received the death sentence (later com-
muted to life imprisonment) Father Mathew suspended preparations for
his own fifty-eighth birthday.[49]

Father John Kenyon had been active in promoting temperance during his curacy in Ennis from as early as 1836, and when he moved to
Tipperary he was still involved, having been introduced to the meeting,

for example, when Father Mathew visited Toomyvara in 1841. While parish priest of Templederry he built up the Confederate Club there to be one of the strongest in the country. With John Mitchel he left the Confederation because it was not militant enough and in the *United Irishman* advocated arming the people and accused Conciliation Hall-type Repealers as being 'part and parcel of the English interest in Ireland'. The same issue of the newspaper reported Varian's speech in Cork recommending passive resistance and an end to acting by constitutional means. Father Kenyon was suspended from his parish for a time by Bishop Kennedy, who also condemned Father James Birmingham of Borrisokane, Father Mathew's friend and first biographer, who by this time was also a supporter of the use of arms.[50]

James Haughton, still active in the temperance movement with Father Spratt in Dublin, had asked to have the Seceders recalled, despite his disapproval of their warlike tones. Bishop Blake of Dromore, long a supporter of Father Mathew's work, had written to O'Connell making the same request, a request which O'Connell asked him to withdraw. Bishop Maginn of Derry, another ardent supporter of teetotalism among the hierarchy in Ulster, was active in attempts at reconciliation. He wrote to Smith O'Brien after his injury at the hands of the mob in Limerick, and helped Thomas D'Arcy Magee escape to America after his attempt to bring volunteers and arms from Scotland to help in the planned insurrection.[51]

Father Mathew would have had little sympathy with Mitchel's call to arms, but Mitchel's insistence, in his letter to the *United Irishman* (which formed part of the evidence for his prosecution) that Irish grain should not leave Ireland while people starved, would have touched a chord of sympathy in Father Mathew at a time when he was working himself towards the point of illness on Famine relief projects. When Mitchel was convicted and sentenced to transportation, Father Spratt was the organiser of a subscription for him and his family, while Lord Cloncurry, another early temperance advocate, made an initial contribution of £100 towards it.[52]

The *Nation* saw Mitchel's conviction as 'the final end of patient endurance' and told its readers it was time to arm, and when Duffy, the editor, was arrested and imprisoned in Newgate, he warned people against giving up their arms. The rising, when it occurred, did not receive the hoped for support, even in Tipperary, where Father Kenyon refused to take the leading part expected of him because of the terms of his

agreement of reconciliation with Bishop Kennedy that permitted him
to resume his duties as a parish priest. Father Mathew's unequivocal
attitude towards the use of arms for rebellion is illustrated a few days
after the skirmish at Ballingarry:

The Teetotallers everywhere remained faithful — You can easily imagine what
the position in Cork would be, were it not for this dragchain — If the people
of Ireland were, as in former days, slaves to drunken habits, our greatest field
would have been deluged in blood.[53]

Father Mathew's evidence at Duffy's trial has been seen as straying
from his usual neutrality in political matters, but his evidence did not
in any way bear witness to the defendant's most recent involvements.
Besides a statement of his good character, the evidence drew attention
to Duffy's continuous interest in those educational aspects of the
Temperance movement which he felt would lead to improvements in
morals and the cultivation of people's minds. By the time of Duffy's acquittal Father Mathew was resolved on going to America, where, on the
issue of slavery, he found neutrality even more difficult to sustain than
on Repeal.[54]

CHAPTER **6**

Reasons and Superstitions

We have seen in Chapter 3 how the Mathewite temperance movement, from a rather modest start in 1838, had gained considerable momentum by the autumn of 1839 and by the middle of the following year, helped by regular missions by Father Mathew to different parts of the country, had become a national movement. While the exact number of adherents throughout the country can never be determined with any degree of accuracy, it is clear that a large proportion of the population became teetotallers for some time at least, with the movement particularly strong in the southern and western counties. The present chapter attempts to explore the reasons why these large numbers were willing to undertake so radical a change in their way of life at that particular time. While determining the motives of so vast a number may indeed be impossible, especially when the temperance movement was so conspicuously lacking in any kind of formulated ideology, an attempt to do so based on what is known of teetotallers' remarks, attitudes and actions may throw some light on why so many were willing to embrace a movement which involved, as Kohl put it, 'infusing into the people a taste for a description of pleasure and enjoyments widely differing from those they formerly enjoyed in the whiskey-shops'.[1]

Emmet Larkin has seen temperance and Repeal as 'revivalist' movements occurring as they did at a time of great anxiety brought about by a precarious economic climate. The meetings at the Horse Bazaar near Father Mathew's house in Cove Street certainly contained elements that resembled revivalist meetings, where converts came forward to narrate their experiences before and after taking the pledge. The Sub Inspector from Gort reported that at the monthly meetings in the temperance room in the town,

many of the members relate in turn what good effects they have individually experienced from taking the pledge. The clergyman then exhorts them to adhere to it, and all others, who are in need of it, to lose no time, but take it, as soon as possible, they then repeat a short prayer calling on God to grant them strength to keep it, after which they break up, and return home.

Norman devotes two pages of his book to exploring the revivalist aspects of temperance and Repeal and concludes that, after 1842, it became difficult to distinguish temperance and Repeal themes in public speeches in Ireland. The connection between temperance and Repeal was examined in the last chapter but it may be noted here that, however correct Norman may have been in seeing elements of revivalism, the tension between the movements, thanks to a great degree to Father Mathew, was always such that the listeners, if not the speakers, would always have been able to distinguish temperance and Repeal themes.[2]

Larkin's reference to the economic climate of the time is appropriate in that attention to economic conditions is seen as increasingly relevant to an understanding of millenarian movements. In her recent study of nineteenth-century millenarianism Anne Taylor has shown that in Swabia in southern Germany, the birthplace of George Rapp, the hope of the millenium was part of local folklore in an area plagued by famine, pestilence and oppression, conditions that bore some resemblance to those in Ireland, which was in addition going through a period of rapid social change — another usual accompaniment to millenarianism. O'Farrell's contention that hatred of the English or Anglo-Irish served as a secular substitute for millenial visions has been questioned by Roberts, who found that in the early nineteenth century such hatreds and grievances were capable of being incorporated into popular millenial visions. O'Farrell's view that Irish teetotallers were 'encouraged towards national and moral regeneration' and so revealed none of the millenialism evident in the anti-drink movement elsewhere may also be questioned insofar as it refers to Father Mathew's work. For while the large number of teetotallers that were Repealers confirms an encouragement towards national regeneration — although the encouragement came as much from local priests as from Father Mathew — and while Father Mathew himself saw temperance as a prerequisite to moral regeneration, the enthusiasm shown for the movement, especially in the early days, does suggest elements close to the hopes for radical changes in the world associated with millenarianism.[3]

The first characteristic of traditional European millenarian movements, writes Hobsbawm, was the total rejection of the present evil world and a longing for another, better one. It is clear from the Temperance Reports and newspaper accounts of the time that when drunkards took the pledge they were not just renouncing drink but the social occasions associated with drinking which, in the context of life in the country or small town, meant a radical change in their lives. Those who enrolled in a temperance society, Father Mathew told his audience at Clifden in the summer of 1840, 'are expected not only to give up intoxicating liquors, but to be more vigilant in governing their passions on all occasions'. Every temperance man becomes a new man, he said at Tralee at the end of the same year. Independent observers like Kohl seem to have been convinced that the old way of life associated with drinking had indeed been abandoned by millions. 'It may be doubted', he wrote in 1842, 'whether history furnishes an example of so great a moral revolution, accomplished in so short a time, and whether any man ever so quickly obtained so great and bright a name as Father Mathew.' James Silk Buckingham travelled in Ireland in August 1842 and claimed at a meeting in Exeter Hall the following January that he had seen 'only three intoxicated persons' there, one of whom was an English soldier, another a Scottish artisan and the third an Irishman. The rejection of the present way of life and the desire for a new is perhaps best reflected in the change of attitudes noticed by Grant. 'Formerly', he wrote for his English readers in 1844, 'a drunken man was a hero among the peasantry, now he is looked upon with a measure of abhorrence of which we in this country can have no idea.'[4]

Father Mathew had formulated no ideology to correspond to Hobsbawm's second characteristic of millenarian movements other than the simple moral necessity to stop drinking alcoholic drinks on the grounds that they were harmful or would lead to harm, either to oneself or by giving scandal to others. There could not be any doubt, he told the Clifden audience, but 'that the Almighty hand is directing this great moral reformation'. If God was directing it, resistance to it must have been from the devil. 'The prejudice that pervades Maynooth College, in favour of strong drink is a mystery to me', he wrote to a priest there, 'and I do not know how to account for the delusion except by attributing it to the machinations of Satan.' Others offered more sophisticated interpretations, Thomas Davis locating the drunkenness of the past as a symptom of political subjection and Father Mathew's work as a hope of freedom. Reduced through cruel treatment and misgovernment to a state near to barbarism, the Irish people, according to Venedey, gradually 'awoke to a consciousness of a higher destiny for which they were fitted', leading to a desire to free themselves from slavery to drink. But the principle of temperance could not have taken root, wrote Carleton in *Art Maguire*, his didactic novel on the harmfulness of drink, if the Irish people had not been ready for it, and to the objection that those on whom it made most impact — the habitual drunkards — were farthest removed from religious influences, he replied that they must have had 'the buried seeds of neglected instruction lying in their hearts'. It was not Father Mathew's eloquence that had brought about such great changes in Ireland, Robert McCurdy told the Belfast Total Abstinence Society early in 1840, rather, it was the conviction people had that the cause he was promoting was a good one 'and would cure the evils under which they were groaning'.[5]

The 'fundamental vagueness' about how the new society was to be brought about, corresponding to Hobsbawm's third characteristic of millenarian movements, was not present in Father Mathew's crusade in that it was clearly to be brought about by getting people to abstain from alcoholic drink for life, but it was present in that he and his followers were unclear as to how temperance was to be promoted and made permanent and how social as well as individual benefits would emanate from it. At the end of 1839 the *Waterford Chronicle* identified the feelings of many who had taken the pledge, resembling in some ways the feelings that several of the police officers and magistrates who wrote the Temperance Reports tried to describe three or four months later:

They say they experience not the slightest difficulty in eschewing their former habits. They feel they have triumphed over their "besotting sin", and now scarcely think of their habitual potations — nay, they profess a positive dislike of whiskey — they hate the scenes of their late abandonment, and loathe their past pursuits, they feel a new life within them, accompanied with an increasing sense of self-respect, and they are determined to make every atonement for their past by their amended habits and well regulated demeanour for the future.

Five years later Carleton described the feelings associated with an expected visit of Father Mathew's temperance mission to a locality:

Wherever it went, joy, acclamation, ecstasy accompanied it; together with a sense of moral liberty, of perfect freedom from the restraint, as it were, of some familiar devil, that had kept its victims in its damnable bondage. Those who had sunk exhausted before the terrible Moloch of Intemperance, and given themselves over for lost, could now perceive that there was an ally at hand, that was able to bring them succour, and drag them back from degradation and despair, to peace and independence; from contempt and infamy, to respect and praise. Nor was this all. It was not merely into the heart of the sot and the drunkard that it carried a refreshing consciousness of joy and deliverance, but into all those hearts which his criminal indulgence had filled with heaviness and sorrow.[6]

While McCurdy was prepared to vouch for Irish people's genuine conviction of the value of Father Mathew's cause, others saw the mass response to him as a symptom of Irish instability, 'the mark of a nation which is guided rather by emotions than convictions', as O'Connor put it later. 'The Irish character', declared a contemporary handbill, possessed 'a greater capacity for good or evil than that of any other country or nation, with a quickness of intellect, a vivacity of fancy, a restlessness of curiosity, that gives a constant thirst for knowledge, a warmth of heart that often induces acts without due reflection . . .' S.C. Hall, who recalled seeing Father Mathew give the pledge to an assembly of poor people in, he thought, Buttevant, county Cork, wondered at their motives. Some, he felt, were 'prompted by reason and reflection, some by superstition, some in accordance with an almost instinctive rule, by which numbers will follow where a few lead'.[7]

What a family might hope to attain from the drunken father taking the pledge is vividly illustrated on the temperance certificates held at the National Library in Dublin. On the left hand side is a picture of a man beating his wife while a child attempts to hold him back; on the other side domestic peace prevails, with a savings bank certificate over the fireplace. The message is simple. If a drunkard would only spend his money on the necessities of life rather than on drink there would be no poverty and domestic violence. When everyone took the pledge poverty would disappear. Speaking at Lismore early in 1840 Father Mathew summed up the beneficial achievements of the temperance movement up to that time — improvements in self-respect, respect for the laws of God and man, domestic happiness and public order — and went on to hope that by continuing in this manner the wounds inflicted on the country by religious and political differences would be healed, that sects and parties would forget their differences and that those belonging to them would 'spend the days that remained to them in the blissful bonds of charity and concord'.[8]

*   *   *

The association of pledge taking with superstitious feelings, something S.C. Hall noticed at Buttevant, was the subject of a specific question in the Inspector General's circular. In Chapter 2 it was noted that an account of Father Mathew administering the pledge in Cork in 1838 referred to it as 'taken under the deep seal of ecclesiastical authority — while the promise is regarded as a compact with the representative of their Creator'. At this stage of the movement, when nearly all of those coming to Father Mathew to take the pledge were Catholics, the fact that he was a priest was obviously helpful, and Birmingham gave his influence as a priest as the first reason for his success. There was nothing specifically Catholic about the wording of the pledge, however, which remained the same from the evening of 10th April 1838 until he visited Limerick at the end of the following year: 'I promise to abstain from all intoxicating drink, except used medicinally, and by order of a medical man, and to discountenance the cause and practice of intemperance.'[9]

George Carr was among those who understood the pledge to be binding for life but when he listened to the wording at the end of 1839 he agreed that he was wrong — the words 'as long as I will continue a member of a Teetotal Temperance Society' had been added, although this condition was removed again a year or so later. The Sub Inspector of Police for Skibbereen reported that in his District the condition of belonging to a teetotal society was accepted: those who found they could not live without alcohol and resigned from the teetotal society were felt to have acted honourably, while those who returned to drinking without formally resigning from the teetotal society were 'regarded generally as persons who have violated a vow as solemn as an oath'. The officer reporting from Kinsale, on the other hand, made no mention of any condition: in his district those who took the pledge were under the impression that if they broke it, whether or not they formally resigned from the Society, 'some immediate manifestation of the Divine judgement would happen them'.[10]

Both replies were in response to a question from the Inspector General of Constabulary on whether or not the pledge was associated with superstitious feelings. The reply from Kinsale was typical of the vast majority of those answering in that it made no mention of an acceptable release from the pledge by formally resigning from the teetotal

society and because it emphasised the widespread belief in divine intervention in the event of its violation. The Sub Inspector from Ennis
gave details of the stories in circulation 'of persons becoming deranged
who broke the Pledge, and of the whiskey they were about to drink being, on approaching their lips, turned into Blood, Maggots, etc.'. A man
told Sister Mary Francis Clare that he went to see Father Mathew out
of curiosity but 'found himself fairly fixed on the place where he stood,
and not one step could he move one way or the other'. Father Mathew
having approached him and advised him to avoid alcohol, he found that
when he was next presented with whiskey punch he was filled with feelings of disgust. Several of the police officers qualified the extent of superstitions associated with the pledge by attributing the expectation of
disaster to 'some few of the lower order' or 'numbers of the country people' or by noting that such beliefs were less widely held than formerly.
The Sub Inspector from Oughterard, himself a Catholic, noted the general
impression among the people that 'the anger of heaven' would follow
the breaking of the pledge. A few restricted their remarks to the offence
being seen as 'a great sin' and one saw it as being associated, not with
superstitious, but with 'religious feelings'.[11]

From Corofin it was reported that parish priests in the area were encouraging people to believe in the stories about divine judgement, but
in Clonmel there were two priests who were opposed to the movement
and went so far as to offer to absolve people from the pledge. Rather
more ambiguous was the attitude of a priest in Dingle, county Kerry,
who, having led the temperance procession through the streets of the
town on St. Patrick's Day, 1840, appeared drunk on the same streets
later in the evening and, for good measure, told a policeman kicked by
a drunk that he deserved it! These events encouraged the Head Constable in his report to venture the opinion that no strong feelings of
superstition regarding the violation of the pledge were apparent among
the people of Dingle![12]

A police officer who witnessed Father Mathew giving the pledge at
Kilkenny and Castlecomer made the point that while the pledge was
indeed associated with superstitious feelings, 'the deportment of Rev.
Mr. Mathew did not create or encourage such'. Maguire quoted Father
Mathew as saying that the pledge 'appears to be as fast binding as the
strongest oath'. While this *could* be taken to mean that the pledge *was*
as binding as an oath, the more likely meaning is that people's adherence
to the pledge was such that it was kept as faithfully as if it had been

an oath. Taking the pledge, he said in Dublin in November 1840, 'constitutes no religious vow whatever: it is simply a moral resolution to abstain from all intoxicating liquors, and thereby avoid evil'. This resolution
or promise, he later wrote, was all that was required from anyone who
wanted to become a teetotaller. In practice, however, the manner in which
it was administered 'imported as much as possible a sacred character
to the pledge'.[13]

While Father Mathew's attitude to individuals who broke the pledge
was compassionate in private, his public disapproval of those who had
lapsed suggests that at times he may have felt the pledge was more binding than a simple promise. Speaking at Toomyvara church in 1841, he
mentioned the small number who had broken the pledge, and added
that they 'must expect a Judas among so many when there was one found
among the apostles'. At Blackpool, Cork, in 1846, he stressed that the
pledge was a promise 'made to God on bended knees . . . No man or
woman who broke the pledge, without repenting and atoning for it, ever
recovered from their degradation, or ever was known to prosper in life.
The judgement of Almighty God falls on the pledge-breaker, as if God
in his mercy wished to protect the faithful teetotaller.' His language on
these occasions was moderate, though, when compared with that of the
newspapers that took it upon themselves to castigate those who had broken
the pledge and didn't intend to renew it. When Father Mathew visited
Waterford early in 1842 some who had broken the pledge availed of his
visit to take it again. Others didn't, and the *Waterford Chronicle* asked
indignantly:

What shall we say of the unrepentant perjurer who still like his prototype the
unclean animal, wallows in the mire of his own filth, and has not availed himself
of the Apostle's recent visit to wipe off the stain of perjury? We leave him to
the gnawings of his own guilty conscience, and the contempt of every honest
man in the community. Those wretched animals are well known, and however
they may brazen out their drunken habits, they are, and will continue to be,
despised, condemned and avoided.[14]

Father Mathew made significantly fewer crusades around Ireland during
1843, something that may have been dictated by his financial state but
may also have been influenced by a reluctance to be seen as in any way
associating his movement with Repeal. He may have been similarly influenced in the timing of his visit to England in the summer of that
year, when Repeal agitation was at its height. While in England he made

it clear that he did not wish to advance the interest of any party and when a man mentioned O'Connell at a meeting at Deptford in London Father Mathew ruled him out of order. The nature of the pledge excited curiosity there, however, and there was speculation about whether it was a vow or a promise and to whom it was made. He said in Leeds that the pledge was 'the simple expression of a determination to be total abstainers . . . a simple resolution'. Dr. Wiseman's view was that

when Father Mathew said 'promise' he said 'you do not promise Almighty God, you promise yourselves, you promise your wives, your families, society in general, and those whom you have degraded by intemperance, and whom it is your duty to elevate to the proper standard of humanity'.

Nothing new was added to the debate, no agreement was reached and Father Mathew refused to consider the question to be of great importance. Even when Frederick Lucas, editor of the *Tablet* and himself a teetotaller, drew attention to the wide variety of interpretations Catholic priests put on the pledge, Father Mathew showed little interest in the arguments, holding that it didn't really matter whether the pledge was a vow or a promise so long as it kept people away from drinking and permitted them to live better lives.[15]

Whether seen as a vow or a promise, some sought release from the obligations of the pledge by finding a doctor who would give dispensations on medical grounds. In April 1840, Father Mathew said in Dublin that he regretted including the words 'except for medical purposes' in the pledge, as he doubted very much whether alcohol was good for any disease. Towards the end of 1841 the words were deleted, but in January 1842 Father Mathew was lightheartedly complaining that he was still 'at war with his friends in the medical faculty, in consequence of their over pliancy in giving dispensations for drink'. Reporting the deletion of the medical clause from the pledge given by Father Mathew in Navan church a couple of months later the *Drogheda Argus* gave as the reason that 'some medical men were getting into the practice of permitting their patients "to take their medicine at the dinner table" '. He was still denouncing their interference with temperance in 1845, when he told the story of an asthmatic in Cork who was recommended by a medical man to drink Drogheda ale and died within a week. They had no right, he said, to prescribe any alcohol for teetotallers. 'Alcoholic drinks as medicine are a delusion', he wrote to a correspondent in England, and even as late as 1847 he had to admit that doctors' prejudices in favour of alcohol was something that could only be removed with time.[16]

Within a few days of Father Mathew leaving Limerick in December 1839 a cleave-boy was arrested when victuallers, indignant at his drunkenness, asked the Stipendiary Magistrate to apprehend him in person. On being charged, the youth said he had been to Cork to take the pledge from Father Mathew some months before and that on the day of his drunkenness he had drunk some 'ginger cordial', adding that 'if there was whiskey in it it was against my knowledge, for I would not drink a drop of it if I thought there was'. His plea of accidental drunkenness was surprisingly accepted, but on his acquittal he was warned that cordials were forbidden to members of temperance societies. Father Mathew condemned them frequently. 'You should not partake of cordials of any kind', he told his audience in Dublin in 1840, and two years later in Clare he was still cautioning teetotallers against them. Despite the fact that they were known to contain alcohol, the manufacture and import of cordials for teetotallers became a prosperous undertaking, with publicans happy to convince teetotallers that such drinks were permitted to them. In September 1840, a boy was arrested for stealing a gallon of cordial intended for teetotallers. The owner was said to have paid 3/6d. a gallon for it in Liverpool and was going to sell it at the substantial profit of 3½d. a naggin, or 9/4d. a gallon. By the beginning of 1842, however, it would seem that the trade in cordials was on the decline.[17]

For many, the greatest scandal associated with the pledge was not that some people broke it, nor that dispensations from its obligations could be obtained from doctors or from Father Mathew himself, nor that some resorted to the self-deception and hypocrisy of the cordial drinkers, but that many took it in a state of near or absolute intoxication. The Inspector General's Circular asked if it were true that people took the pledge in a state of intoxication, or at least got drunk when they decided to take it. About two thirds answered in the affirmative, although many did not make clear which of the two parts of the question they were affirming, or if they were saying both parts were true. Some, like the Sub Inspector for Enniscorthy, spelt it out clearly. He 'saw numbers take the pledge in a beastly state of intoxication and hundreds took (as they called it) their "farewell drop" immediately before receiving it'. With an ear to the worst impressions of the movement, the Sub Inspector for Arthurstown was willing to believe that many took the pledge in such a state of drunkenness that they returned again to take it, having forgotten they had already done so! Some of the reports made the distinction between getting drunk on deciding to take the pledge, which was common, and actually taking it while drunk, which was less so. Of those who denied that the pledge was taken in a state of drunkenness in their districts, a few conceded that this had been the case formerly but was no longer so. The Sub Inspector for Gort reported that while no one in his area now took it while drunk, it had previously been thought by 'the lower classes here that to render it useful, the pledge should be taken by persons while intoxicated'. Even from America it was reported that some were thought 'none too steady of step' as their friends urged them to take the pledge in Boston, while in Stratford in Essex, Father Mathew actually refused to give the pledge to a woman who was, the *Morning Chronicle* wrote, 'so drunk as to be scarcely able to maintain her perpendicular'.[18]

The 'farewell drop', it would seem, was extended over a long period for some. Reports from Sub Inspectors mentioned intending teetotallers getting drunk before they left for Cork to take the pledge, and the *Cork Constitution* was concerned about crowds arriving in the city from all parts of the country 'often in a state of inebriety'. This was in the autumn of 1839, but by the middle of 1841 there was an indication that Father Mathew was himself concerned about these final drinking bouts. At Toomyvara church he told the story of two people about to take the pledge who went into a public house to take their 'farewell drop'. They stayed there until they were turned out, whereupon they met a man whom they murdered and they were imprisoned in Kilkenny gaol.[19]

*   *   *

Regaled with outlandish stories about the fairies, the much-travelled Kohl had to admit that the Irishman was 'one of the most believing fellows I have ever met'. Many of the beliefs about cures went back to pre-Christian times and were, as Wood-Martin wrote of the Killery straining stones, a 'survival of the semi-Christianization of a pagan custom'. While the origin of belief in the curative power of the water of holy wells may have been older than Christianity, in practice such wells were often associated with a saint who had lived nearby. Not everyone going to holy wells was looking for a cure, as Hardy recorded from Ardmore, where the majority were doing penance rather than seeking cures. But the expectation of cures, perhaps fired to some extent by the relief from poverty and despair that the excitement associated with miracles could bring about, was an important element in keeping devotions at the wells alive. Living in what

Lady Wilde called 'an atmosphere of the supernatural' people had more confidence in traditional charms and incantations as defences against ill-health than in medicines prescribed by doctors. 'Of all the superstitions', her husband William Wilde wrote in 1849, 'the medical lingers longest', noting also that such superstitions were by no means confined to the countryside: fortune tellers and fairy doctors 'of repute' were to be found in and around Dublin.[20]

However ancient the origin of the beliefs relating to miraculous cures, they were, in the middle of the nineteenth century in Ireland, held by a population that was in fact Catholic and however adept people may have been in maintaining traditions of superstition alongside that of orthodox religion, it is hardly surprising that there was considerable overlapping of the two ways of confronting the supernatural. Writing at the beginning of the present century Wood-Martin drew attention to the difficulty of defining where superstition might be said to end and religion begin, and, with regard to miracles, the borderline may be particularly difficult to locate. Sectarianism could add further complications. When Archbishop Murray of Dublin issued a pastoral letter in 1823 announcing that one of the nuns at St. Joseph's convent, Ranelagh, had been miraculously cured of paralysis, one pamphlet dismissed it as an attempt to prove that the Catholic church 'is the exclusive church of the God of Nature'. Another, noting that the claimed cure took place during mass and the taking of communion, saw it as an attempt 'to prove that by the sacrifice of the Mass was the clemency to be obtained'. However much it might be dismissed as 'Popery', the fact that the Archbishop was unanimously supported by his clergy, and this in a diocese that included the largest urban area in Ireland, suggests that the belief in direct divine intervention in human affairs was in accordance with what Connolly has called 'long standing and deeply held traditions'. But an acknowledgement of miracles did not imply a sanction for credulity. While belief in some miracles has been sanctified by the Church and the expectation of others has not been forbidden, 'the proposal of false miracles' is listed among the sins of superstition.[21]

In this context it is not surprising that priests, especially those of particular sanctity, were often thought to possess special powers with regard to cures, to the extent that the clay from their graves mixed with water, for example, was used for healing in some parts of the country. Croly was no doubt exaggerating the credulity of country people's attitude to priests when he pronounced it as 'the prevailing notion' in 1834 'that the visible and invisible world is under their control, that they can at their will and pleasure make sick or make well'. But there is evidence of belief in a wide variety of healing powers ascribed to priests. Lady Gregory has recorded the tradition that they could cure strokes and madness. Elizabeth Andrews' book on folklore in Ulster quoted the words of a man from Donegal about a priest who had cured a twisted face supposedly caused by the fairies. ' "He was", the man added, "one of the old sort, who could work miracles, of whom there are not many nowadays" .' Evidence from the Irish Folklore Commission archives confirms traditions of the healing power of priests in different parts of the country. These include curing severe pain, healing a child (both county Waterford), curing an insane woman (Kerry), transferring a sore from a man to a hen (county Cork) and one manuscript tells of a priest who 'could cure whatever he liked and bring the dead to life' (Wexford). It was not only practising priests that were thought to have miraculous powers: the clay from the graves of others thought to have led lives of particular sanctity was sought after. Suspended priests were thought to possess particular powers and the Mayo ascetic Bernard Cavanagh, to whom many miracles were attributed, was in fact hostile to priests and often preached against their vices.[22]

While the church was having some success at this time in encouraging a movement away from traditional beliefs and practices towards something resembling modern Irish Catholicism, Kohl gave no hint of any changes in attitudes towards miracles when he put those attributed to Father Mathew in their historical context. 'In former days', he wrote,

Ireland had her St. Patrick, who banished toads and serpents from the island. At the present day she has her Father Mathew, who is banishing the spirit of drunkenness from her shores. Between both, there has been a multitude of miracle-workers of a similar kind. By these remarks I do not in the least wish to blot the fame of this worthy man, but only to show how the Irish are wont to encircle such individuals with the halo of saints.[23]

Before looking at some of the miracles attributed to Father Mathew it may be useful to consider briefly some of the weaker senses of the term 'miracles' used by contemporaries in referring to his achievements. The weakest and almost metaphorical use of the term was when it referred to the 'miracle' of making Ireland a temperate country. What was meant here was that, given the extent of drunkenness in the country, his success in curing it was an extraordinary achievement, as was his success in breaking down the resistance of individual notorious drunkards to taking the pledge.

A slightly stronger sense of the term is discernible in a statement by the Protestant nationalist William Smith O'Brien, who felt himself able to ascribe Father Mathew's success to 'none of the ordinary operations of human agency' and regarded him as 'specially deputed on a divine mission by the Almighty'. By this he probably meant that Father Mathew was carrying out God's will in saving Ireland from drunkenness, a view expressed by Pope Gregory XVI when told about it and by Father Mathew himself, when he said the results of the temperance movement 'are allowed by all to be the work of God'.[24]

There was also a widespread belief from an early date in his mission that Father Mathew had been told in a vision to take up the temperance cause, that he had a special divine-given gift for curing drunkenness and that the pledge, therefore, when administered by him, had a miraculous effect which left the recipient free from the wish to drink intoxicating liquor again.[25]

This was a mere two steps away from believing that Father Mathew could perform miracles in the full sense, and the intermediate step was encouraged by the common observation that many people who had taken the pledge had shown obvious improvements in their health. The undisciplined mind is prone to superstition, wrote Michael Quin of the *Dublin Review*, and this weakness led many to believe the improvements in health had come from the miraculous powers transmitted by Father Mathew through the temperance pledge, rather than from the improved constitution that could reasonably be expected in a body previously abused by heavy drinking.[26]

The Temperance Report from Loughrea found it 'melancholy and disgusting in the extreme to witness the credulity and superstition evinced by persons of every rank and station, possessing the Roman Catholic religion' who believed Father Mathew could perform miracles, and described the spectacle of boys pretending to be cripples and throwing away their crutches when Father Mathew gave them his blessing. When magistrates and members of the Grand Jury for the county could be taken in by such faked miracles, it sadly concluded,

it is not to be wondered at, that the lower ranks should be duped into this belief, and it is shocking to relate, but it is nonetheless true, that there is scarcely a single person amongst the lower orders who is not firmly persuaded that he has the power of working miracles. Mr. Mathew did not appear to openly encourage this erroneous superstition, but at the same time, he took scarcely any pains to disabuse the persons who had conceived this idea. It is likely he rather encouraged this opinion, knowing that it would be a great means of making them keep the pledge inviolate.

As will be seen later Father Mathew did in fact deny he had the power to perform miracles, though not as forcibly as some would wish. And while there were clearly other cases of deception like those at Loughrea, some of his reported miracles do in fact merit more serious consideration.[27]

In Waterford early in 1841 Father Mathew was credited with curing a young man from Wexford who was paralysed and dumb. Having taken the pledge and received Father Mathew's blessing, 'to the astonishment of everyone in the chapel where he took the pledge he threw away his crutches, walked off with his friends, and was able to speak with them, but in an extremely low key. This circumstance was witnessed by thousands.' More convincing than the evidence of the 'thousands' who would have been predisposed to believe it, was the evidence of the Poor Law Guardians for the City who confirmed that the man had indeed been a cripple, having applied to them for relief some time before.[28]

A case was reported in the Limerick newspapers, similar to that in Waterford in that the man cured was officially reported to have had the disease (Barrington's hospital was supposed to have given him treatment for it) and in that a large number of people saw him cured. It was different, however, in that the illness was said to have come on following his breaking the pledge.[29]

When a cripple was reported to have been cured by Father Mathew in Donegal, his landlord decided to investigate the claim 'to trace the matter and expose any imposture that might mislead the people'. Here again there seemed to have been no doubt about the man having been a genuine cripple before meeting Father Mathew, nor about the evidence that he was actually cured. He did, however, reveal an extraordinary strong faith, not in Father Mathew's power of healing but in God's power to cure him by means of Father Mathew's prayers.[30]

The Protestant press, not surprisingly, were first to denounce what they saw as attempts to promote Father Mathew's work by preying on the ignorance and superstitions of the people rather than by giving them rational explantions of why they should not drink. The *Dublin Evening Mail* was unhappy with the 'miracle-mongers' at the beginning of December 1839, and a few weeks later the *Tipperary Constitution* wrote that Father Mathew should openly declare that it was not in his power to perform miracles. Returning to the attack early in the new year the *Mail* claimed that many were attending Father Mathew's meetings around the country to be cured of lameness, blindness and other bodily ailments.[31]

No doubt fully aware of these criticisms and that his words and actions in Dublin would be given close scrutiny, Father Mathew said at a meeting at Beresford Place at the end of March 1840, that he had no powers of healing, and on the following day denied that he could perform miracles. Richard Allen later recalled that when a sick man was carried before him he asked that he be taken away, quoting Father Mathew's actual words, 'I have no more power than you.' These denials satisfied the *Dublin Evening Post* that Father Mathew had, while in Dublin, made every effort to dissuade people from the error of believing he could perform miracles, but with little success. The *Dublin Evening Mail* felt a stronger denial of the miracles attributed to him was required, and blamed the Catholic church, rather than Father Mathew himself, for allowing such ignorance to persist among its members that such things could be thought possible.[32]

It was clear that a simple denial that he could perform miracles was never going to be enough to convince his followers he had no such power. Towards the end of 1840 Thomas H. Edwards noted in his diary that when Father Mathew came to Carlow it was said that he could cure all sorts of diseases, so that 'Numbers of the most wretched-looking creatures are parading the streets, some in carts and others supported by their friends.' His followers attributed his denials to his modesty: he may deny that he has the power of healing, one of them told Kohl, 'but we know well he has it for all that'. The Halls noted that Father Mathew made very little effort to deny he had special powers and quoted a letter from him which said that he knew such superstition existed, but that if he were to publicly deny he had such power it would have impeded the progress of the movement. He even acknowledged that the cause of temperance and the superstition about his powers 'are so closely entwined, that the tares cannot be pulled out without plucking up the wheat also'. In some cases, accounts of his miracles were used as publicity for his meetings, although it is unlikely that he approved of this. The *Dublin Evening Mail* drew attention to a handbill distributed at the fair at Ballymahon, county Longford, which claimed that Father Mathew had performed 400 miracles and went on to announce his imminent arrival at Athlone. The *Mail* added, however, that it felt Father Mathew had nothing to do with the handbill.[33]

Did Father Mathew himself believe he could heal people? In the Donegal miracle referred to earlier he told the cripple he had no power to cure him or anyone else, that he would indeed pray for him, but that often those for whom he had prayed remained crippled or sick. This might be taken to suggest he believed that *some* of those for whom he prayed or to whom he gave his blessing *had* been cured. Jonathan Simpson watched him touch people who were carried before him at New Ross in expectation of cures, and asked him if he believed his touch would cure them. Father Mathew replied that he did not, but that if the people he touched thought it did them good, what was wrong with that?[34]

His refusal to deny strongly enough that he could work miracles and his continuing to touch invalids and give them his blessing or, as he put it, to ask God to bless them, left a sufficiently large grey area for people to react in whatever way suited their predispositions. 'I defy you', a man wrote to him in 1840, 'to show me a single man or woman or child relieved by you from any bodily or mental defect or infirmity.' On the other hand, a letter from a Protestant in the *Cork Constitution* in 1844 was pleased to note that in the case of Father Mathew there had never been any attempt at mock miracles even though no one could have had 'a greater opportunity of working on the superstitions of the peasantry than he'. The ambiguity about his attitude which permitted people to believe that he could perform miraculous cures while he regularly denied that he had the power to do so bore resemblance to that of O'Connell, who, while continuing to condemn violence, did so with an ambiguity that permitted people to believe that he was going to lead an armed revolt.[35]

The Protestant *Irish Ecclesiastical Journal* was concerned not so much that people were prepared to believe that he could work miracles but that so little effort was being made to see if miracles were in fact being performed. Surely, in the case of the Limerick man, the surgeons at Barrington's hospital could say whether or not the man had been suffering from paralysis? Or, in the case of a reported healing of blindness, it must be easy to find out if the person concerned had been blind and could now see? Both Catholics and Protestants were to blame, it went on, for not resolving such matters. The Catholic church should investigate such claims and expose them if they are false, and Protestants, for their part, should not 'suffer such statements to pass quietly into admitted and undisputed facts, without a single effort to arrive at the truth, on the spot and at the time'.[36]

Many Catholics were also unhappy about the expectation of miracles. Dr. Foran, Bishop of Waterford, who was one of Father Mathew's earliest supporters among the hierarchy, told people taking the pledge that Father Mathew had no power to cure diseases and infirmities 'and that if he thought he had and attempted to exercise it, he would not permit him'. In Philadelphia, Bishop Kenrick noted that many people brought their sick and blind to Father Mathew, who prayed for them and blessed them. The bishop's lack of enthusiasm for the matter is reflected in his laconic conclusion that he did 'not know whether any wonderful cures were wrought'.[37]

How important a factor in the success of his movement was Father Mathew's reputation for being able to work miracles? Mary Moore's grandmother saw him when he was in Navan

'I can see him again', said my grandmother, 'with his arms raised high above the heads of the people, whose cheers were hard to stop. It had gone out that he could work miracles. He knew it had and he said, "Do not think that I can work miracles, this arm is but an arm of flesh". Yet, many who took the pledge from him at that time felt that, as the result of the promise, they would see their third generation.'

There is a suggestion here that all who attended, and not just the sick and infirm, had hopes of supernatural benefits in some way derived from Father Mathew's miraculous powers, and to this extent his reputation helped the movement enormously. The position with the large numbers who came to his meetings in expectation of miraculous cures of particular infirmities also helped, for it not only swelled the numbers attending meetings but satisfied a need in sick and healthy alike. People did not wish 'the delicious delusion of restoration to health and strength' to be destroyed, wrote the Dublin correspondent of the *Nenagh Guardian* about Father Mathew's denial that he could heal the sick. It was seen almost as a form of entertainment. The overall good achieved by his crusade was seen by some newspapers as a reason for acquiescing in a form of behaviour they would otherwise deplore. The *Sligo Journal*, noting that Father Mathew 'so far complied with their superstitions as to touch each of them with his hand' would have preferred if he had not thus sanctioned people's ignorance, but concluded that 'where so much real and unquestionable good has been done, it becomes us not to censure too harshly'.[38]

His local supporters exploited the public's desire to see supernatural happenings as we have seen in the case of the handbill distributed at Ballymahon fair. When Father Mathew departs from a town or arrives in one, wrote the Sub Inspector from Arthurstown,

Placards are posted in all quarters detailing an account of the wonderful *Cures* and works he performed where he *last visited*, and this is a great cause of his being followed by such numbers and the Irish people, although shrewd and cunning in many particulars are as far as superstition is concerned especially in a case like this on a par with the Inhabitants of a less favoured country or perhaps the most uncultivated nation of the earth.

The expected miracles not having taken place, he noticed that afterwards many were disappointed, especially friends of the afflicted, and some had their confidence in Father Mathew shaken. It may be wondered if, as time went on and it became clear that not many were going to be cured of their afflictions, others, too, lost confidence in him and drifted away from the movement. It is interesting to note, in conclusion, that as perceptive an observer of Irish life as William Carleton blamed the lame, deaf, dumb and blind for bringing discredit on the temperance movement by claiming mock miracles. Though the superstitions associated with miracles, then, may have initially helped the rapid spread of the movement, they may also have contributed to some extent to its decline.[39]

Wearing the scapular was already a common exercise in piety in pre-Famine Ireland and in 1842 a hostile critic went so far as to affirm that there were more copies extant of a devotional booklet on the scapular than of any other work ever published in Ireland. Resembling the scapular in that it was hung around the neck and distributed by one whose reputation for working miracles was widely believed, it is not surprising that a priest in 1840 found his flock believing the medals from Father Mathew to be 'superseding the necessity of scapulars and other safeguards against danger'.[40]

Belief in its actual powers varied widely. Directly relating to temperance was the belief reported from Arthurstown that the light of the medal could banish all thirst — presumably the reference was to thirst for alcoholic drink. From Kilfinnane district an account was given of a man who would never go out at night for fear of ghosts, but, armed with his medal, he was no longer afraid to travel anywhere in the dark. In Galway it was thought that no evil could touch the person possessing the medal and in Abbeyleix a man thought that anyone wearing it could not be shot by policemen or soldiers. Kohl also found that the medals were worn as an amulet or talisman. The Sub Inspector's report from Abbeyleix contained a story illustrating another aspect of the medal's power: to commit a crime while wearing it led to madness. Most important, though, was the medal's supposed power to cure diseases, the Temperance Reports usually referring merely to the fact of this belief within their area but sometimes, as in the report from Cahir, explaining that the healing was effected by rubbing the medal to the diseased part of the body. In county Limerick W.R. Le Fanu saw medals that had been blessed by Father Mathew used in this way for curing rheumatic pains and, besides, had 'known one to be tied on the back of a man's hand to cure a boil, and I have seen opthalmia treated by hanging two of these medals over a girl's eyes'. More wide-ranging powers were attributed to medals and scapulars on the Aran Islands where, during a severe storm in 1841, a 'woman sent a boy, to immerse in the sea a bag containing two temperance medals and a scapular, believing they would calm the troubled waters'.[41]

The belief in Father Mathew's power to perform miracles persisted to the end of his life and people were still taken to him for cures at Lehenagh during his retirement. Maguire, while not committing himself to believing that Father Mathew could actually perform miracles, described several of the cures that were supposed to have been effected by him. One of these seems to have been witnessed by him and others were based on evidence that he considered reliable. He saw Father Mathew, with his obvious goodness and piety, not to mention his success in persuading so many to stop drinking, as fitting into the type of man that people would have expected to perform miracles: this in itself was a help in effecting cures of maladies where 'the mind could in any way become a useful agent'. As if unsatisfied that this explanation could not have accounted for all the alleged cures, he introduced the evidence of Dr. Barter, a Protestant who ran a hydropathic centre patronised by Father Mathew towards the end of his life. Barter was often a witness to the relief experienced by people who came to Father Mathew for cures and he was convinced that this was possible because Father Mathew possessed a large amount of what he termed 'animal magnetism'. Moreover, he believed Father Mathew's own paralysis was brought about by overusing this power, thereby draining his own nervous powers and bringing his life to an early end. This corresponds to some extent with what non-professional people believed about his paralysis: in response to his protests that if he had the power of healing he would surely cure himself, they would reply that he was afflicted with paralysis because he had taken the sickness of others upon himself. This in turn is in line with a tradition recorded by Lady Wilde, that healers 'must lose something when they do cures — either their health or something else.'[42]

The explanations of Maguire and Barter carried little weight with another of Father Mathew's biographers. Sister Mary Francis Clare, the 'Nun of Kenmare', while submitting to the authority of the church as having the final say in such matters, nevertheless felt certain that his cures were indeed miracles, that natural causes could not explain them and that, considering his life of incessant toil, it might be wondered, not that he died so young, but that he lived as long as he did. Besides, she added, how would Barter's explanation account for the miracles at Father Mathew's grave? For belief in his miraculous powers continued after his death. Maguire, writing seven years after Father Mathew died, noted that people went to his grave in St. Joseph's Cemetery seeking cures and, according to the evidence of the sexton there, many cures were effected. In 1914 the Bishop of Cork signed a statement in the presence of the Provincial of the Irish Capuchins to the effect that during his life Father Mathew 'was held in reverence by the people of Cork, as a priest of exceptional sanctity, and many people attributed cures to his prayers and blessings. After his death people were wont to pray for favours at his tomb.'[43]

A recent work on Father Mathew has suggested that a possible reason why he has not been canonised as a saint could be that Irish people have not been sufficiently persistent in putting forward his case to Rome. However this may be, it is of interest to note in conclusion that a contemporary American non-Catholic observer of Father Mathew's work, Dr. Channing, a man not given to emotional responses, held the following view: 'However much as Protestants we may question the claims of departed saints, here is a living minister, if he may be judged from one work, who deserves to be canonized, and whose name should be placed in the calendar not far below the Apostles.'[44]

CHAPTER 7

The Catholic Clergy

When he heard that Pope Gregory XVI's acceptance of one of the temperance medals had led to a rumour that he had become a teetotaller, Father Mathew was reluctant to issue a denial, as to do so might cause some to break the pledge.

The belief that his holiness has thus sanctioned our Sacred Society, has softened down the violent opposition of many of the clergy, who deep drinkers themselves, have openly encouraged the People to follow their example.[1]

As mentioned in Chapter 1, a small number of priests were active in the temperance movement before Father Mathew, though with rather limited success. A letter from one of them to Father Mathew in 1840 is worth quoting from at length in that it shows the difficulty of the task confronting such priests and the hope that Father Mathew's success must have given them.

It is now 20 years nearly since I commenced my missionary labours and though I have been a strenuous advocate of temperance during that period, and incessant in my exhortations, you have effected more good, in one short hour, than I have been able to achieve during the whole of my ministry. I have scarcely brought one parish to sobriety while you have persuaded a nation to abandon drunkenness and vice for temperance and virtue . . . When I came amongst them 15 years ago, the degrading vice of drunkenness was so habitual with persons of every class, grade and persuasion that it ceased to be considered discreditable before men or sinful before God. Ardent spirits were an indispensable offering upon every occasion of festivity, thanksgiving or business. All rejoicings ended in drunkenness, services were acknowledged by a trial to liquor

and no bargain was considered lucky unless it was consecrated and cemented
by a libation ... They began 12 years ago to make St. Patrick's Day, a day
of total abstinence and the next year ... to abstain from ardent spirits during
the whole of Lent ... many of the prime drunkards became teetotallers and
most of the rest confined themselves to a certain small allowance which, it was
supposed, would not injure them. And though some few broke out occasionally,
on the whole temperance was practised to such an extent that it would be difficult to find so many as five persons going home drunk from any of our fairs
or other public meetings. Thus far is the ground broken in this remote and
isolated district and with your help and God's blessing I hope my parishioners
will now universally pledge themselves to strict and total abstinence.[2]

Which was the more typical Irish priest of the time ? The heavy drinker,
happy for his parishioners to be as indulgent as he was, or the abstemious
priest from Belmullet, happy to see the battle against drunkenness being won? In his commitment to temperance before Father Mathew, Father
Lyons from Belmullet was certainly among a minority of priests. The
Cork Constitution, irritated by a suggestion in the *Dublin Evening Post*
that few Catholics were engaged in temperance work before Father
Mathew because of concerns over proselytising, drew attention to the
fact that not a single Catholic priest in Cork helped in the cause introduced into the city by a Protestant clergyman. Taking up the debate
locally, the Catholic *Southern Reporter* was unwilling to admit that the
clergyman, Rev. Nicholas Dunscombe, could really have been active before
Father Mathew, claiming that the latter had been a silent but effective
worker in the cause of temperance before making his commitment public
in 1838. Though the *Reporter* resented what it saw as the *Constitution*'s
'indirect thrust at the Catholic clergy', it did not deny the claim that
no priests had been publicly involved in promoting temperance in Cork.
But priests, like everyone else, had to reconsider their attitudes in the
light of Father Mathew's success. Before considering the role of Catholic
priests in the movement it may be appropriate to first look at the attitudes of Catholic bishops to Father Mathew's work.[3]

Commentators on the connection between Repeal and temperance were
usually concerned with explaining Repeal rather than temperance. Alison
believed the Catholic hierarchy was responsible for channelling into
Repeal agitation the surplus incomes of Irish labour that had previously been spent on drink. While abstinence from drink would indeed have
permitted repealers to respond more generously to church-based political
collections it might be questioned whether this was the hierarchy's main

interest in the temperance work of Father Mathew. In their recently published books Theodore Hoppen and Elizabeth Malcolm, while differing in their interpretation of the attitude to temperance of a few bishops, agree that the majority of them approved of the movement, although Malcolm adds that most of their support for it was only nominal, 'five or six at most being active and committed teetotallers'. The evidence would seem to suggest that the hierarchy's support for the cause may have been greater than she implies.[4]

As related in Chapter 3, it was invitations from Bishop Ryan of Limerick and Bishop Foran of Waterford that first enabled Father Mathew to extend his teetotal work outside Cork and Dr. Murray, when he asked him to come to Dublin, confirmed the movement as a national one. Besides these three prelates, early enthusiasm for his work was shown by Bishop Keating of Ferns, who invited him to Enniscorthy and sent a circular to the clergy in his diocese asking them to publicise the visit, 'that such as wish may attend on the occasion, and begin the good work of reformation.' Such was the enthusiasm at Oulart, a few miles from Enniscorthy, that priests were themselves giving the pledge to those who had not been able to go to Father Mathew in person. Keating was thought by a contemporary to have had reservations about the movement later, although Father Augustine, in his biography of Father Mathew, insisted that this was not the case, pointing to an invitation Father Mathew received to come to Keating's diocese as late as 1847.[5]

Bishop Browne of Galway had favoured teetotalism from at least 1836, had invited Father Mathew to Galway and continued his enthusiasm for his mission when he was transferred to the diocese of Elphin in 1844 — in Sligo in 1847 he praised Father Mathew for the benefits his work had brought to the diocese of Elphin. Like Browne, the commitment of Bishop Blake of Dromore pre-dated that of Father Mathew, having been active while a priest in Dublin in the early eighteen thirties, as noted in Chapter 1. He invited Father Mathew to Newry where large numbers became teetotallers, many of whom, according to an account written nearly fifty years later, kept the pledge for life. The enthusiasm of Bishop Cantwell of Meath may be gauged from a statement by Father Mathew at Ardmore in 1842 to the effect that more than half the priests in the diocese of Meath were teetotallers.[6]

Another supporter, Bishop Feeney of Killala, was either less enthusiastic than Cantwell or exercised less influence over his priests, for at a temperance meeting in Ballina in the middle of 1840 a toast was proposed to the health of the chairman, Rev. Peter Quinn, 'accompanied by the equivocal compliment that he was the only priest in the diocese to have taken the medal'. Bishop McGettigan of Raphoe took the pledge from Father Mathew at Letterkenny but must not have kept it as he was later described as a man who drank too much. Bishops Coen of Clonfert, Egan of Kerry, Haly of Kildare and Leighlin, Kernan of Clogher and Kinsella of Ossory all invited him to their dioceses, although the strength of their enthusiasm is difficult to determine. The last four named continued to support him at least into 1843, as their names appeared on the requisition for the Theatre Royal for the Mathew Testimonial. Kinsella's supposed opposition to the movement was, he explained in the autumn of 1840, based on the fact that he refused to bless temperance medals on the grounds that it might deter non-Catholics from joining what he, like Father Mathew, wanted to be a movement for all Irish people, irrespective of their religious beliefs.[7]

The *Catholic Directory* for 1842 recorded that almost every part of Dr. Browne's diocese of Kilmore had been visited by Father Mathew and the clergy and people 'have erected in every parish the glorious standard of temperance'. The bishop's commitment was illustrated in 1841 when he accompanied Father Mathew around his diocese every day for a fortnight. Perhaps the most enthusiastic of all Father Mathew's supporters among the hierarchy was Edward Maginn, who took over the diocese of Derry when Bishop McLaughlin had a breakdown, and was appointed Coadjutor Bishop in 1845. In a speech during one of Father Mathew's visits to Derry he argued that temperance had enabled Ireland to take her place among the peoples of the world. A letter from a mourner following Maginn's death in 1849 related how he campaigned against using barley for distilling during the Famine while people starved, how 'he hastened through his diocese preaching total abstinence from all intoxicating drinks, and animating his clergy and people in this holy warfare, adding example to precept, by first taking the pledge of total abstinence himself'.[8]

Of the remaining dozen or so archbishops and bishops in Ireland, two, Bishop Murphy of Cork and Bishop French of Kilmacduagh and Kilfenora, were on friendly terms with him. Father Mathew lodged with French when he was in Gort in 1846 and the Vicar General of the diocese, Dr. Nagle, was listed by Birmingham among the 30 earliest clerical supporters of the movement. Coming from a family engaged in the drink trade, Murphy was no supporter of teetotalism, but at the same time seemed to have offered no particular opposition to Father Mathew's temperance activities in Cork beyond the light-hearted teasing that Ullathorne witnessed when he went with Father Mathew to meet him. Murphy gave Father Mathew his blessing, to loud applause, in the course of the 1842 temperance procession through Cork attended by Daniel O'Connell.[9]

Archbishop Slattery of Cashel, Bishop Kennedy of Killaloe and Bishop Higgins of Ardagh voiced opposition to Father Mathew's nomination for the vacant seat of Cork when Bishop Murphy died in 1847. Despite having been elected as the favoured candidate by the parish priests of the diocese, he was passed over in favour of Father Delany, parish priest of Bandon. With Egan of Kerry, Slattery is listed as a 'non-temperance' bishop by Hoppen and is described by Malcolm as having been sceptical about Father Mathew's work while putting no obstacles in his way. Father Mathew was in Clonmel before the end of 1839, went on missions to, and stopped while passing through those parts of Tipperary within the diocese of Cashel on many occasions during the following six years. The Temperance Reports suggest great enthusiasm for the movement in the diocese, with 8,000 having pledged themselves in the Cahir district alone by March 1840. When Father Mathew came on one of his many visits to Thurles in 1844 he was reported to have been 'specially invited by his Grace the Archbishop of Cashel' and on the cover of the 1845 edition of the rules of the Thurles Total Abstinence Society Dr. Slattery is named as the Patron. That Slattery did not take a more conspicuous role in promoting Father Mathew's work in his archdiocese may have been as much attributable to his introspective and retiring nature as to any scepticism he may have had about its benefits.[10]

As noted in Chapter 1 Bishop Kennedy's involvement in the temperance movement in his diocese dated from 1838. Few dioceses could have more frequently appeared on Father Mathew's itinerary, including as it did such prominent towns in the temperance movement as Kilrush, Ennis, Nenagh and Borrisokane. At a dinner in Kennedy's honour in 1842, attended by Father Mathew, it was said that he was among the first to invite him into his diocese and give his co-operation and sanction to his temperance mission. While the opposition of Slattery and Kennedy to Father Mathew as Bishop of Cork were probably based on the overenthusiasm of the priests and laity in the diocese in promoting his candidature rather than on any hostility towards his temperance work, Bishop Higgins' opposition, which took the form of a letter to Cullen in Rome, expressed the view that, as recipient of a government pension, he would act as 'a check and a spy' in the deliberations of the Irish Bishops. Higgins, however, was not opposed to the temperance movement. Father Mathew would have been welcomed in his diocese if, after paying for medals and cards and other expenses, the proceeds of his work in the diocese would be put to the fund for building Longford cathedral. Following Father Mathew's failure to agree to this, Higgins began to administer the pledge himself, although some preferred to travel outside the diocese to take it from Father Mathew. A letter from a priest in Athlone who had tried to mediate between Bishop Higgins and Father Mathew makes it clear that the disagreement was purely over money:

It is unnecessary for me to assure you of the great value Dr. Higgins sets on your unparalleled labours in this holy cause. His Lordship has this day as well as at Moate panegyrised them in the most emphatic language to the people and earnestly invoked their fervent prayers for you and all other zealous clergymen who distinguish themselves in this holy war against the too long national vice of intemperance.[11]

It is rather ironic that the disagreement between them should have centred on the 'profit' made once expenses had been covered, as events seem to have shown that a loss rather than a profit was normally sustained on Father Mathew's crusades around the country. It is interesting, however, that Higgins should have believed that money was being made from the movement despite Father Mathew's many denials. The suspicion of regular priests bleeding parishes dry had been long held by secular clergymen, and there was more than a hint of it too in Archbishop MacHale's purported reference to Father Mathew as a 'vagabond friar'. Father Mathew wrote to Dr. Cullen, then Rector of the Irish College in Rome and agent of the Irish bishops there, thanking him for securing for him the office of Commissary Apostolic, which confirmed him as a missionary directly answerable to the Holy See. In his letter he referred to MacHale's renewed hostility, which most recently had taken the form of an attack on Father Mathew which, besides referring to him as a 'vagabond friar', accused him of going around the country with a woman and making an enormous profit from selling temperance medals which he spent on brandy, 'laughing at the poor dupes, whom he robbed'. It is clear from his reply that Cullen valued the work Father Mathew was doing, but while regretting the hostility it evoked in some ecclesiastics, he recommended that he suffer in silence. MacHale's hostility did not go completely unchallenged. A letter from 'A Teetotaller of Galway' in the *Connaught Journal* at the end of 1840 suggested that MacHale's attitude was damaging his reputation and in 1843 a faction fight in county Galway was blamed on the Archbishop preventing Father Mathew from crusading in his diocese.[12]

But MacHale actually approved of teetotal societies, though he favoured a shorter pledge than that for life insisted upon by Father Mathew. The Tuam Temperance Society had 150 members in 1840 and when Father Kileen came from Galway seeking funds for the completion of the Augustinian chapel he gave the pledge to 400 people, mostly women. Hope was expressed that Father Mathew would visit Tuam when he was next in the West but that was not to be. Many in the Tuam diocese had taken the pledge and bought medals. MacHale's complaint was that while Father Mathew had collected a large amount of money for medals in his diocese he had made no contribution to the Archbishop's schools, set up in opposition to the government's national system of eduction. Matters were not helped when a letter from Father Mathew to John Kernan of the Tuam Temperance Society, which expressed wonder at MacHale's opposition to teetotalism, found its way into the *Galway Advertiser*. In 1841 teetotallers in Westport, angry at MacHale's attitude towards Father Mathew's work, resolved to support only those clergymen that were favourably disposed towards the Temperance Society. The resolution was condemned by the *Galway Vindicator* as 'most unwise, most presumptuous and most unjust'. It added that MacHale was not hostile to temperance societies and hoped that other temperance societies would follow Father O'Connell of the Metropolitan Total Abstinence Society, who had condemned the Westport teetotallers. Father Mathew expressed his disappointment at O'Connell's condemnation; O'Connell, in turn felt that however important the success of temperance might be, he could not countenance anything in its promotion that would 'sever the attachment between the priesthood and the people'. MacHale's attitude changed in due course, perhaps realising from the publicity Father Mathew's debts received that he could not have been making all that much money from his temperance medals. In 1852 Forbes noticed that MacHale had become 'reconciled to lay schools as well as to the system of Father Mathew . . .'[13]

Archbishop Crolly of Armagh and Bishop Denvir of Down and Conor (which included Belfast) were opposed to Father Mathew visiting their dioceses because, they claimed, the peace might be disturbed by

Orangemen. Crolly promised to review the situation when Father Mathew had visited other parts of Ulster. He did visit Ulster on many occasions, and though there was occasional opposition shown, in general he was welcomed with enthusiasm by Protestants and Catholics alike. His warm reception in towns like Cootehill, Carrickmacross (where 80,000 were reported to have taken the pledge), Monaghan, Castleblaney and Newry was such as might be thought sufficient for Crolly and Denvir to invite him to Armagh and Belfast, but no invitation came. That Crolly probably had little real interest in Father Mathew's crusade may be inferred from the fact that in his speech at a banquet in honour of the hierarchy who were meeting in Cork city in the autumn of 1839 he made no reference to temperance, despite the fact that hundreds of teetotallers were arriving daily in the city to take the pledge from Father Mathew and that Daniel O'Connell, in an earlier speech at the same banquet, had spoken of the great moral change that had been brought about by the temperance movement. It needs to be remembered, on the other hand, that Crolly and Denvir were very much aware of religious tensions within their dioceses, where Catholics were becoming sufficiently numerous to present a threat to Protestant domination — Crolly himself, while parish priest in Belfast, had seen his presbytery windows broken by Orangemen. They might possibly have had some sympathy with Father Mathew's work, but thought the risks of promoting it within their dioceses too great. They would have known, also, that Father Mathew was certain to receive invitations to the diocese of Dromore and to give the pledge in towns within easy reach of Belfast and Armagh. Indeed, an estimated 10,000 people from Belfast were thought to have taken the pledge when he was in Moira in 1842.[14]

About twenty bishops, then, invited Father Mathew to their dioceses, with about half that number showing support that could be considered enthusiastic, with the remainder, insofar as it can be determined, showing little interest beyond allowing him to preach temperance and give the pledge in their dioceses. A few lost their enthusiasm as time went on. Of those who did not invite him, two were specifically opposed to the profit they thought he was making on temperance medals sold, money which they felt ought to go to projects within their dioceses. Two others claimed not to have invited him in order not to risk initiating religious strife, and neither seems to have put any obstacle in the way of large numbers from their dioceses going to neighbouring dioceses to take the pledge from him. Of the few bishops remaining, none seems to have made any public pronouncement disapproving of Father Mathew or the temperance movement and one, Bishop Crotty of Cloyne and Ross, seems to have had no objection to Father Foley carrying out his temperance mission in part of his diocese.

A speech made by Rev. B.J. Roche, P.P., at a reception for Father Mathew when he was in Galway in 1846 shows how difficult it would have been for a bishop to disassociate himself from Father Mathew, even if he had reservations about the temperance crusade. Having praised Bishop O'Donnell, Father Roche concluded:

He had no doubt their Bishop would be found willing to co-operate with the temperance movement, and to encourage their distinguished guest in his arduous labours — he well knew that a temperate people would be more obedient to the pastor's voice and submissive to the authority placed over them.

A bishop who was not sympathetic to the teetotal movement, he seemed to be telling O'Donnell (who was not present), could not expect to have an obedient flock.[15]

That the movement had close links with the Catholic clergy is evident from the Temperance Reports. The teetotallers in Enniscorthy met in a chapel, those from Kilfinnane had mass said regularly in the room they rented for their meetings and at Abbeyleix mass was said once a month for each member and five when a member died. St. Mary's Temperance Society in Limerick city had a rule that enjoined every Catholic member to go to confession at least every six months. In Enniscorthy priests refused the rites of the church to anyone who would not join the local temperance society and the same was threatened in Corofin, where priests were said to have had complete control of the temperance societies. When a slater broke the pledge in Galway, the local paper reported, the parish priest went to his employer and had him dismissed, and the man was only able to get his job back when he took the pledge again.[16]

Evidence from contemporary sources about the extent of priests' involvement in Father Mathew's work needs to be qualified by the consideration that some of them may have gone along with it in order not to alienate their teetotal parishioners. The support, however, does seem to have been considerable. In response to an Orange jeer that the Catholic clergy were careful to abstain from the practice of temperance, the *Waterford Chronicle* claimed at the end of 1839 that priests not only preach Father Mathew's temperance principles but 'practise them with scrupulous observance'. The cause of temperance prospers in Ireland, Richard Allen wrote around the same time, because as many as 300 Catholic clergymen were among its subscribers. The extent of clerical support revealed in the Temperance Reports, written a few months later, suggests that the figure of 300 may not have been an exaggeration — certainly McCurdy's contention that 'not more than a dozen' priests had adopted Father Mathew's principles by March 1840 was an underestimation. On his visit to Connaught alone, Father Mathew told his Dublin audience at the end of March, 'not less than fifty clergymen had taken the pledge'.[17]

Writing in April or May 1840, Birmingham listed the names of 30 priests who joined the movement 'in the early stages of the progress of temperance', though he added that many more might have joined since Father Mathew went to Dublin. Two thirds of those listed were from the dioceses of Killaloe, Waterford and Clonfert. That support among priests was strongest in those dioceses where the bishop was enthusiastic was to be expected. We have already noted the large number of priests who were teetotallers in the diocese of Meath, and it was claimed at the dinner to honour Bishop Kennedy at Nenagh that there were more clerical teetotallers in Killaloe than in any other diocese in Ireland. The Temperance Report from Waterford city announced that the priests there were 'strenuously endeavouring to maintain and extend' the principle of total abstinence. The Sub Inspector at Rathkeale in the diocese of Limerick reported that the clergy there 'advise them in the confessional, exhort them from the Altar and in their cabins' to keep the pledge. In an addendum to his report the Sub Inspector from Oughterard in the diocese of Galway predicted that as the presidents of most temperance societies were likely to have been parish priests,

an immense power will be added to the great influence these functionaries already possess — a power that will appear (unlike that exercised in Politics), to belong to them legitimately, as the great ostensible object of these Societies is the prevention of vice, and the promotion of virtue and morality amongst the people. The disciplined regularity and steady habits produced by these Societies will become also active auxiliaries to their ordinary influence; as it is a well ascertained fact that in proportion as the Catholic population become moral and regular, they become more connected with their priests, and more amenable to their councils.[18]

By the time that Birmingham was writing the Introduction to another edition of his book on Father Mathew at the end of 1840 he was able to claim that about 500 Catholic clergymen had joined the movement. This constituted about a quarter of the priests in the country at the time. Father Mathew confined himself to a statement in the autumn of 1840 to the effect that the Catholic clergy had 'in numerous instances' been assisting the promotion of temperance. At a temperance meeting in Cork the following February it was announced that 700 priests had joined. Father Mathew must have been encouraged when he was in Ballyshannon at the beginning of 1841 and saw temperance societies from Fermanagh, Leitrim and Donegal come into the town 'headed by their Parish Priests and musicians' and when, a few months later, back again in the diocese of Raphoe, he saw thousands come into Letterkenny from surrounding districts led by their priests, nine of whom were named.[19]

An appeal from James Haughton around the middle of 1841 calling on clergymen to help make Father Mathew's revolution permanent suggests that the involvement of priests may have been decreasing, although at one time in 1842 Father Mathew claimed he was holding 70 invitations from bishops and priests to administer the pledge in different parts of the country. A letter he wrote to Dr. Kirby in Rome in May of the same year seemed to confirm that clerical support was still largely confined to those diocese where the bishop was well disposed towards the cause. When he was in Nenagh the following month he must have been encouraged by a humorous allusion to the benefits ambitious priests might derive from the silver medal he gave each of them who took the pledge:

Hints began . . . to be thrown out that a silver medal would be no bad recommendation to a good curacy, as the Parish Priests were determined to give a decided preference to curates of that caste . . . all the talent of the Church was enlisted at the side of the great moral reformation.

The speaker, a local priest, went on to say how the Catholic clergy had secured a more disinterested and permanent gain from Father Mathew's work, in that their teaching was now producing a greater effect on the lives of their parishioners. This was in the diocese of Killaloe, of course, and may not have been an accurate reflection of the situation with priests throughout the country and indeed, later the same year, Father Mathew told an American visitor that the Catholic clergy 'were not generally favourable' to his work.[20]

In 1843 there was disagreement among visitors about the role of the clergy in the promotion of temperance, although there was unanimity about their advocacy of Repeal. Venedey felt that as the Irish people were already accustomed to being guided by their priests, Father Mathew's employment of them to promote his movement 'was to advance on a road that was already prepared and made smooth for him'. Kohl, his compatriot, thought it was the movement that had swept the priests along in the first place:

The Roman Catholic priesthood of Ireland, though, at first, they beheld with jealousy the movement originated by the exertions of a simple monk, have allowed themselves to be borne along by the stream; nay, have even partially placed themselves at its head, and the entire matter has thus assumed a Catholic-religious character. [21]

Did Father Mathew want the movement to be a specifically Catholic one? As noted in Chapter 3, the Temperance Reports indicated that some Protestants had taken the pledge in most police districts in the southern counties and a considerable number had done so in a few. It has also been seen that Father Mathew's reluctance to give the pledge in Catholic churches in the early days of his crusade was to prevent the movement from getting a 'sectarian tinge'. On his return from a successful trip to Ulster in 1841 he said he was proud that sectarian feeling 'had disappeared wherever he had gone — at least there had been no manifestation of it'. In the presence of Protestants, too, there seems to have been efforts to discourage aspects of the movement that might meet with their censure. At Nenagh in March 1840, for example, when the Protestant rector of Nenagh was present, invalids were discouraged from soliciting cures and Father Mathew was seen to withdraw his hand when people attempted to kiss it. Speaking at Enniskillen in 1843 he was able to assure his audience that while it was true that the greater proportion of his teetotallers were Catholics, people of all religions belonged, with many Protestants enrolled, for example, in the Bandon Temperance Society. Cullen, in response to Father Mathew's complaint about MacHale, noted that Father Mathew's known anti-sectarianism was being interpreted by some critics as indicating 'sentiments too liberal towards Protestants in matters of religion'.[22]

But if Father Mathew clearly wished to make Protestants as welcome within his temperance campaign as Catholics, and often went out of his way to emphasise this, there were Catholic clergymen among his supporters who saw the movement purely in Catholic terms. Many priests felt those who took the pledge were better Catholics, Father Scanlan of

Nenagh going so far as to say that they were exemplary in their piety and that 'religion had a new conquest in every convert to teetotalism'. Father Mathew himself, in a rare attempt to spell out what temperance might actually achieve, said that it paved the way to morality, religion and social improvement. There is evidence of a similar connection between temperance and religion in England and Wales. In 1838, 170 of the 177 members of the Birmingham Total Abstinence Society were found to be regular church attenders, and the Abergavenny Total Abstinence Society claimed in 1840 that intemperance was preventing thousands from hearing the gospel.[23]

The support that priests gave to Father Mathew in Ireland was in fact substantial when compared to that given by clergymen to the temperance movement elsewhere. There was initially little support for teetotalism among ministers of religion in Wales, although this did grow substantially, especially among Calvinist Methodists. Lists of ministers committed to teetotalism in England in 1837 and 1848 showed that while support for the movement doubled in eleven years, it came mainly from Independents and Congregationalists, with only a small number of the clergymen of the Church of England listed. In Lower Salesia in Germany in 1847 only about one twentieth of the Protestant clergymen took any active interest in the temperance movement.[24]

Granted the acknowledgement of a close association between temperance and religion and the relatively substantial support that was forthcoming from the hierarchy and priests, it may be wondered why Father Mathew did not make more use of them to extend and consolidate his work. 'The results of the great Temperance movement are allowed by all to be miraculous, and no one ought to interfere', he wrote to Dr. Kirby in Rome in 1842, having condemned Bishop Kenrick of Philadelphia for forming the teetotallers in his city into a confraternity and other clergymen in America for permitting such dispensations from, or dilutions of the pledge as they considered appropriate to local circumstances. This, and his claim in the same letter that people do not consider themselves teetotallers until they have received his blessing suggests he was opposed in principle to any organisational structure to promote the cause. Two years later he emphasised that the temperance movement was directed by the finger of God. This could hardly have been encouraging to any priest who might have ideas about how to promote the movement locally or who wanted assistance or advice on how to deal with a local problem related to temperance.[25]

His conviction that the divine will was somehow acting itself out through him and his apparent hostility to the efforts of others who did not adhere strictly to his methods in the promotion of temperance is evident in his controversy with Father Spratt in 1846. Spratt had been giving the pledge to Dubliners in considerable numbers but when he arranged one of his meetings for Finglas on the same day as Father Mathew was holding one at Sandyford he was accused of creating a division among the temperate and having 'other objects, besides the promotion of teetotalism'. When, later in the year, Spratt visited Belfast and Drogheda to give the pledge, he was reprimanded by Father Mathew for doing so without the permission of the parish priests and, in the case of Drogheda, against the known wishes of the parish priest. He felt obliged to distance himself from Spratt's activities, Father Mathew argued, because there was an impression that Spratt was acting with his 'approbation'. Had he been silent, Father Mathew wrote, 'all the Bishops in Ireland would have become opposed to the Temperance movement'. It was his policy, he wrote in another letter, not to hold a temperance meeting in any parish unless invited to do so by the parish priest.[26]

Given the state of ecclesiastical discipline in the Catholic church in Ireland at the time and the fact that Father Mathew held the title of Commissary Apostolic from Rome permitting him to preach anywhere in Ireland, it is to be doubted whether countenancing a temperance meeting in a city or town without the approval of the parish priest would have turned the hierarchy of Ireland against the temperance movement. His attitude towards Spratt and his successful campaigns — he gave the pledge to 5,000 in Belfast — and his lack of enthusiasm for the kind of organisational structure which might consolidate the gains made against drunkenness, suggest that he was reluctant to relinquish personal control of the movement. Whether he was influenced in this by motives of vanity or jealousy or from a genuine conviction that God was acting directly through him is something that will never be known, but it is in any case clear that what was needed was some kind of national body, perhaps with representatives from each temperance society or group of societies. That the basis for such a body existed in 1840 is clear from the Temperance Reports which show priests involved in almost every district in the counties surveyed by the Inspector General of Constabulary. To have given these priests access in some way to a national temperance organisation would have enabled them to influence the direction the movement might take, an influence based on experience of promoting the cause locally, which in turn could have been enriched by their shared experiences on a national level. Far from encouraging any such development, Father Mathew would almost certainly have opposed it, and there seems to have been no serious effort to establish any kind of national structure beyond entering all teetotallers' names on a register kept in Cork. Whether such a national organisation, had it been formed, would have been able to withstand the upheaval of the Famine years is debatable, but, had it done so, the isolated efforts of priests recorded by Forbes in 1852 might have been drawn together to give the movement a new lease of life.

CHAPTER **8**

Conclusion

The year 1845 opened with Father Mathew in an optimistic mood. There was only one backslider in every 500 teetotallers, he wrote, and all 'the rising generation are being educated in the strictest habits of temperance; and in a few years, dunkenness will be a thing passed away, never to return'. His optimism was still evident in October, when, speaking of a visit to Blessington, county Wicklow, he noted that only a tiny number of those who had taken the pledge when he first went there five years before had violated it. Even when press reports showed that nearly twice as many drunkards had been committed to Cork Bridewell during September 1845 than during the same month in 1844, he continued to argue that drunkenness had been banished, and that there were more teetotallers than ever in the city. Had there not been races in Cork during September, and had not the recent increase in the numbers employed given heavy drinkers the opportunity to indulge themselves even more? The comparison should have been made, he concluded, not with a year before, but with a period before he began his temperance mission.[1]

By this time the partial failure of the potato crop, first noticed in September, had been confirmed as being 'extremely extensive' by the Mansion House Committee, who had based their report on information received from all parts of the country. Among the Committee's recommendations to meet the expected scarcity of food were the closing of Irish ports to the export of all foods and the suspension of the use of grain for distillation. The extent of the disaster was quantified by a report from the Scientific Commission set up to suggest remedies for the potato

168

TABLE 8.1

**THE NUMBER OF DRUNKARDS COMMITTED TO CORK CITY
BRIDEWELL, ENDING 1 APRIL EACH YEAR, 1841-46**

1841	2,087	1843	1,607	1845	3,374
1842	2,842	1844	2,452	1846	6,622

Source: *Cork Constitution,* 14 April 1846.

failure: more than half the Irish potato crop had been lost. Speaking to farmers at Golden chapel at the end of 1845 Father Mathew drew attention to the 'threatened scarcity' and recommended a more extensive system of flax cultivation. This, and other advice for improving agriculture was, in the opinion of the local newspaper, more likely to influence the farmers than the advice of professionals.[2]

Back in Cork, he had to defend the movement there against more accusations of backsliding. He was able to answer most of them with reasonable conviction, although a set of figures appeared in the *Cork Constitution* in April (Table 8.1) which caused him considerable concern. Faced with such an enormous increase in the number committed for drunkenness — it had almost doubled during the last year — he had to concede, in a letter to the *Constitution*, that drunkenness did indeed still occur in Cork city. But most of those taken up were 'poor sinful females', he went on, who were often taken into custody several times in the course of the year. One unfortunate woman had been arrested 161 times during the previous year, and she and six other women had been taken up so often that they represented nearly 1,000 of the arrests for drunkenness in that year. 'Others have been taken up sixteen times in a fortnight, others twenty five times a month, others ten times a month. It is easy, then, to see how the list of six thousand has been made out.' He concluded by agreeing that the existence of even one Christian drunkard was to be deplored and that everything should be done to prevent it. In a comment the *Constitution* asked if the seven had not been equally 'sinners' the previous year, and suggested that as the figures had always been collated in the same way, a reason for the recent increase still had to be found. The comment concluded by reminding Father Mathew of the numerous cases of drunkenness that never reached the eye of the police.[3]

Perhaps a clearer indication of the decline of the influence of temperance in Cork may be gleaned from the returns for drunkenness for the city over the decade from 1841 to 1851 (Table 8.2). The increase in drunkenness that was recorded in the years 1844-51, taken together with the national increase in the consumption of legally distilled spirits during the same period (despite a decrease in population amounting to nearly two million), are but a sample of the statistical evidence available to show that, however much the movement may have been in decline before the Famine, such decline was certainly further accelerated during the Famine years.

The ways in which the temperance movement was affected by the Famine will be considered under three headings: those associated with Father Mathew himself, those associated with the large scale social disruption of the time and finally, those associated with emigration.

Though involved in Famine relief work from an early date, Father Mathew continued to travel around the country to promote temperance. Sometimes, as at Galway in January 1846, he was able to combine preaching a charity sermon to raise money for victims of want with pledging and re-pledging teetotallers. As conditions worsened, increasing demands were made on his time by the food crisis. He took on the role of unofficial but highly respected adviser on Irish conditions. General Hewetson, a government official in Cork, described him as 'well acquainted with the country and the habits of the lower orders, [who] gave me a good deal of interesting information'. Father Mathew was also useful to the officials who were trying to carry out such relief measures as the Government organised. Hewetson found him helpful, not only in gauging the poor's response to the Government's Indian corn, but in combatting prejudice against it. Sir Randolf Routh of the Relief Commission

TABLE 8.2

DRUNKENNESS IN CORK CITY 1841-51

1841	2,018	1845	6,513	1849	6,508
1842	1,685	1846	6,246	1850	8,855
1843	2,345	1847	4,148	1851	8,185
1844	3,378	1848	5,532		

Source: *Return . . . Drunkenness.* P.P. 1852-3 (531), lxxxi, pp. 300-301.

had written a pamphlet on the various dishes that could be prepared using Indian corn, and Father Mathew made his contribution to combatting prejudice by writing to the local newspapers enclosing a sample of a loaf and stirabout made from Indian corn, together with instructions on how to use the unfamiliar meal. Both the *Cork Examiner* and the *Cork Constitution* agreed on the 'palatableness' of the food, and Maguire recalled in his book how Father Mathew at this time used to stand at his door eating a piece of cake made from the yellow meal and giving the impression that he was enjoying it.[4]

He was always prepared to take the side of the starving poor against those who were ready to make profits from their misery. When food prices rose at the end of 1846 Father Mathew complained to Trevelyan, Secretary at the Treasury in London, that the people had been abandoned to the corn and flour traders who were making up to 100 per cent profit on transactions. Cargoes of corn were bought up before the ships even reached Cork 'and are sold like railway shares, passing through different hands before they are ground and sold to the poor'. The extent of his personal involvement in the sufferings of the poor may be appreciated in an extract from a letter to Trevelyan the following summer:

My residence is near the part of the suburbs of Cork occupied by market gardeners. Several of these industrious people rushed into my parlour at an early hour this morning in an agony of terror exclaiming that the blight was come again in that the potato field of their neighbour Flynn was destroyed last night, and that they would be all ruined. Incredulous, I went in person to the stricken field, and found with deep sorrow that the statement was not exaggerated. A dense, wet fog continued to envelop the district . . . After its disappearance, the gardener's wife . . . found a large portion of the garden drooping, wilted and of a dark brown colour. She hurried into her house with loud cries and her husband rushed to the field and . . . discovered that another plot of potatoe ground, separated for the farmer by a most luxuriant crop of wheat, was also blighted. We are all panic struck, waiting in every house in this rural district. A few days more will decide the destiny of thousands . . .[5]

His advice to government agencies, his appeals to them on behalf of the needy, as well as his attempts to harness the sympathy of the public in Ireland and abroad engaged only a part of his energies. At a more practical level he was on the Relief Committee for Cork city and for a time turned his own home into a soup kitchen for the starving. During the winter of 1846-7 he was also trying to establish a public bakery and to organise relief through the schools. There was opposition from the tradesmen bakers, and his aim of producing a 4lb. loaf for sale at 6d. or 6½d. was not realised, although the public bakery managed to produce one for 8¼d., compared to 9¾d. to 10d. in the shops. When he gave the charity sermon for Peacock's Lane and Sullivan's Quay schools the large sum of £120 was raised, and a note on the proceedings in the local press said that the schools were spending £4 per week on bread. Up to the autumn of 1846 he was maintaining his commitment to temperance, as may be witnessed from his 'schedule for the coming weeks' which appeared in the *Cork Examiner* in September:

Left town last evening, as one of the Poor Relief deputation to his Excellency, and will return on Friday. On Saturday evening, he will leave for Kilfinnane, in the county of Limerick, where he is to preach and administer the total abstinence pledge, on Sunday the 6th inst. On the 13th he is to be at Borrisokane. On the 20th in Dublin, to advocate the claims of the Christian Schools. On the 27th to Killarney. On the 3rd of October at Ballinasloe. On the 11th, at Loughmore, near Limerick, and on the 25th at Kilgass, near Longford.[6]

As conditions grew worse he concentrated his entire energy on relief work, although in October 1847 he made a tour that took him as far away from Cork as Sligo and Derry and the following month he was at Omagh and Strabane. As ever, he refused to accept that there was any decline in the temperance movement, attributing reports of lapses to exaggerations and distortions of the truth. When he went to Limerick at the beginning of 1848, however, he was told by the local temperance society that there were indeed some who had 'violated their sacred pledge'. He insisted that despite the increase in public houses, two thirds less spirits were consumed in Ireland in 1847 than in 1838. Nor did the small number who attended meetings at the temperance rooms, he told his audience at one of these rooms in Cork in February, mean that those not attending had abandoned temperance. And he had heard from Bishop Maginn of Derry that not a single pledge-breaker was to be found in the district of Inishowen, a stronghold of the movement in his diocese.[7]

Early in April 1848, Father Mathew suffered an attack of paralysis, probably brought on by over-work and fasting. Though he made a relatively quick recovery, his doctor would not allow him to resume his punishing work schedule, and it was against his advice that Father Mathew agreed to visit America the following year. He spent two and a half years travelling around America promoting temperance, mostly, but not entirely, among the Irish there. When he returned to Ireland he was no longer strong enough to resume the crusade. From 1846 onwards, then, he had been unable to conduct his temperance mission in the way he had developed, namely, by making regular tours around the country, exhorting teetotallers to remain loyal to the pledge, pledging new members and re-pledging those who had lapsed and wished to rejoin. As so much of the impetus of the movement was centred on him, it is not surprising that, in his absence, many lost their original enthusiasm for teetotalism. Even with some national structure, the movement would have been bound to suffer from the enforced withdrawal of so charismatic a leader. Without it, a decline was inevitable.[8]

Even more significant than Father Mathew's inability to devote the necessary attention to the temperance movement during the Famine was the great number of his supporters among the fatalities. Assessments of the number that died have varied but a recent account that used the most up-to-date statistical methods for enumerating fatalities put the figure above a million. The excess mortality (the number that died over and above those that would have been expected to die under normal circumstances) in the period 1846-50 showed a distinct east-west pattern, as Cousens has pointed out, with Mayo, Galway, Clare, Kerry and Cork showing an excess mortality figure greater than one eighth of the population. With the exception of Mayo, much of which lay within the diocese of Tuam where the Archbishop was hostile to Father Mathew's crusading methods, all these counties were prominent among the areas that showed great enthusiasm for teetotalism from an early date, as noted earlier in Chapter 3 and Chapter 4. County Tipperary, which had an excess mortality rate over the period of one tenth of the population, had a particularly high rate for 1850, when Clare, Limerick and Kerry were also among the highest in the country and when the influences of the Famine in parts of Ulster, for example, had almost disappeared. Queen's County, perhaps the most prominent county in Leinster in the early days of Father Mathew's crusade, had a particularly high excess mortality rate for that province in 1850.[9]

Many of the counties worst hit by the Famine, therefore, corresponded with the counties where the teetotal movement was strongest. This is not of course to suggest that there was any connection between teetotalism and famine conditions, but it does seem to indicate that the movement flourished best in those parts of the country most vulnerable to the Famine, areas now understood to have been characterised by poverty, 'whether measured by dependence on wage labour or by reliance on in-adequate landholdings'. A disproportionate number of teetotallers may therefore have been among the fatalities although some, by saving money rather than spending it on drink, may have been able to afford the passage money for America.[10]

Not only counties, but particular towns and suburbs that had become closely identified with the teetotal movement featured among places par-ticularly badly affected by the Famine. Perhaps the best known of these was Skibbereen, where the first teetotal society in Ireland had been founded and where Father Mathew's work was embraced with enthusiasm. The sufferings of the people of Kilrush were made worse by evictions and Nenagh, another prominent town in the teetotal movement, had nearly 15,000 people on relief towards the end of 1849. So many people emigrated from the Claddagh during the Famine that part of Boston was called Claddagh 'after their ancestral village'.[11]

Besides a disproportionate number of teetotallers among the fatalities, the Famine was likely to have contributed to the decline of Father Mathew's movement in a number of other ways. The general demoral-isation of the population that was the inevitable accompaniment of their suffering could only have had an adverse effect on loyalty to the pledge. Shortly before departing for America in 1849 Father Mathew told a meeting in Cork that though the cause was still strong, 'some of our people have been rendered so dispirited and so reckless by the pressure of the times, by the fearful famine that afflicted this country, that in a moment of flair and frenzy they gave up the pledge'. Two years earlier he had written to a correspondent in America to say that, much as he would like to go there, he felt he could not abandon the people of Ireland lest they 'drown their agonies in drink'.[12]

In the social disruption that accompanied the Famine customs and traditions that had prevailed for centuries were abandoned, with the dead, for example, remaining unburied by their relatives in some afflicted areas. If forms of behaviour, dating from the dawn of civilisation and sanc-tioned by society, were abandoned before the horrors of the Famine, it is hardly surprising that the recently acquired habits of abstinence from alcohol were not always strong enough to withstand the pressures of the times and that many broke their pledge. Those who might have encour-aged them to persist were often unable to spare the time needed for temperance work. Many teetotal societies stopped holding meetings altogether and many of the local officers, usually priests, were working long hours on relief work.

A final way in which the Famine may have contributed to the decline of Father Mathew's movement was through the number of people who were forced to emigrate. Some of the areas from which large numbers of people left Ireland during the Famine years coincided with areas where a large part of the population had been enthusiastic teetotallers. The diocese of Kilmore, where Bishop Browne had been a keen supporter, sometimes even personally accompanying Father Mathew on his missions to his diocese, was among the areas from which a high percentage of the population left the country between 1846 and 1851. Many also emigrated from Cork and Tipperary during that period, though other counties where Father Mathew's movement was strong like Galway, Clare, Limerick and Kerry, despite their impoverishment, were not among the counties from which the highest proportion of the population emigrated. Clifden, county Galway, Ballyvaughan, county Clare, Newcastle, county Limerick, for example, all had as many as 70 per cent of the population on relief, but with such a high incidence of pauperism, few were able to save the fare to emigrate.[13]

*   *   *

Despite the blow dealt to his work by the Famine, Father Mathew has been seen by a modern historian as an 'apostle of modernisation'. While he accepts that superstitions played a part in Father Mathew's success, for Kearney this is only half the story. The other half is that of a man who believed that the condition of Ireland could be improved and that a means to this was the teetotal movement, with 'its emphasis upon such values as literacy, thrift, and insurance against illness and its involvement in politics in some places', which linked it with other forces at the time that were trying to come to terms with 'the new problems of a changing world'.[14]

Malcolm feels Kearney's account of the crusade underestimates the influence of Father Mathew's personal appeal to his followers and the extent to which the movement's expansion was aided by superstitious beliefs. The millenial and superstitious aspects of the movement have been explored in Chapter 6, but here it may be observed that while these were indeed important in the spread of teetotalism, as early as 1840 superstitious aspects of the movement were seen by police officers as being relevant to some only of those who were taking the pledge. Observers like S.C. Hall, while acknowledging that many of those taking the pledge were guided by superstition, were convinced that many were 'prompted by reason and reflection'. As striking as the superstitions and excitement which surrounded the adoption of teetotalism in many instances was the fidelity with which it was adhered to in the years before the Famine. The Temperance Reports testify to the small number who broke it in the early days of the crusade, sometimes putting the figure at two or three out of several thousands in particular districts. While there was undoubtedly a decrease in the number taking the pledge after 1841, this was partly determined by the fact that such a large proportion of the population had taken it already, and there is no convincing evidence that the pledge was abandoned in any great numbers until the Famine. The Repeal Reports of 1843, newspaper reports and figures for the consumption of legally distilled spirits offer no evidence for a large-scale decline in the movement. In 1842 and 1843 less than half the amount of legally distilled spirits was consumed in Ireland than in 1838 and in 1844 the figure was only slightly over half (Table 4.1). There was an increase in detections for illegally distilled spirits in 1842 and again in 1843, but the fact that these decreased again when the duty was reduced on legally distilled spirits suggests that the increased consumption of poteen in 1842 and 1843 was by regular drinkers unable to afford the price increases on legal whiskey rather than by newly lapsed teetotallers.[15]

Father Mathew himself, in encouraging people to take the pledge or to remain loyal to it, dwelt not on the superstitions associated with it but on the advantages of sobriety over drunkenness, domestic harmony over family rancour and thrift over dissipation. At St. Patrick's Temperance Hall, Cork, in 1849, he told his audience that he had never known anyone addicted to drinking to have got on well, 'whilst he could assert, that the fortunes made by the rich, were chiefly owing to their habits of temperance'. Though perhaps more exaggerated than usual, the sentiments were those he had been expressing for eleven years: the sober succeed and the drunkards fail. His reluctant acceptance of an element of superstition in teetotallers' attitude towards himself and towards the pledge were determined largely by his wish to use every means to ensure that people kept the pledge. In this he may have revealed not so much a sympathy for the receding world of superstition as a willingness to engage himself and his movement in the modern world of pragmatism.[16]

Central to Kearney's argument is that Father Mathew's movement was urban-based. Though the main modernising force of the movement was in the towns, it had an influence on the surrounding countryside analogous to the influence of the money economy of the towns on the bartering system of their hinterlands in the model of the dual economy first formulated by Lynch and Vaizey and subsequently modified by other economic historians. Malcolm counters this by pointing out that the majority of the recruits to teetotalism came from the countryside, not from the towns, and that country people formed the majority of those who took the pledge at Father Mathew's great meetings in cities like Cork, Limerick and Waterford.[17]

As the vast majority of the people of Ireland lived in the countryside and as most of the population took the pledge, it follows that the majority of teetotallers are likely to have lived in the countryside. It has been noted in Chapter 3 that at Father Mathew's great meetings in Limerick, Waterford and Galway in the winter of 1839-40 the vast majority of those taking the pledge came from the surrounding counties. Some would have come from small towns but the majority no doubt came from rural areas. A newspaper report on his visit to Limerick at the end of 1839 drew attention to the fact that many who had come in from the surrounding countryside had never seen Limerick city before and that 'their astonishment was evident, while gazing at every corner — some at the public buildings, at the quays, bridges, and shipping in the river, with intense admiration'. But Kearney was more interested in impact than in numbers', and the Temperance Reports would seem to bear him out in his claim that the movement was most influential in the towns. They contain a wealth of information about the progress of the movement in the towns, of teetotal societies with their rooms and meetings, processions and parades, ideas for retaining members, benefit schemes and an interest in savings banks in some areas. There is little reference made to the activities of teetotallers who lived outside the towns, though it is clear from newspaper reports that great numbers of them came into the towns for teetotal processions and parades on St. Patrick's Day, for example. Active membership, though, in the sense relevant to modernisation, may have been largely confined to the towns. Though impossible to prove, two observations suggest that this may have been the case.[18]

When Bishop Foran of Waterford had to renew the pledge of several hundred lapsed teetotallers who lived outside the city towards the end of 1841, he noted that none of them had belonged to benefit societies. It is unclear whether this meant that they belonged to teetotal societies which did not have benefit societies as part of their programme of activities or that they had never joined a temperance society at all. In either case it reflects an attitude towards teetotalism quite different from the intensity with which teetotal society membership was conducted by their counterparts in the towns, as recorded in the Temperance Reports.[19]

While it has been shown in Chapter 4 that the influence of Father Mathew's movement on the reduction of crime was not nearly as great as some of the temperance advocates at the time were prepared to claim, it is nevertheless clear that for a time at least it was one of the factors that helped bring about a reduction in crime. In the context of the present discussion it is of interest to note that the reduction in crime that accompanied Father Mathew's work in the counties of Limerick and Waterford between 1838 and the outbreak of the Famine was substantially less than the reductions in the cities of the same names. Bearing in mind the many other factors that could have influenced variations in crime figures and the difficulty of establishing a causal link between drinking and crime, it would of course be rash to suggest that teetotallers in the cities of Limerick and Waterford took their teetotalism more seriously than their contemporaries in the countryside. But, taken with Bishop Foran's concern over lapsed teetotallers in the countryside not belonging to benefit societies, there may be grounds here for questioning the largely rural character of the movement, despite the greater numbers living in the countryside who had taken the pledge. Though substantially less in numbers, it may well have been the urban teetotallers who made the greater impact.[20]

*   *   *

Father Mathew's timing of his long intended visit to America could not have been worse. When the movement, disrupted beyond recognition by the social upheaval that accompanied the Famine, needed a nationally recognised spokesman to keep the question of teetotalism to the forefront in the reconstruction of the country, he left Ireland for two and a half years. Though he accomplished much for teetotalism in the United States, especially among the Irish there, his reputation in progressive circles in Ireland, England and America suffered because of his refusal to publicly associate himself in America with the abolitionist cause that he had supported before he went there. While he was in America Father O'Regan was the mainstay of the movement in Cork. He was often assisted on teetotal platforms by Richard Dowden or by a local priest. Meetings were held in the city temperance halls and in towns like Kinsale,

Passage, Ballintemple, Glanmire, Douglas and Carrigtwohill. Father Mathew wrote to Dowden from America to say he was proud of the efforts of Father O'Regan, his 'steadfast friend and disciple'.[21]

It may be wondered if, had he been in Ireland at the time, the Synod of Thurles in 1850 could have concluded without mentioning teetotalism. The synod aimed at restoring the Catholic church in Ireland to a more strictly disciplined institution insofar as this was compatible with the existing state of society. In his address, Cullen, now a Cardinal and Archbishop of Armagh since Crolly's death the year before, condemned the 'godless colleges', secular education, proselytising, and encouraged the workhouse authorities to treat the poor with consideration and mildness. The poor in their turn should be encouraged to 'respect the right of property, to honour the rank and station of the great and powerful, to be obedient to those in authority, to be grateful for favours received, and to pour forth fervent prayers for their benefactors'. An appeal to the principles of teetotalism would not have seemed amiss in the context of this passive role for the poor. Cullen, who had shown a guarded approval of Father Mathew's work in 1842, may have felt the subject of teetotalism might have had a sufficiently long enough airing by 1850 as to make mention of it superfluous. But Father Mathew must surely have been disappointed that the subject did not even merit a passing reference.[22]

When John Forbes, a doctor and teetotal advocate, travelled around Ireland in 1852 he found many of the urban societies still in existence, though with greatly reduced numbers. The society in Killarney had been split by a dispute and had suffered further through the emigration of no less than 100 young men belonging to it within the space of four years. Priests were active in some areas, though the number was small when compared to the number who supported, or claimed to support the movement before the Famine. In Ballina and Galway the movement was undergoing something of a revival and in the former, as well as in Westport and Sligo, the Sisters of Mercy had taken up the cause and accepted the one year pledge.[23]

The involvement of the Catholic clergy, including nuns, and the kind of pledge that would be most effective in reducing drunkenness were questions that were to become relevant again in the Catholic temperance movement later in the century. Father Cullen, in his progress towards forming what was eventually to become the Pioneer Total Abstinence Association, gave a central role to priests and nuns in the organisation of the movement. Besides the more effective involvement of the clergy, Father Cullen was committed to associating the teetotal cause with Catholic spiritual practices in a way that Father Mathew, with his more liberal form of Catholicism and his wish to include Protestants and Dissenters under his banner, would not have found acceptable. Some of the priests involved with his crusade seem to have thought differently.[24]

At the end of 1854, when Father Mathew was in Madeira for treatment for his paralysis, a meeting of the Globe Lane Temperance Society, Cork, was addressed by a local priest, Father McNamara. The *Cork Examiner* reported him as saying

that people ought to crown their moral efforts by the support of religion. Religion was the parent and pure sustainer of moral conduct: if we depended on our strength alone we were always in danger of a fall; but if we made a religious feeling accompany every exertion, we took to ourselves the most effective support. Surely you who take the pledge ought to make a daily remembrance of your solemn promise, and pray to the Father of all goodness to sustain your effort at goodness.[25]

Some twenty years after Father Mathew's death it was claimed by a priest who had known and supported his work that his anti-sectarianism was a contributory factor in the decline of the movement, in that the presence of so many creeds 'prevented him from grafting his pledge upon the religious life of the people, and from thus securing for it a principle of supernatural strength and permanence.' In an attempt to meet this point Father Augustine argued in his book that it was up to the local clergy to connect the pledge with religious practices.[26]

Some Catholic clergymen, both in Ireland and England, questioned the wisdom of a pledge for life and the need for a total abstinence pledge except for 'confirmed drunkards'. Nevertheless, when the League of the Cross was founded in England in the eighteen seventies and spread, with only modest success, to Ireland, it was the pledge of total abstinence that was adopted by Cardinal Manning in London and Father Nugent in Liverpool. 'Total abstinence, sanctioned and enforced by a religious sentiment', wrote a Liverpool journal, applauding Father Nugent's efforts in converting several thousand to teetotalism, 'is the only efficacious means of checking intemperance amongst the poorer class of Catholics in Liverpool. It is useless to rely upon a middle course', because they lacked 'the power of regulating their indulgence in drink by the rules

of prudence'. While such a sweeping generalisation about the Catholic
poor of Liverpool may be questioned, it is clear that Manning and Nugent
were both greatly influenced by Father Mathew's methods. Indeed, some
of those who helped Manning in London had taken the pledge from Father
Mathew thirty years earlier and in Liverpool the first to join Father
Nugent's movement was John Denvir, who had taken the pledge as a
boy from Father Mathew when he visited England in 1843.[27]

Though inspired by Father Mathew's work, Father Cullen was careful
to avoid its shortcomings and, while not despairing of the ideal of universal sobriety, saw more value in a small number of total abstainers committed to the seriousness of the pledge than the large numbers enrolled
by Father Mathew, many of whom had given little or no thought to what
they were undertaking. In this he was more patient than Father Mathew,
who yearned to have all Ireland sober and invariably numbered his
adherents in millions. But in another way Father Mathew was the more
patient. As Father Cullen's essentially elitist movement progressed towards
its final form the individual drunkard was left by the wayside, with
membership restricted to those, to use his own words, 'who had never
taken strong drink at all, or had taken it in strict moderation, or who,
by long probation, had proved their stability in the practice of total
abstinence'. It was the individual drunkard who presented Father Mathew
with his greatest challenge, and his patience with him contributed to
his reputation for individual piety. Maguire recorded many examples of
his sympathy for human weakness and another contemporary observer,
Justin McCarthy, recalled that no matter how often a man might have
broken the pledge and returned to drunkenness, 'Father Mathew was
ever ready with forgiveness and renewed hope, never despairing of the
weakling's possible redemption'.[28]

Besides the exclusively Catholic nature of Father Cullen's movement,
its alignment with religious practices and its concentration on the
temperate rather than on drunkards, it was also more closely associated
with the cultural aspects of Ireland's struggle for independence than
Father Mathew ever allowed his movement to become with Repeal. But
it was in their organisation that the two movements revealed the greatest
differences, with Cullen's movement characterised by efficient and pur-
poseful organisation. Father Mathew's claim, in a letter to Edward Bullen,
that he was opposed to 'anything like organisation' among teetotallers
because this would be playing into the hands of the movement's enemies
is difficult to understand. One would have thought that, with Father

Mathew's reputation for political neutrality, the more formal the structures for his controlling the movement, the more happy the authorities would have been. It may be that, having no organisation, he felt able to absolve himself from responsibility for the actions of teetotallers, or it may even be that, lacking any formal structure, the movement must necessarily revolve round himself.[29]

Though by all accounts a rather shy and unassuming man there is a suspicion that, despite his regular disclaimers that the success of the teetotal movement was attributable to providence and not to him, he enjoyed his role as the central figure in and undisputed leader of the movement. Granted that in the conditions of the time and in order to better promote the cause he had to accept a certain degree of adulation from his followers, some reported incidents in his presence would seem to have called out for a disclaimer that did not come. At a banquet in his honour in Cork in February 1843, the following lines occur in a song sung by a Mr. Hackett:

> Then hail our Glorious Apostle
> Whose presence this evening we prize,
> Who shed blessings unnumbered on Erin
> And made her sons temperate and wise.
>
> And when monarchs and deeds of past ages,
> Are from memory's tablet effaced,
> Illumin'd on History's pages
> Shall the bright name of Mathew be traced.

When Father Mathew rose to address the meeting he made no attempt to disassociate himself from the exaggerated adulation of the song.[30]

A few months later at Kilrush, in the course of a temperance meeting, Kohl noticed the chairman bowing respectfully every time he mentioned Father Mathew's name and used expressions about him like 'the great Apostle of Temperance' and 'the great God-gifted man'. Kohl commented:

I thought of Christ, who, when his disciples praised him, said that no one was good but God in heaven, and I fancied that Father Mathew, who repudiates the miracles which the people ascribe to him, should likewise have disclaimed the gross flatteries which the orator uttered in his presence.

But he did not. Kohl appreciated that it may have been necessary for Father Mathew to accept such 'pompous and exaggerated expressions' in order to maintain his influence with the people but, on recalling that when Father Mathew entered the hall the band had played 'See, the conquering hero comes!' he wondered how it was possible 'to countenance such arrant flattery!'[31]

A friend of Father Mathew wrote of him that with the earnestness of Christianity 'he combined the simplicity of a child'. There is evidence that, far from revealing such simplicity, he was very conscious of what today would be termed his 'image'. Despite permitting himself to get into serious debt he wrote to Father Spratt that 'I do not charge myself with improvidence'. When he was offered a £100 (later raised to £300) pension by the government he wrote to a correspondent in London:

The affair of the £100 a year pension is scarcely known in Cork. I was too much troubled by it, to mention the circumstances to more than two or three.

It is more likely that he did not mention the matter because, once it became generally known, it might have influenced some teetotallers with nationalist feelings to mistrust a man who, long committed to political neutrality, could nevertheless accept a government pension. Maguire's assurance that granting Father Mathew a pension 'met with the universal approval of the country' must be questioned. As we have seen in Chapter 7, Bishop Higgins' objection to Father Mathew's appointment to the see of Cork was because he feared that, as a recipient of a government pension, he would keep the government informed of the deliberations of the Irish hierarchy.[32]

Father Mathew was emphatic that, despite his acceptance of the pension, he had not violated his principle of not interfering in religion or politics. This was in response to a suggestion that accepting such a pension represented devotion to the British government. Another view was that the pension was acceptable as a means of paying off debts that had their origin in his socially beneficial activities rather than in his private means. For, as he himself wrote, the debts 'have been contracted in establishing the Great Temperance Movement and not for my own individual benefit'. To some of the Irish in America, however, his acceptance of such a pension seemed yet another humiliating defeat in the wake of the failure of Repeal, the devastation of the Famine and the abortive rising of 1848. In presenting him with $150 which they had collected before his arrival in America, the Roman Catholic Temperance Association Benefit Society of New York expressed the hope that their gift would help towards 'freeing you for ever from any dependence on the British government which we, as Irishmen, detest and abhor'.[33]

Whatever the shortcomings of Father Mathew's crusade when compared to those who came after him in the temperance movement among
Irish Catholics, there can be no doubt that he made the path easier for
later campaigners in the field like Manning, Nugent and Cullen. While,
as we have seen in Chapter 1, a few Catholics were involved in the
temperance movement before Father Mathew, it was largely the preserve
of Protestants. Father Mathew may not have fully banished the idea that
temperance was associated with Protestantism but, by engaging such
a large part of the Catholic population in the crusade, he made it an
acceptable concern for Catholics.

In a letter to G.W. Carr at the end of 1839, to which reference has already
been made in Chapter 2, Father Mathew, having considered the reasons
why Irish people engaged in drunkenness and the role temperance societies
might play in addressing the problem, concludes with the hope 'that the
day will come when the Drunkard will be regarded as an object of abhorrence and contempt by all classes of Society'. Did he achieve this object?[34]

Shortly before he died in 1856 Father Mathew told Richard Dowden
that they had achieved one great victory:

we have turned the tide of public opinion; it was once a glory for men to boast
of what they drank; we have turned that false glory into shame; we have also
given to the timid temperance man, to the teetotaller, the protection of his virtue, and a large share of public sympathy for his sacrifice in the cause of the
first of virtues, sobriety.[35]

When he died a couple of months later the *Cork Constitution* included
in his obituary the regret that so little of his work was likely to survive
him. Two days later the *Times* reproduced the *Constitution*'s obituary
in full, acknowledging it as having come from a 'respectable and
thoroughly Protestant journal'. More interestingly, the Catholic *Cork Examiner* reproduced it without comment, which suggests that the *Examiner*
may have shared the *Constitution*'s fear that little of Father Mathew's
work would survive him. Eight years later, at the unveiling of Father
Mathew's statue in Cork, James Haughton noted that while there had
indeed been relapses 'even yet the degrading evils caused by drink are
not so glaring as formerly'. S.C. Hall thought Father Mathew's aim had
been realised. Writing fifteen years after his death, Hall believed that
though drunkenness still persisted in Ireland

that which was formerly a glory is now a degradation. The sin of drunkenness
was rather an honour than a shame before . . . it has become a shame and

a reproach, not alone among the peasantry and the lower classes of the towns, but among the gentry . . .[36]

Other influences, like the increasing power of the Catholic church, nationalist aspirations, the movement for legislation to restrict drinking times and the work of the police no doubt all played a part in bringing about the change in attitudes that Hall has attributed to Father Mathew alone, and evidence could never be found to determine the exact contribution of Father Mathew's crusade. The evidence does, however, suggest that it was considerable, enough, perhaps, to justify the *Cork Examiner*'s hope expressed at his burial in the cemetery he provided for the poor of Cork, that though he had ceased to exist in this world, his memory would never die.[37]

Notes and References

The full title and publication details of books are given in the first entry for each book cited and abbreviated thereafter; the abbreviations for official publications and newspapers are listed on pages 225-29.

I found much of Father Mathew's handwriting in his Draft Correspondence difficult (and often impossible) to read. I am grateful to John Quinn of Notre Dame University for putting transcripts of many of the draft letters at my disposal; these are identified in the notes where the letter Q follows the citation.

Newspaper dates are for the nineteenth century unless otherwise indicated, e.g. 3 Mar. 40 means 3 Mar. 1840.

Cited newspapers carry the day and the month, except those that came out monthly, which carry the month only.

INTRODUCTION

1 State Paper Office, Dublin, H.O.M.A. 131/10 'Replies to Chief Inspector of Constabulary's Temperance Enquiry of March 1840' (hereafter 'Temperance Reports' in text, 'T.R.' in Notes); Liverpool Record Office, Papers of the Earl of Darby (Box 34), *Circular addressed by order of the Irish Government to the stipendiary magistrates in Ireland, with the several answers received from these officers* (1843) and *Circular addressed by order of the Irish government to the county inspectors of the constabulary force with the several answers received from those officers* (1843) (hereafter 'Repeal Reports' in text, *Magistrates* and *Constabulary* in Notes); Capuchin Archives, Dublin, Father Mathew Draft Correspondence (hereafter 'Mathew Draft Correspondence'); Rev. James Birmingham, *A Memoir of the Very Rev. Theobald Mathew, with an account of the rise and Progress of temperance in Ireland* (Dublin, 1840). A second edition, with additional material, came out the following year.
2 John Francis Maguire, M.P., *Father Mathew: A Biography* (London, 1863).
3 Sister Mary Frances Clare (M.F. Cusack), *The Life of Father Mathew, the People's Soggarth Aroon* (Dublin, 1874). For her cure see William O'Malley, *Glancing Back. 70 Years Experience and Reminiscences of Press Man, Sportsman and Member of Parliament* (London, 1933), p. 28.
4 J.H. Olivier, *Vie du Père Mathew* (Saint-Dizier, 1878).
5 Frank J. Mathew, *Father Mathew. His Life and Times* (London, 1890).
6 Katharine Tynan, *Father Mathew* (London 1908); Sean Ua Ceallaigh, *Beatha an Athar Tioboid Maitiu* (Dublin, 1907).
7 Rev. Patrick Rogers, *Father Theobald Mathew. Apostle of Temperance* (Dublin, 1943).

187

8   Rev. Father Augustine, *Footprints of Father Theobald Mathew, O.F.M. Cap.* Apostle of Temperance (Dublin, 1947).

9   *Times*, 1 Aug. 1843.

10   Jane Welsh Carlyle, *A New Selection of her letters*. Arranged by Trudy Bliss (London, 1949), p. 129.

11   H.F. Kearney, 'Fr. Mathew: apostle of modernisation' in Art Cosgrove and Donal McCartney (eds.), *Studies in Irish History Presented to R. Dudley Edwards* (Dublin, 1979), pp. 164-175.

12   Elizabeth Malcolm, 'Temperance and Irish Nationalism' in F.S.L. Lyons and R.A.J. Hawkins (eds.), *Ireland Under the Union: Varieties of Tension* (Oxford, 1980), pp. 69-114. Elizabeth Malcolm, *Ireland Sober, Ireland Free: Drink and Temperance in Nineteenth-Century Ireland* (Dublin, 1986).

CHAPTER 1: IRELAND IN THE EIGHTEEN THIRTIES

1   Brendan M. Walsh, 'A Perspective on Irish population patterns' in *Eire-Ireland*, iv, 3, Autumn 1969; Kevin Whelan, 'The Famine and Post-Famine Adjustment' in William Nolan (ed.), *The Shaping of Ireland: The Geographical Perspective* (Cork, 1986), p. 154; K.H. Connell, *The Population of Ireland 1750-1845* (Oxford, 1950), p. 90; Michael Drake, 'Marriage and Population Growth in Ireland, 1750-1845' in *Economic History Review*, 2nd ser. xvi, 2 (1963), p. 312; Salaman has listed 20 failures of the potato crop in Ireland between 1800 and 1842. Redcliffe N. Salaman, *The History and Social Influence of the Potato* (Cambridge, 1949), pp. 605-7; E.L. Almquist, 'Pre-Famine Ireland and the Theory of European Proto-industrialization: Evidence from the 1841 Census' in *Journal of Economic History*, xxxix (1979), p. 718.

2   (Sir John Burgoyne), *Ireland in 1831. Letters on the state of Ireland* (London, 1831), p. 10. Burgoyne was made chairman of the Board of Works in 1831 and later served on the Irish Railway Commission; Gustave de Beaumont, *Ireland: Social Political, and Religious* (London, 1839), i, p. 262. Liberal newspapers welcomed de Beaumont's account of Irish misery 'corroborated by every impartial writer on the name subject'. *S. Rep.*, 5 Sep. 39. Mansergh felt his statements about peasants and landlords alike needed qualification. Nicholas Mansergh, *Ireland in the age of Reform and Revolution* (London, 1940), p. 33.

3   *Third Poor Inq.*, p. 3; de Beaumont, *Ireland*, i, p. 292; J.G. Kohl, *Travels in Ireland* (London, 1844), p. 86. Kohl is generally considered a reliable witness 'singularly free from prejudice'. Constantia Maxwell, *The Stranger in Ireland* (Dublin, 1969 edn.), p. 295.

4   J.E. Bicheno, *Ireland, and its Economy* (London, 1830), pp. 34, 51. Bicheno was a sympathetic observer of Irish life, who later served as a

commissioner on the Irish Poor Inquiry; John Barrow, *A Tour round Ireland, through the sea-coast counties, in the autumn of 1835* (London, 1836), p. 53; Alan Gailey, 'Changes in Irish rural housing' in Patrick O'Flanagan, Paul Ferguson and Kevin Whelan (eds.), *Rural Ireland 1600-1900: Modernisation and change* (Cork, 1987), pp. 95-100.

5 Kohl, *Ireland*, pp. 80, 88; L.M. Cullen, *An Economic History of Ireland since 1600* (London, 1981 edn.), p. 106; Kevin O'Neill, *Family and Farm in Pre-Famine Ireland. The Parish of Killashandra* (Madison, 1984), p. 117; *Sir Walter Scott's Tour of Ireland* described by D.J. O'Donoghue (Glasgow, 1905), p. 24, Bicheno, *Ireland*, p. 37; Barrow, *Ireland*, p. 329; Timothy O'Neill, *Life and Tradition in Rural Ireland* (London, 1977), p. 52; Jonathan Binns, *The Miseries and Beauties of Ireland* (London, 1837), i, pp. 31-2, 187; de Beaumont, *Ireland*, i, p. 270; *The Irish Journals of Elizabeth Smith*, edited by David Thompson with Moyra McCarthy (Oxford, 1980), quoted 'Introduction', p. xvi.

6 S.J. Connolly, 'Marriage in Pre-Famine Ireland' in Art Cosgrove (ed.), *Marriage in Ireland* (Dublin, 1985), pp. 80-85; O'Neill, *Family and Farm*, p. 45; W.W. Simpson to Lord Lieutenant 24 Feb. 1840, printed *D.E.P.*, 29 Feb. 40.

7 Good health may also have been due in part to a system of public dispensaries set up early in the nineteenth century on a local basis, where free medical attention was available for the poor. Because raising a local subscription was a condition of obtaining a grant, provision was inadequate in poor areas like Connaught. Helen Burke, *The People and the Poor Law in Nineteenth Century Ireland* (Littlehampton, 1985), pp. 5-10. Cullen, *Economic History*, p. 129; Brian Walker, 'Ulster Society and Politics, 1801-1921' in Ciaran Brady, Mary O'Dowd and Brian Walker (eds.), *Ulster. An illustrated history* (London, 1989), p. 159; *Third Poor Inq.*, p. 5; James O'Flynn, *The Present State of the Irish Poor, with outlines of a Plan of General Employment* (London, 1835), p. 5; David Fitzpatrick, *Irish Emigration 1801-1921* (Dublin, 1984), pp. 4, 27.

8 William Carleton, *The Black Prophet* (Shannon, 1972 edn.), p. 87; John Keegan, *A Young Irishman's Diary (1836-1847)*, edited by Rev. William Clare (printed for the editor, 1928), p. 38; William Nolan, *Fassadinin: Land, Settlement and Society in Southeast Ireland 1600-1850* (Dublin, 1979), p. 148; de Beaumont, *Ireland*, i, p. 293; Joel Mokyr, *Why Ireland Starved. A Quantitative and Analytical History of the Irish Economy 1800-1850* (London, 1983), p. 133; James S. Donnelly, *The Land and the People of Nineteenth Century Cork* (London, 1975), pp. 69-71; W.A. Maguire, *Living Like a Lord: The Second Marquis of Donegal 1769-1844* (Belfast, 1984), pp. 77-9.

9 Patrick Lynch and John Vaizey, *Guinness's Brewery in the Irish Economy 1759-1876* (Cambridge, 1960), pp. 9-26; Joseph Lee, 'The Dual Economy

in Ireland, 1800-1850' in T. Desmond Williams (ed.), *Historical Studies*, viii (1971), pp. 191-201; Mokyr, *Why Ireland Starved*, pp. 20-24; Raymond J. Raymond, 'A Reinterpretation of Irish Economic History (1730-1850)' in *Journal of European Economic History*, xi, 3 (1982), pp. 663-4.

10 Robert Lowery, *Robert Lowery: Radical and Chartist*, edited by Brian Harrison and Patricia Hollis (London, 1979), p. 148. When Cobbett visited the poorhouse in Dublin in 1834 he found the inmates there dressed worse than the scarecrows in his native Hampshire. Dennis Knight (ed.), *Cobbett in Ireland*. A warning to England (London 1984), pp. 43-5, 59-60; H.S. Thompson, *Ireland in 1839 and 1869* (London, 1870), p. 11; Burke, *People and Poor*, p. 34; Timothy P. O'Neill, 'The Catholic Church and the Relief of the Poor 1815-45' in *Archivium Hibernicum*, xxxi (1973), pp. 133-4.

11 Lowery, *Radical*, p. 148; Binns, *Miseries,* i, p. 83; Anthony Trollope, *An Autobiography* (Oxford, 1980 edn.), p. 65; Elizabeth Fry and Joseph John Gurney, *Report Addressed to the Marquess Wellesley, Lord Lieutenant of Ireland, respecting their late visit to that country* (London, 1827), p. 56; Lady Chatterton, *Rambles in the south of Ireland during the Year 1838* (London, 1839), i, p. 10; Kohl, *Ireland*, p. 90; Samuel Wilderspin, *Early Discipline Illustrated, or, the Infant System progressing and successful* (London, 1840 edn.), pp. 65, 75.

12 De Beaumont, *Ireland*, i, p. 258; Lowery, *Lowery*, p. 148; Ann McKernan, 'In Search of the Irish Town: Re-discovery of a Source for Bandon, Cork' in *Bandon Historical Journal*, ii (1985), p. 25.

13 T. Jones Hughes, 'The Estate System of Landholding in Nineteenth Century Ireland' in Nolan (ed.), *The Shaping of Ireland*, p. 145; Nolan, *Fassadinin*, p. 141; T.W. Freeman, 'Irish Towns in the Eighteenth and Nineteenth Century' in R.A. Butlin (ed.), *The Development of the Irish Town* (London, 1977), pp. 121-22; Kohl, *Ireland*, p. 225; Burgoyne, *Ireland*, p. 17; Patrick J. Corish, *The Irish Catholic Experience*. A Historical Survey (Dublin, 1985), p. 153.

14 D.H. Akenson, *The Irish Education Experiment*. The national system of eduction in the nineteenth century (London, 1970), pp. 57-8; Ignatius Murphy, 'Primary Education' in Patrick J. Corish (ed.), *A History of Irish Catholicism* (Dublin, 1971), v, pp. 6-7; Map 78A by K.M. Davies and Map 79 by Brian O'Cuiv in T.W. Moody, F.X. Martin and F.J. Byrne (eds.), *A New History of Ireland* (Oxford, 1984), ix, pp. 66, 71; L.M. Cullen, *The Emergence of Modern Ireland 1600-1900* (London, 1983 edn.), p. 132; Brian O'Cuiv, 'Irish Language and Literature' in T.W. Moody and W.E. Vaughan (eds.), *Eighteenth Century Ireland 1691-1800* (Oxford, 1986), pp. 377-86, 418-21.

15 S.J. Connolly, *Priests and People in Pre-Famine Ireland 1780-1845* (Dublin, 1985 edn.), pp. 33, 172.

16 Connolly, *Priests and People*, pp. 88-91; Emmet Larkin, 'The Devotional Revolution in Ireland, 1850-75' in *American Historical Review*, 77, 3 (1972), p. 630; David W. Miller, 'Irish Catholicism and the Great Famine' in *Journal of Social History*, ix, i (1975), pp. 84-7; Corish, *The Irish Catholic Experience*, pp. 167-68; Desmond Keenan, *The Catholic Church in Nineteenth Century Ireland* (Dublin, 1983), p. 119; K. Theodore Hoppen, *Elections, Politics and Society in Ireland, 1832-1885* (Oxford, 1984), p. 205. In Killashandra, Co. Cavan, Protestants as well as Catholics stayed away from church because of their poor clothing. O'Neill, *Family and Farm*, p. 117.

17 Connolly, *Priests and People*, p. 117; de Beaumont, *Ireland*, ii, p. 88; Alexis de Tocqueville, *Journeys to England and Ireland*, trans. G. Lawrence and K.P. Mayer (London, 1958), p. 130.

18 Elizabeth Longford, *Wellington: Pillar of State* (Panther, 1975 edn.), p. 192. For the role of priests in the Waterford election of 1826 see Oliver MacDonagh, *The Hereditary Bondsman*: Daniel O'Connell 1775-1829 (London, 1988), p. 224; Bicheno, *Ireland*, p. 138; Donal A. Kerr, *Peel, Priests and Politics*. Sir Robert Peel's Administration and the Roman Catholic Church in Ireland, 1841-1846 (Oxford, 1984 edn.), pp. 68-70; K.B. Nowlan, 'The Catholic Clergy and Irish Politics in the Eighteen Thirties and Forties' in *Historical Studies*, ix (Belfast, 1974), pp. 122-24. John F. Broderick, *The Holy See and the Irish Movement for the Repeal of the Union with England 1829-1847* (Rome, 1951), p. 62; Baptist Wriothesley Noel, *Notes on a Short Tour through the Midland Counties of Ireland in the Summer of 1836, with observations on the condition of the peasantry* (London, 1837), p. 285; Count Cavour, *Thoughts on Ireland: its present and its future*, trans. W.B. Hodgson (London, 1868), pp. 41-2. Barrow, *Tour*, p. 344; Henry D. Inglis, *A Journey throughout Ireland during the Spring, Summer and Autumn of 1834* (London, 1838 edn.), p. 90; D.O. Madden, *Ireland and its rulers since 1829* (Dublin, 1843), p. 253.

19 Angus MacIntyre, *The Liberator*: Daniel O'Connell and the Irish Party 1830-1847 (London, 1965), pp. 139-66; Oliver MacDonagh, *The Union and its aftermath* (London, 1977 edn.), p. 54. For Catholic appointments to higher posts in law, legal administration and the police up to March 1839, see Hansard xlvi, p. 1007, 21 Mar. 1839.

20 Denis Gwynn, *Daniel O'Connell: The Irish Liberator* (London, 1930), p. 238; M.A.G. O'Thuathaigh, *Thomas Drummond and the Government of Ireland 1835-41* (Dublin, 1978). In the three years following the 1836 Police Act two thirds of the recruits to the force were Catholics, and during those same years the force had been particularly successful in suppressing faction fights and preventing Orange Processions. By 1840 their number had exceeded 8,000 and the number of troops in the country had been reduced

from 19,000 in 1835 to 14,000. Stanley H. Palmer, *Police and Protest in England and Ireland* (Cambridge, 1988), pp. 240-43, 255-6, 362; Hansard li, p. 949, 31 Jan. 1840. It was perhaps from the reform of the 'self-elected and irresponsible' municipal corporations that Catholics living in towns gained most from Whig reforms. R.B. McDowell, *Public Opinion and Government Policy in Ireland 1801-1845* (London, 1952), pp. 180-84.

21   (Prince Pückler-Muskau) *Tour in England, Ireland and France in the years 1826, 1827, 1828 and 1829 . . . in a series of letters* (Philadelphia, 1833), p. 418; *S.C. Drunkenness*, p. 401; Cullen, *Econ. History*, pp. 172-3; *Rev. Comm. Tables*, pp. 431, 441; *Lic. Dist. Irl.*, p. 659; Binns, quoted Peadar O'Flanagan, 'Pre-Famine Westport 1825-1845' in *Cathair-na-Mart*, Journal of the Westport Historical Society, iii (1983), p. 46; K.H. Connell, 'Illicit Distillation' in *Irish Peasant Society*, Four Historical Essays (Oxford, 1968), p. 18; William J. Fitzpatrick, *The Life, Times and Correspondence of Right Rev. Dr. Doyle, Bishop of Kildare and Leighlin* (Dublin, 1861), ii, p. 181.

22   John Dunlop, *The Philosophy of Artificial and Compulsory Drinking Usages in Great Britain and Ireland* (London, 1839), *passim*; *S.C. Drunkenness*, pp. 396-7; *Fifth Poor Inq.*, p. 58; Dunlop, *Philosophy*, p. 113; *Third Poor Inq.*, pp. 108-111.

23   Richard Stivers, *A Hair of the Dog*. Irish Drinking and American Stereotype (University Park and London, 1976), p. 18; James R. Barrett, 'Why Paddy Drank: The Social Importance of Whiskey in Pre-Famine Ireland' in *Journal of Popular Culture*, xi, Summer 1977, pp. 159/21; Chatterton, *Rambles*, ii, p. 143-44; *Temp. Int.*, 8 Feb. 40.

24   Samuel C. Hall, *Retrospect of a long life: From 1815 to 1883* (London, 1883), i, p. 485; Mr. & Mrs. S.C. Hall, *Ireland: its scenery, character* (London, 1841-3), i, p. 34; Thackeray, *Sketch Book*, p. 65; Binns, *Miseries*, i, p. 341; *Third Poor Inq.*, pp. 104-107.

25   Dr. Speer, quoted in W.R. Wilde, 'Report Upon the Tables of Deaths' in *Census 1841*, pp. 645-6; *Gal. Vin.*, 29 Dec. 41; *Nat.*, 28 Jan. 42; W.E. Channing, *An Address on Temperance* (Boston, 1837), pp. 24, 29.

26   J.F. Maguire, M.P. 'The Life and Labours of Father Mathew' in *Irish Penny Readings* (Dublin, 1879), p. 123. The speech was actually made in 1857.

27   Lynch and Vaizey, *Guinness's*, p. 89; for problems with beer statistics see E.B. McGuire, *Irish Whiskey*. A History of Distilling, the Spirit Trade and Excise Controls in Ireland (Dublin, 1973), pp. 229-300; for beer figures for England, George B. Wilson, *Alcohol and the Nation*. A Contribution to the Study of the Liquor Problem in the United Kingdom from 1800 to 1935 (London, 1940), p. 369; population estimates are from B.R. Mitchell and P. Deane, *Abstract of British Historical Statistics* (Cambridge, 1962), p. 8; statistics for European beer consumption are from

B.R. Mitchell, *European Historical Statistics 1750-1975* (London, 1981 edn.), p. 492.

28 *Spirits 1800-1845*, p. 427; Michael G. Mulhall, *The Dictionary of Statistics* (London, 1899), p. 544.

29 For population estimates, Mitchell and Deane, *Historical Statistics*, p. 8.

30 See, for example, evidence of G.W. Carr, *S.C. Drunkenness*, p. 577. Irish distillers were as much concerned about the evasion of duty by licensed distillers as by illicit stills, *Seven Ex. Comm.*, p. 79. For the gauger's corruptibility, S.C. Hall, *Retrospect*, i, p. 485, and for his integrity and tenacity, 'Bob Pentland, or the Gauger Outwitted' in *Carleton's Stories of Irish Life*, introduction by Darrel Figgis (Dublin, n.d.), pp. 187-99; Samuel Morewood, *A Philosophical and Statistical History of the Inventions and Customs of Ancient and Modern Nations in the Manufacture and Use of Inebriating Liquors* (Dublin, 1838), p. 676. C(aesar) O(tway), *A Tour in Connaught, comprising Sketches of Clonmacnoise, Joyce Country and Achill* (Dublin, 1839), p. 8.

31 *Hibernian Temperance Society, Paper B* (Dublin, 1830), p. 1; Hibernian Temperance Society, *Proceedings of the first annual meeting held at the Rotunda on the 7th April 1830* (Dublin, 1830), pp. 3, 52; J(ames) H(enry), *Observations and Advice addressed to the mechanic and industrious classes, on the use of ardent spirits* (Dublin, 1830), pp. 14-15. James Henry, *Essays on Intemperance addressed to the benevolent inhabitants of cities, and especially of Dublin* (Dublin, 1830), p. 31.

32 Anonymous, 'A Few of Ireland's Temperance Worthies' in Fredk. Sherlock, *Fifty Years Ago* (Belfast, 1879), p. 107; W.D. Killen, *Memoir of John Edgar, D.D., LLD* (Belfast, 1867), pp. 28-32; John Edgar, *The evils, cause and cure of drunkenness* (Belfast, 1830), p. 19; Hibernian Temperance Society, *Proceedings*, pp. 10-11.

33 Dawson Burns, *Temperance History* (London, 1889-91), i, p. 32; Hibernian Temperance Society, *Paper A* (Dublin, 1830), p. 31; *I.T.L.G.*, 12 Nov., 24 Dec. 1836; Malcolm, *'Ireland Sober'*, pp. 63-5; George Cornelius III Bretherton, 'The Irish Temperance Movement: 1829-47', unpublished Ph.D. Thesis, Columbia University, 1978, p. 144; Ann Jane Carlile to Alexander Mayne, 12 Jan. 61, printed Fredk. Sherlock, *Ann Jane Carlile. A Temperance Pioneer* (London, 1897), pp. 16-21; T.J. Barron, 'Ann Jane Carlile: A Temperance Pioneer' in *Breifne*, Journal of Cumann Seanchais Breifne, ii, 6 (1963).

34 Malcolm, *'Ireland Sober'*, pp. 68-9, 79, 84-5; Amhlaoibh O'Suileabhain, *The Diary of Humphrey O'Sullivan*, trans. Rev. M. McGrath (London, 1936), ii, pp. 125, 251; Fitzpatrick, *Doyle*, ii, pp. 181-3. George W. Carr to Judge Crampton, printed *Irish Temperance Banner*, 1879 (copy pasted to p. 509 of N.L.I.'s bound 'Hibernian Temperance Pamphlets') .

35 Morewood, *Liquors*, p. 708; John Barclay Sheil, *History of the Temperance Movement in Ireland* (Dublin, 1843), p. 28; Barrow, *Tour*, p. 231; Bretherton, 'Irish Temperance', p. 103; *I.T.L.G.*, 12 Nov. 36; *Temperance Penny Magazine*, iii, 38.

36 *I.T.L.G*, 12 Nov. 36, 14, 21 Jan. 37; *P.T.A.*, July 37; Keegan, *Diary*, p. 18; Noel, *Short Tour*, pp. 21-2; Charlotte Elizabeth, *Letters from Ireland 1837* (London, 1838), p. 96.

37 Hibernian Temperance Society, *Paper A*, p. 4; John Edgar, *Scriptural Temperance. A discourse preached at Fisherwick Place Church* (Belfast, c.1830), p. 3; Malcolm, *Ireland Sober*, pp. 70-71; William Urwick, *The Life and Letters of William Urwick, D.D. of Dublin*, edited by his son, (London, 1870), p. 118; Charles Haliday, *An Inquiry into the influence of the excessive use of spirituous liquors in producing crime, disease, and poverty in Ireland* (Dublin, 1830), p. 41.

38 Brian Harrison, *Drink and the Victorians: the Temperance Question in England 1815-1872* (London, 1971), pp. 113-14, 130-34; Malcolm *Ireland Sober*, pp. 72-73; Norman Longmate, *The Waterdrinkers: A History of Temperance* (London, 1962), pp. 42-88.

39 Harrison, *Drink and the Victorians*, p. 137; for vice-presidents in 1839, *The Dublin Almanac and General Register of Ireland* (Dublin, 1839), p. 275; Malcolm, *Ireland Sober*, pp. 72-73.

40 There is disagreement about the significance of the Skibbereen Society in the history of the temperance movement. Brian Harrison, *Drink and the Victorians*, p. 103; Malcolm, *Ireland Sober*, pp. 77-8; James Coombes, 'Europe's First Total Abstinence Society' in *Journal of Cork Historical and Archaeological Society*, lxxii, Jan.-Dec. 1967, pp. 52-7; William Logan, *Early Heroes of the Temperance Reformation* (Glasgow, 1873), p. 81; *S. Rep.*, 23 Jan. 41; Dublin Temperance Society, *Address of the Dublin Temperance Society to their fellow-citizens* (Dublin, 1830), pp. 3-4.

41 R.B. Rose, 'John Finch, 1784-1857: A Liverpool Disciple of Robert Owen' in *Transactions of the Historic Society of Lancashire and Cheshire*, 109 (1957), pp. 159-84; Longmate, *Waterdrinkers*, p. 47; P.T. Winskill, *The Comprehensive History of the Rise and Progress of the Temperance Reformation* (Warrington, 1881), p. 169; *P.T.A.*, June, July 37; *I.T.L.G.*, 18 Mar. 37.

42 *P.T.A*, June 37; Killen, *Memoir*, pp. 94-5.

43 *Hib. Temp. J.*, May 36; Samuel Haughton, *Memoir of James Haughton, with extracts from his private and public letters* (Dublin, 1877), p. 37. See also, T. Wilson Fair, 'The Dublin Total Abstinence Society' in Sherlock, *Fifty Years Ago*, pp. 74-7, and E. McDowel Cosgrave, *Brief History of the Dublin Total Abstinence Society* (Dublin, 1897).

44 *P.T.A*, July 37; *I.T.L.G.*, 7 Jan. 37, 19 May 38; Dawson Burns, *Temp. History*, i, p. 130; *Br & F.T.I.*, 25 Apr. 40.

45 Bretherton, 'Irish Temperance Movement', p. 91; Noel, *Short Tour*, p. 22;
    Winskill, *Rise and Progress*, p. 170; *Temp. Reg.*, 1 Feb. 40.
46 *I.T.L.G,* 12 Nov. 36; *P.T.A*, July 37; *I.T.L.G.*, 12 Nov. 36, 8 Apr., 3 Jun. 37,
    24 Feb. 38; *Cork Stan.* 9 Apr. 38; *Nen. Gaz.*, 22 June 42. For temperance
    in Ennis before Father Mathew, see Ignatius Murphy, 'Ennis Temperance
    Society, 1835-1839' in *North Munster Antiquarian Journal*, xxvii (1985),
    pp. 88-9.
47 In the same year the secretary of the Hibernian Temperance Society regret-
    ted 'the want of co-operation on the part of the Roman Catholic clergy'
    as well as the clergy of other denominations. *Temp. Penny Mag.*, June 1838.

CHAPTER 2: FATHER MATHEW

1 Sir Bernard Burke, *Genealogical History of the Dormant, Abeyant, Forfeited
   and Extinct Peerages of the British Empire* (Baltimore, 1978, reprint of
   1883 edn.), pp. 360-1; *Dictionary of Welsh Biography down to 1940* (London, 1959), p. 618; Croker, *Researches*, p. 227; Morewood, *Liquors*, p. 589;
   Pückler-Muskau, *Tour*, p. 405; Mathew, *Father Mathew*, p. 98.
2 Burke, *Genealogical*, p. 361; Rev. David Mathew, 'Father Mathew's Family:
   The Mathews in Tipperary' in *Capuchin Annual*, 1956-7, p. 149; Stephen
   Gwynn, *Saints and Scholars* (London, 1929), p. 174. The ruins of
   Thomastown Castle were bought by Father, later Archbishop, Mathew, great
   grandson of Father Mathew's brother Charles and son of Frank Mathew.
   That a strain of eccentricity remained in the family may be inferred from
   the entry for Archbishop Mathew in the most recent volume of the *D.N.B.*,
   on reviewing which John Gross called the Archbishop 'The most fantastic
   single character in the current volume.' *Observer*, 26 Oct. 1986. *D.N.B.
   1971-1980* (Oxford, 1986), pp. 552-54. Frank Delaney was born across the
   fields from the castle and in an article in the *Sunday Press* (27 Jan. 1983)
   drew attention to a haunting photograph of the ruins in D. McLaren (ed.),
   In Ruins: the Once Great Houses of Ireland (London, 1980), p. 25. The
   ruin still stands today, visible from the Tipperary-Cashel road. Neither road
   nor path leads to it, but a walk through Mr. John O'Neill's fields that sur-
   round it is rewarded with closer contact with what may be regarded as a
   shrine to extravagance and excess and paradoxically, because of Father
   Mathew's birth there, to their opposites. For a detailed description of the
   house see Mark Bence-Jones, 'Thomastown Castle, Co. Tipperary' in *Country Life*, 2 Oct. 1969, and more briefly, Mark Bence-Jones, *Burke's Guide
   to Country Houses* (London, 1978), i, p. 272. My thanks to Joe Gleeson,
   formerly Local Studies Librarian, Thurles, for information on Thomastown
   House.
3 Moira Lysaght, *Father Theobald Mathew OFM Cap: the Apostle of
   Temperance* (Dublin, 1983), pp. 12-13; Burke, *Genealogical*, p. 361.

4   Maguire, *Father Mathew*, pp. 4-5, 11-12; a grand aunt Hannah McGrath, who nursed him until he was seven, later remembered that he had never shed a tear as a child. (Michael Quin) 'The Temperance Movement in Ireland' in *Dublin Review*, viii (1840), p. 467; M. 0'C. Bianconi and S.J. Watson, *Bianconi: King of the Irish Roads* (Dublin, 1962), p. 29; Fearghus O'Fearghail, *St. Kieran's College Kilkenny 1782-1982* (Kilkenny, 1982), pp. 16-17, 28.

5   Maguire, *Father Mathew*, pp. 12-22; Fr. Augustine, *Footprints*, p. 28.

6   Fr. Cuthbert, *The Capuchins: a contribution to the history of the counter-reformation* (London, 1928), p. 330; Maguire, *Father Mathew*, pp. 39-42. 'He was the first confessor I ever had and a most excellent one', wrote John O'Neill Daunt in *A Life Spent for Ireland*. Selections from the Journals of W.J. O'Neill Daunt, edited by his daughter (Shannon, 1972, reprint of 1896 edn.), p. 132. When Richard T. Cook visited the chapel in 1984 he found it used as a storehouse for shoe-boxes. *Ev. Ech.*, 24 Sept. 1984.

7   Fr. Augustine, *Edmund Rice and Theobald Mathew* (Dublin, 1944), p. 11; *First Poor Inq.*, p. 350; Sir John Pope-Hennessy at Centenary Celebrations, *Cork Ex.*, 10 Oct. 90.

8   Maguire, *Father Mathew*, 74-76; Lewis, *Dictionary*, i, p. 411; John B. O'Brien, *The Catholic Middle Classes in Pre-Famine Cork* (Dublin, 1979), pp. 7-8; *Morning Chronicle*, 16 Dec. 39.

9   (Archbishop Ullathorne), *From Cabin-Boy to Archbishop*. The autobiography of Archbishop Ullathorne (London 1941), p. 106; M.B. Buckley, *The Life and Writings of the Rev. Arthur O'Leary* (Dublin, 1868), p. 21; Maguire, *Father Mathew*, 70-71. The clerk to the chapel is quoted in Patrick J. Hamell, 'Father Mathew Centenary Sermon' in *Fr. M. Rec.*, Jan. 1957.

10 W.M. Thackeray, *The Irish Sketch Book and Notes of a Journey from Cornhill to Grand Cairo* (London, 1869 edn.), p. 62; Maguire, *Father Mathew*, p. 63; for Catholic Association, Father Mathew to Rev. Mr. Devereaux, 8 Dec. 1824 (2), Mathew Draft Correspondence (Q).

11 Madden, *Ireland and its Rulers*, p. 280.

12 Gwynn, *Saints and Scholars*, p. 168; A. Nicholson, *Ireland's Welcome to the Stranger* (London, 1847), p. 254; O'Neill Daunt, *A Life*, p. 132; Maguire, *Father Mathew*, p. 49. A modern Capuchin has traced the influence of St. Francis as Father Mathew's secret. Father James, 'Secret of Theobald Mathew — Capuchin' in *Capuchin Annual* 1956-7, p. 115.

13 *Annual Report of the House of Recovery or Fever Hospital of the City of Cork for the year 1826* (Cork, 1827), p. 7; John Phelan, *A Statistical Inquiry into the present state of the medical charities of Ireland* (Dublin, 1835), p. 124; Maguire, *Father Mathew*, pp. 78-82.

14 J. Windele, *Historical and descriptive notices of the City of Cork and its vicinity, Gaugaun Barra, Glengariff, and Killarney* (Cork, 1839), p. 106; G.L. Smyth, *Ireland: Historical and Statistical* (London, 1844-9), iii, p. 304.

Maura Murphy, 'The Economic and Social Structure of Nineteenth Century Cork' in David Harkness and Mary O'Dowd (eds.), *The Town in Ireland* (Belfast, 1981), p. 127. From 1834 onwards production at Guinness's was substantially greater than at Beamish and Crawford. Lynch and Vaizey, *Guinness's*, p. 260. Production figures for Beamish and Crawford were kindly put at my disposal by Beamish and Crawford plc; Inglis, *Journey*, p. 108; John B. O'Brien, 'Agricultural Prices and Living Costs in Pre-Famine Cork' in *Journal of the Cork Historical and Archaeological Society*, lxxii, Jan.-June 1977, pp. 9-10; Maura Murphy, 'The Working Class of Nineteenth Century Cork' in *Journal of the Cork Historical and Archaeological Society*, lxxxv, Jan.-Dec. 1980, pp. 27-29; *Third Poor Inq.*, p. 80.

15 *Third Poor Inq.*, p. 74; *First Poor Inq.*, p. 40; S.F. Pettit, *This City of Cork 1700-1900* (Cork, 1977), p. 139.

16 *Third Poor Inq.*, p. 62; Murphy, 'Catholic Education', p. 10; Desmond Rush, *Edmund Rice: the man and his times* (Dublin, 1981), pp. 59-60; *Third Poor Inq.*, p. 62; Ian D'Alton, *Protestant Society and Politics in Cork 1812-1844* (Cork, 1980), p. 34; *A Report of the Proceedings of the Cork Reformation Society . . .* (Cork, 1828), p. 12; *Report of the Cork Auxiliary Church Missionary Society for the year ending December 31, 1851* (1851), p. 3; Murphy, 'Economic and Social Structure', p. 146.

17 Rachel O'Higgins, 'Irish Trade Unions and Politics' in *Historical Journal*, iv (1962), p. 212; *Third Poor Inq.*, pp. 61-4; Murphy, 'Economic and Social Structure', p. 146.

18 O'Brien, *Catholic Middle Class, passim*; MacIntyre, *Liberator*, pp. 53-4; D'Alton, *Protestant Society, passim*.

19 O'Brien, *Catholic Middle Classes*, pp. 7, 10; D'Alton, *Protestant Society*, p. 35; *Third Poor Inq.*, p. 76.

20 James Fraser, *Guide Through Ireland* (Dublin, 1837), p. 87; *Proceedings of the Cork Scientific and Literary Society* (Cork, 1838), *passim*. The speakers included several people (John Francis Maguire, Richard Dowden, Isaac Varian, Denny Lane and Nicholas Dunscombe) that were to become supporters of Father Mathew's temperance work; William Bates, *The Maclise Portrait Gallery of 'Illustrious Literary Characters'* (London, 1883), p. 41. Father Prout was also active in the fight against cholera in Cork in 1832. Anonymous, 'Father Prout', *Journal of the Cork Historical and Archaeological Society*, i (1892), p. 77.

21 *Min. St. Pet., N.L.I.*; Logan, *Early Heroes*, pp. 174-5. Used to going against the established customs of society, Quakers were less inhibited than others in confronting the obstacles involved in advocating temperance. Elizabeth Isichei, *Victorian Quakers* (Oxford, 1970), p. 237. For possible Skibbereen influence in Cork, *S. Rep.*, 23 Jan. 41. For Dowden card, Day Pap., U 140 D2.

22 *Third Poor Inq.*, p. 62; *D.W.H.*, 8 Feb. 40

23 *Seventh Exc. Comm.*, pp. 233-4. Distilleries at Bandon and Riverstown are included in the Cork figures. McGuire, *Irish Whiskey*, p. 355; *Third Poor Inq.*, p. 63; Lynch and Vaizey, *Guinness's*, p. 90. A nineteenth century historian of breweries thought Beamish and Crawford's 'the most ancient porter brewery in Ireland'. Alfred Barnard, *The Noted Breweries of Great Britain and Ireland* (London, c.1890), ii, p. 353; the Cork Total Abstinence Society counted 502 pubs in 1836. *I.T.L.G.*, 24 Dec. 36; other counts for 1838 include 600 (Windele, *Historical and descriptive*, p. 105) and 763 (*D.W.H.*, 16 Feb. 39); *Third Poor Inq.*, p. 61.

24 Desmond Bowen, *The Protestant Crusade in Ireland, 1800-1870* (Dublin, 1978), p. 205; *Min. St. Pet.*; *Free*, 17 Dec. 38; *D.E.P.*, 12 Nov. 39.

25 *P.T.A.*, July 37; for Blackrock, *I.T.L.G.*, 4 Mar. 37, and Anonymous, *The South of Ireland and her poor* (London, 1843), p. 103; for numbers, Rogers, *Father Mathew*, p. 34; Rogers was quoting from James McKenna, 'Manuscript History of the Temperance Reformation in Ireland, England and Scotland', which has been missing for some years. For McKenna's eccentricity, Thomas Hudson, *Temperance Pioneers of the West* (London, 1887), pp. 289-90; for Martin, W.R. Martin, 'William Martin', typescript, Friend's Lib. (London). For festival, *I.T.L.G.*, Jan. 38.

26 Martin, 'William Martin', p. 3; Birmingham, *Memoir*, p. 16; Michael Hurst, *Maria Edgeworth and the Public Scene* (London, 1969), fn. p. 113. The interview with O'Connell apeared in *Cork Ex.*, 12, 13 Sept. 1890.

27 The pre-1890 view is in Maguire, *Father Mathew*, pp. 106-7; A.M. Sullivan, *New Ireland*. Political Sketches and Personal Reminiscences of Thirty Years of Irish Public Life (Glasgow, 1877), p. 49; Sister Mary Francis Clare, *Father Mathew*, p. 57; and Mathew, *Father Mathew*, pp. 34-5. The amended version is in Fr. S(tanislaus), 'Father Mathew and Temperance' in *Capuchin Annual*, 1930, pp. 162-8; Rev. Patrick Rogers, 'Father Mathew: A Biography' in *Bonaventura*, Spring 1939, p. 182; Rev. Patrick Rogers, *Father Mathew*, p. 39; Father Augustine, *Footprints*, p. 90; Lysaght, *Father Mathew*, p. 24; and Malcolm, *Ireland Sober*, p. 110. The clergyman was almost certainly Rev. John E. Lombard, who answered the questions on St. Nicholas's parish in reply to the Poor Commissioners' circular. *First Poor Inq.*, p. 983. An unidentified English visitor to Cork in 1835 found Lombard 'a delightful man in every sense of the word'. C. Moore, 'Cork City as seen by an English visitor in 1835' in *Journal of the Cork Historical and Archaeological Society*, viii (1902), p. 204.

28 *Cork Ex.*, 13 Sep. 90; Fr. Augustine, *Footprints*, pp. 97-8.

29 *Br. Temp. Her.*, Jan. 45; Maguire, *Father Mathew*, pp. 111-13; Fr. Augustine, *Footprints*, pp. 99-103.

30 *Cork Stan.*, 11, 13 June 38. For Hockings, Longmate, *Waterdrinkers*, pp. 48-9, and Brian Harrison, *Dictionary of British Temperance Biography*

(Coventry, 1973), p. 64; for the influence of Hockings' work in Ireland, Malcolm, *Ireland Sober*, pp. 92-3; for Father Mathew's financial problems see Chapter 3.

31 *Cork Stan.*, 23 July 38; Ullathorne, *Cabin Boy*, p. 195.

32 Maguire, *Father Mathew*, pp. 112-13; Justin McCarthy, *The Story of an Irishman* (London, 1904), p. 35; Father Mathew (to George Whitmore Carr) 8 Dec. 1839. Miscellaneous Letters, Friends' Lib. Dublin.

33 *D.W.H.*, 13 Apr. 39; Gen. Return Magistrates, 260-62, P.R.O. (L.); Smyth, *Ireland*, iii, p. 79. Three years later, when the movement had spread throughout Ireland, Father Mathew was to complain that only 20,000 had taken the pledge in the city of Cork, a much smaller proportion of the population than had taken it in other places. Fr. Augustine, *Footprints*, p. 181. Writing in March 1840 the R.M. for Thurles said drunkards began going to Cork 'almost one year ago'. T.R., Thurles, county Tipperary. For drunkenness on the way to Cork, see T.R., Tralee and Kilgarvan, county Kerry.

34 *Cork Ex.*, 13 Sep. 90; *Lim. Rep.*, 15 Nov. 39.

35 *Cork Stan.*, 11 Apr. 38, 23 July 38; *D.W.H.*, 7 Dec. 39.

36 Malcolm, *Ireland Sober*, pp. 114-15; *Temp. Int.*, 29 Feb. 40; *Wat. Chron.*, 12 Oct., 30 Nov. 39; Father Foley had enrolled 769 members in Dungarvan alone by October 1839, and had particular success among the miners of Bunmahon, who had a great reputation for drunkenness. By the end of November he was given the credit for converting nearly 30,000 to teetotalism in Waterford and in north and east Cork. *D.E.P.*, 7, 9, 25 Nov. 39. Drunkards from Limerick were reported to be travelling to Cork to take the pledge from the summer of 1839. *Lim. Rep.*, 12 July 39.

37 T.R. Rathkeale, county Limerick; *Cork Con.*, 23 Oct. 39; *D.E.P.*, 5 Nov. 39; Father Mathew's letter to Belfast T.A.S. is printed in Fr. Augustine, *Footprints*, p. 109.

38 Birmingham, *Memoir*, p. 16; *P.T.A.*, July 37; *I.T.L.G.*, 7 Oct. 37; *D.E.P.*, 31 Mar. 40; *Clare J.*, 1 Aug. 39; *Lim. Rep.*, 8 Nov. 39. Father Mathew preached at the dedication ceremony at the opening of Kilrush church. Rev. I. Murphy, 'Pre-Famine Passenger Services on the Lower Shannon' in *North Munster Antiquarian Journal*, xvi (1973-4), p. 81; for benefit system, *Lim. Chron.*, 22 Jan. 40; for money on spirits, *Temp. Rec.*, Nov. 42; Kohl, *Ireland*, pp. 93-106. The meeting Kohl attended was reported in *Clare J.*, 6 Oct. 42.

CHAPTER 3: THE TEMPERANCE CRUSADE

1 *I.T.L.G.*, 12 Nov. 36; 'Rules of St. Mary's Temperance and Mortality Society' in T.R., Limerick City.

2 G.H. Fitzgerald, Mayor of Limerick, to Rev. Theobald Mathew. This appeared in many newspapers and was quoted in W.J. Battersby, 'Biographical Sketch of Very Rev. T. Mathew' in *Catholic Dir. 1841*,

pp. 246-7. The letter was printed and sold as a poster at 4d. per dozen by the Irish Temperance Union. There is a copy of one in Day Papers, U 140, Scrapbook 2, p. 128. Father Mathew acknowledged the assistance the letter gave his movement at a dinner in his honour in Limerick in 1841; see *Tuam Her.*, 23 Oct. 41; *D.E.P.*, 19, 29 Oct., 14 Nov. 39.

3   *Clare J.*, 2 Dec. 39; *Lim. Rep.*, 3 Dec. 39; *Lim. Chron.*, 27 Nov., 4 Dec. 39.

4   *Lim. Rep.*, 3 Dec. 39; *Lim. Stan.*, 3 Dec. 39. The *Limerick Standard* differed from other accounts in saying that Father Mathew was already accompanied by dragoons on his way to the Court House. It also reported a large number of injuries received when part of a ballustrade along the river collapsed and several people fell in. The *Lim. Chron.* confirmed this last point and an English Quaker visiting the city some time afterwards noted that 100 feet of iron railing was still on the ground. See Cyrus Clark in *British Temperance Herald*, quoted by Sheil, *Temperance Movement*, p. 13.

5   The lowest figure was in *Times*, 17 Dec. 39; most biographers gave 150,000; see, for example, Maguire, *Father Mathew*, p. 133; John Begley, *The Diocese of Limerick. From 1691 to the Present Time* (Dublin, 1938), p. 386, gave 180,000; *D.E.P.* was told it was 200,000, and McKenna, according to Shaw, said it was 250,000. H.B.P. Shaw (later Fr. Nessan, O.F.M. Cap.), 'The Life and Times of Fr. Theobald Mathew', unpublished M.A. Thesis, U.C.C., 1939. For injured, *Lim. Chron.*, 4 Dec. 39; *Times*, 17 Dec. 39; *Free J.*, 5 Dec. 39; *Lim. Stan.*, 3 Dec. 39.

6   *Evening Packet*, reprinted *Lim. Stan.*, 10 Dec. 39; *Wat. M.*, 7 Dec. 39; *D.E.M.*, reprinted *Lim. Stan.*, 6 Dec. 39; *Kill. Mod.*, 7 Dec. 39. For Father Mathew and miracles, see Chapter 6. For a more detailed account of Father Mathew's first visit to Limerick see Colm Kerrigan, 'Father Mathew in Limerick' in *North Munster Antiquarian Journal*, xxvii (1985), pp. 62-69.

7   For agreement to come to Waterford see Father Mathew to D.J. Murphy, printed *Wat. Chron.*, 30 Nov. 39; *Wat. Mir.*, 11, 14 Dec. 39; *Wat. Chron.*, 14 Dec. 39; *D.E.P.*, 5 Jan. 40.

8   *Wat. Mir.*, 14 Dec. 39; Bishop Foran quoted Maguire, *Father Mathew*, p. 117; T.R. Waterford City; *Wat. Chron.*, 14 Dec. 39.

9   *Tipp. F.P.*, 14 Dec. 39; *Wat. Mir.*, 16 Dec. 39; Bianconi and Watson, *Bianconi*, p. 123; *Wat. Chron.*, 30 Nov., 21 Dec. 39; Inglis, *Journey*, p. 133; Anthony Marmion, *The Ancient and Modern History of the Maritime Ports of Ireland* (London, 1855), pp. 559-60; *P.T.A.*, July 37; *Tipp. F.P.*, 28 Sept., 2 Oct., 18, 21 Dec. 39; *D.E.P.*, 6 Feb., 3 Mar. 40; Birmingham, *Memoir*, pp. 32-7, 43.

10 For Gort, *D.E.P.*, 15, 18, 20 Feb. 40 and T.R. Gort, county Galway, *Gal. Adv.*, 4 Jan. 40. For Mechanics rules see *Con. Jour.*, 4 June 1840. For origins of Mechanics, Mary Casteleyn, *A History of Literacy and Libraries in Ireland* (Aldershot 1984), pp. 161-62.

11 *Con Jour.*, 5, 19 Mar., 40; *D.E.P.*, 19 Mar. 40; *B.F.T.I.*, 4 Apr. 40. For Claddagh teetotallers, *Gal. Adv.*, 4 Jan. 40. According to Birmingham, Father Mathew's invitation to Galway came from Bishop Browne. *Memoirs*, pp. 37-41. For Loughrea numbers, *Gal. Adv.*, 21 Mar. 40, T.R. Loughrea, county Galway. For a more detailed account of Father Mathew's visits to Galway see Colm Kerrigan, 'Temperance and Politics in Pre-Famine Galway' in *Journal of the Galway Archaeological and Historical Society*, 43 (1991), pp. 82-94.

12 On Hockings' influence see Haughton, *Memoir*, pp. 38-9. *D.E.P.*, 19 Mar. 39, 5, 17, 19 Mar. 40; *D.W.R.*, 19 Mar. 40.

13 *Free Jour.*, 30, 31 Mar. 40; *D.E.P.*, 31 Mar., 2, 4, 7 Apr., 17 Nov. 1840; Superintendent Rice to commissioners, Dublin Metropolitan Police, 4 April 1840. P.R.O. (Lon.) H.O. 100 263.

14 *D.E.P.*, 31 Mar. 40. For a rumour that only Father Mathew's pledge was efficacious, see *Kilk. Jour.*, 1 Apr. 40.

15 Father Mathew to S.C. Hall, n.d. (83); Father Mathew to Dr. Spratt, n.d. (1089), Mathew Draft Correspondence (Q).

16 Birmingham, *Memoir*, pp. 81-2.

17 T.R. City of Limerick, City of Waterford, Thurles, Nenagh, Clonmel and Roscrea, county Tipperary.

18 T.R. City of Limerick, City of Waterford, Cahir, Thurles, county Tipperary; Loughrea, Portumna, Gort, county Galway. If a Temperance Report was written for Galway town, it has not survived.

19 T.R. City of Limerick, City of Waterford. Olivier, *Père Mathew*, p. 54; *Nen. Guar.*, 4 Apr. 40; *Tipp. Vin.*, 10 Apr. 44.

20 McCarthy, *Irishman*, p. 35; John Denvir, *The Life Story of an Old Rebel* (Shannon, 1972 edn.), p. 13; for Susan Dowden, *I.T.L.J.*, 2 Jan. 99; Keegan, *Diary*, p. 34; *Gal. Adv.*, 30 May 40; Father Mathew to Peter Purcell, 23 July 1844 (1247), Mathew Draft Correspondence (Q). While Father Mathew emphasised the importance of parents practising as well as preaching temperance to their children, Father Foley 'receives no father or mother without previously engaging them to enrol their children'. For Father Mathew, *S. Rep.*, 2 Jan. 41; for Father Foley, *Wat. Chron.*, 21 Dec. 39.

21 T.R. Thurles, Newport, Cashel, Nenagh, county Tipperary, City of Limerick; 'Diary of Joseph Tabuteau, R.M.', S.P.O., vii-1-39, 3/4/5 April 1839, 26/27/28 Feb. 1840. Tabuteau was later transferred to Nenagh (*Tipp. Vin.*, 20 Mar. 44) and the following year became Superintendent Magistrate for the county. E. Lucas to Magistrates at Petty Sessions at Borrisokane, 3 Feb. 1845, P.R.O. (L.) H.O. 45 OS/1148.

22 *D.E.P.*, 4 Feb. 40; the Claddagh report is in the second edition of Birmingham's *Memoir*, pp. 50-52. Halls, *Ireland*, i, p. 310. Extracts from the Waterford Temp. Soc. report are in James Haughton, *A Plea for*

Teetotalism, and the Maine Liquor Law (London, 1855), pp. 80-83; T.R. City of Limerick; *Wat. Chron.,* 22 Jan. 42; Kohl, *Ireland,* p. 101; *S.Rep.,* 8 Apr. 41; Richard Allen to William Lloyd Garrison, 17 Nov. 1841, printed *Lib.,* 17 Dec. 41; *Temp. Rec.,* Nov. 42.

23   T.R. Clonmel, Nenagh, Roscrea, Cahir, county Tipperary, City of Waterford, Loughrea, county Galway; *Temp. Rec.,* June 44.

24   *Sligo Jour.,* 22 Jan. 41; Hely Dutton, *A Statistical and Agricultural Survey of the County of Galway* (Dublin, 1824), p. 367; *Census 1841,* pp. 484, 498; *Lic. Dist. Ire.,* p. 659; *Temp. Rec.,* Aug., Nov. 42. I am grateful to John H. Pierce for information on Charlton and Cadbury. Smyth, *Ireland,* iii, p. 309, carried a report for 1843 that showed the steam engines in the distillery were 'now idle'. Work was resumed at the distillery in 1845, Marmion, *Ports of Ireland,* p. 492; Kohl, *Ireland,* p. 189; Maguire, *Father Mathew,* p. 145; Father Mathew to Mr. Russell, n.d. (1796), Mathew Draft Correspondence (Q). For Father Mathew's family and distilling see also Birmingham, *Memoir,* p. 69, Maguire, *Father Mathew,* pp. 145, 293-4, and John B. O'Brien, 'The Hacketts: Glimpses of Entrepreneurial Life in Cork 1800-1870' in *Journal of the Cork Historical and Archaeological Society,* xc (1985), pp. 152, 156. Some took their losses good humouredly, like the brewer in Waterford who, seeking Father Mathew's blessing, said the least he could do, having put him out of business, was to give him his blessing! *Wat. Chron.,* 14 Dec. 39.

25   *Wat. Chron.,* 13, 22 Jan., 29 Sept. 42; *Times,* 26 Aug. 43. For opposition to his work in London see Colm Kerrigan, 'Father Mathew and Teetotalism in London, 1843' in *London Journal,* 11, 2 (1985), pp. 111-12. After his visit to Huddersfield, local brewers distributed free beer in an apparent attempt to undo his work. Harrison, *Drink and the Victorians,* p. 135. Father Mathew to James Haughton, n.d. (1602), Mathew Draft Correspondence (Q); James S. Roberts, *Drink, Temperance and the Working Class in Nineteenth Century Germany* (London, 1984), p. 25.

26   Kohl, *Ireland,* p. 189; Walter Thomas Myler, *Saint Catherine's Bells: an autobiography* (London, 1870), ii, p. 99; G.L. Barrow, *The Emergence of the Irish Banking System* (Dublin, 1975), p. 195.

27   T.R. Clonmel, Nenagh, Carrick-on-Suir, county Tipperary.

28   *I.T.L.G.,* 29 July, 26 Aug. 37; *North. Adv.,* 30 Oct. 6, 13 Nov. 41; *Wat. Chron.,* 27 Aug. 42; J. Grant, *Impressions of Ireland and the Irish* (London, 1844), p. 143; *D.E.P.,* 22, 29 Aug. 44; Fergus A. D'Arcy, 'The Decline and Fall of Donnybrook Fair: moral reform and social control in mid-nineteenth century' in *Saothair,* 13 (1988), pp. 7-21.

29   Kohl, *Ireland,* pp. 100-101; Elizabeth Malcolm, 'Popular Recreation in Nineteenth Century Ireland' in Oliver MacDonagh, W.F. Mandle and Pauric Travers (eds.), *Irish Culture and Nationalism* (London, 1983), p. 48; Harrison, *Drink and the Victorians,* p. 116.

30 T.R., Portumna, Gort, county Galway, Pallasgreen (Pallas Green), county Limerick, Carlow, Dingle, county Kerry, Kildysart, county Clare; *D.W.H.*, 18 Apr. 39; *Lim. Rep.*, 8 Nov. 39; *Free Jour.*, 7 Aug. 40.

31 *Wat. Mir.*, 30 Jan. 42; Malcolm, 'Popular Recreation', p. 40; *Nat. Temp. Adv. & Her.*, 16 Jan. 43; for Galway, *Gal. Vin.*, 6 Apr. 44; for programme, *Ir. Temp. Chron.*, Oct. 46; McCarthy, *Irishman*, pp. 36-42. For tickets, Day Papers, U 140 D.

32 T.R. Mountmellick, Queen's County, Carrick-on-Suir, county Tipperary, Kildysart, county Clare, City of Waterford; *D.E.P.*, 29 Feb., 24 Mar. 40; *D.W.H.*, 1 Feb. 40; *Wat. Chron.*, 23 Nov. 39; *S. Rep.*, 29 Dec. 40. For Nenagh and Carrick-on-Suir incidents, *Wex. Ind.*, 11 Apr. 40; *Mayo Con.*, 21 July 40.

33 *D.E.P.*, 17 Nov. 40, 2 Mar. 43; McCarthy, *Irishman*, p. 37; Irish Folklore Commission, MS. S 587, p. 168.

34 *D.W.H.*, 16 Nov., 7 Dec. 39; Windele, *City of Cork*, p. 140; for *Tipperary Free Press*, William P. Burke, *History of Clonmel* (Waterford, 1907), p. 554; for circulation figures, *Mayo Mer.*, 15 Aug. 40.

35 *Free Jour.*, 31 Mar. 40; *Gal. Vin.*, 10 July 41, 12 Jan. 42; for Meany, see Brian Dinan, *Clare and its People* (Cork, 1987), p. 133; *Ath. Sen.*, 31 Aug. 40; *Con. Journ.*, 20 Aug. 40; *Tab.*, 15 July 43; Harrison, *Drink and the Victorians*, p. 152. Two draft letters survive from 1847, where Father Mathew informs the editors of the *Tipperary Vindicator* and the *Tipperary Free Press* that he intended to hold a temperance meeting at Kilfeacle. Father Mathew to Maurice Lenihan, 7 June 1847 (2031), and Father Mathew to D.F. O'Leary, 7 June 1847 (2032), Mathew Draft Correspondence (Q).

36 Harrison, *Drink and the Victorians*, p. 115; *Free Journ.*, 1 Apr. 40; *Wex. Ind.*, 11 Apr. 40; T.R. Pallasgreen (Pallas Green), county Limerick. Adams thought Father Mathew's work proved a valuable aid to emigration in that it both helped the poor to save the fare and helped the immigrants' chances of doing well in America. Its value to prospective emigrants was certainly known in Ireland. In 1840 an American visitor told a temperance gathering at Sandyford, Dublin, that an immigrant ship had recently arrived in New York and all those who had temperance medals were employed straightaway at good wages while the others were left starving in the streets. William Forbes Adams, *Ireland and Irish Emigration to the New World from 1815 to the Famine* (Baltimore, 1980 edn.), p. 215; *D.E.P.*, 1 Sept. 40.

37 *S. Rep.*, 29 Dec. 40; *Nen. Gaz.*, 22 May 41; *Cork Ex.*, 23 Nov. 48; Kohl, *Ireland*, p. 101; John Miley, *Will Teetotalism Last?* (Dublin, 1840), p. 18; *Morning Register* piece reprinted *Mor. Chron.*, 26 Mar. 40; *Free Jour.*, 19 Mar. 41; *Wat. Chron.*, 24 Dec. 41.

38 T.R. Nenagh, Clonmel, county Tipperary, City of Limerick, City of Waterford; for Dublin, *Dublin Monthly Magazine*, Jan.-June 1842; *Wat. Chron.*,

204   *Notes to Pages 78-83*

Jan., 29 Sept. 42; *Temp. Rec.,* Feb. 43 Supplement, and June 44. Savings banks were 'established for the safe custody and increase of the small savings of the industrious classes of society' and for the funds of charitable societies. *Pass Book with the Cashel Savings Bank* (Clonmel, 1846), p. 7, N.L.I.

39   T.R. City of Waterford, City of Limerick, Ennis, county Clare; *Lim. Chron.,* 14 Jan. 42; for 1843 report, *Temp. Rec.,* June 44.

40   *Free. Jour.,* 1 Apr. 40; Ullathorne, *Cabin Boy,* pp. 193-4; Draft letter marked 'not sent' from J. McKenna to Editor of *Tablet,* 5 Nov. 44 (92); Father Mathew to Peter Purcell, 23 July 44 (1247), Mathew Draft Correspondence (Q).

41   Father Mathew to Joseph Sturge, 25 Jan. 1845. Papers of Joseph Sturge, M.P., B. Lib. Add. MS. 43845; Maguire, *Father Mathew,* pp. 316-22; Richard Webb to Richard Dowden. Day Papers, U 140 C 107. O'Connell was sympathetic, see Daniel O'Connel to James Haughton, 26 Oct. 1844. Maurice R. O'Connell (ed.), *The Correspondence of Daniel O'Connell* (Dublin, 1978), vii, pp. 281-2. O'Connell's 'warm-hearted imprudence' might be thought to resemble that of Father Mathew. Oliver MacDonagh, *The Hereditary Bondsman: Daniel O'Connell 1775-1829* (London, 1988), p. 155-7. In Dublin Fr. Spratt encouraged temperance societies and individuals to respond to the appeal. *Free. Jour.,* 6 Nov. 44. For England see Father Mathew to Mr. Hunter, 12 April 1845, printed *N.Y.D.T.,* 30 June 49. For London meeting at St. George's Temperance Hall and Exeter Hall (attended by Lord John Russell, S.C. Hall and J.S. Buckingham) see *Temp. Rec.,* Jan., Feb. 45.

42   *Nen. Guard.,* 7 Mar. 40. Smith gave 63,037 as the total number who took the pledge at twenty venues in London. The details are in Frederick Sherlock, *Illustrious Abstainers* (London, 1879), p. 142. At least one newspaper noticed him as a 'counter'. *Mor. Her.,* 7 Aug. 43. For Dublin see notes 13 and 14; *Nen. Guar.,* 4 Mar. 40. That the number of those taking the pledge at particular meetings can tell us little about the total number of teetotallers is further suggested by a report from Clonmel when Father Mathew was there at the end of 1839 which noted that one man took the pledge *eleven* times! *Tipp. Con.,* 20 Dec. 39.

43   Malcolm, *Ireland Sober,* p. 126; for Clark, *D.E.P.,* 18 Feb., 5 Mar. 40. Logan wrote that the *names* of teetotallers had been entered on the roll book of teetotallers when he was in Cork in 1848. Logan, *Early Heroes,* p. 186.

44   *S. Rep.,* 20 Feb. 41; for Boyle, *D.E.P.,* 26 Sept. 40; the *Kilkenny Journal* report was reprinted in *D.E.P.,* 23 Jan. 40.

45   Kohn, *Ireland,* p. 98; Grant, *Impressions,* ii, p. 231; *Tipp. Vin.,* 31 Jan. 46; Malcolm, *Ireland Sober,* p. 125; *Magistrates, Constabulary, passim.*

46 *Gal. Vin.*, 10 Apr. 44, 20 July 45, 17, 21 Jan. 46; *Gal. Mer.*, 28 Mar. 45. That drunkenness had again become a feature of life in the town is suggested by the 750 taken into custody for this offence and for disorderly conduct during 1845, a figure that represents an increase of 331 over the previous year, or nearly three times the figure for 1841. *Drunkenness ... 1841 to 1845*, pp. 300-301. For Cork speech, *Cork Ex.*, 30 Mar. 46.

47 *D.E.P.*, 30 May 44; *Pilot*, 6 Oct. 45.

48 *Tipp. Vin.*, 20 Mar. 44, 9 Apr., 24 May 45.

49 *Cork Ex.*, 3 Jan. 45; *Tipp. Vin.*, 9 Apr. 45, 31 Jan. 46. *Spirit Lic. (Ir.)*, p. 565; I. Slater, *National Commercial Directory of Ireland* (Manchester, 1846), p. 317; *S. Rep.*, 11 Feb. 45.

CHAPTER 4: DRINKING AND CRIME

1 T.R. Kilkenny, Lismore, county Waterford, Skibbereen, Kanturk, county Cork, Ballickmoyler, Queen's county, Bruff, county Limerick.

2 *S.C. Drunkenness*, p. 395; *I.T.L.G.*, 8 Apr. 37; *Cork Ex.*, 2 Jan. 43; for judges views, *Tipp. Vin.*, 16 Sept. 43; *Cork Ex.*, 22 Nov. 48; *Catholic Luminary and Ecclesiastical Record*, 20 June 40; *D.E.P.*, 1 Sept. 40.

3 *The Parliamentary Gazetteer of Ireland, 1843-44* (Dublin, 1844), i, p. cxiv; P.R.O. (L.) Return of Offences before Magistrates (Ireland) H.O. 100 259-262. The figures are for the city *and* county of Limerick, as these were not distinguished until March 1840.

4 The population increase in the years preceding the Famine may in fact have been less than previously thought. See J.M. Goldstrom, 'Irish Agriculture and the Great Famine' in J.M. Goldstrom and L.A. Clarkson (eds.), *Irish Population, Economy, and Society* (Oxford, 1981), p. 165. *S.C. Constab.*, p. 369.

5 The rate of duty was raised from 2/8d. to 3/8d. in March 1842. *Spirits 1800 ... 1845*, p. 427.

6 *Spirits (Ire.)*, p. 555.

7 Lynch and Vaizey, *Guinness's*, pp. 140, 260.

8 G. Pearson, *Hooligan: A History of Respectable Fears* (London, 1983), p. 213; J.J. Tobias, *Crime and Industrial Society in the Nineteenth Century* (London, 1967), p. 21; V.A.C. Gatrell and T.B. Hadden, 'Criminal Statistics and their Interpretation' in E.A. Wrigley (ed.), *Nineteenth Century Society: Essays in the Use of Quantitative Methods for the Study of Social Data* (Cambridge, 1972), p. 339; S. Breathnach, *The Irish Police from earliest times to the present day* (Dublin, 1974), pp. 36-40; T.A. Critchley, *A History of Police in England and Wales* (London, 1978 edn.), pp. 105, 126.

9 Gatrell and Hadden, 'Criminal Statistics', p. 351.

10 Maguire, *Father Mathew*, pp. 200-201.

11   R.B. O'Brien, *Thomas Drummond, Under Secretary in Irealnd 1835-40: Life and Letters* (London, 1889), p. 351; *S.C. . . . Crime*, p. 215.

12   Maguire's figure of 20 faction fights for 1839 forms 19.42% of the 103 'Riots and faction fights' for that year, and 19.42% of the 175 for 1837 gives the figure of 33.99, evened up to 34.

13   *Lim. Chron.*, 7 Dec. 39; Irish Temperance Union Report quoted Haughton, *Plea for Teetotalism*, p. 73.

14   Croker, *Researches*, pp. 230-31; Le Fanu, *Irish Life*, p. 32; *S.C. . . . Crime*, p. 586; George Cornwall Lewis, *On Local Disturbances in Ireland and on the Irish Church Question* (London, 1836), pp. 279-95; de Tocqueville, *Journeys*, p. 143; Breathnach, *Irish Police*, p. 39; Patrick O'Donnell, *The Irish Faction Fighters of the nineteenth century* (Dublin, 1975), p. 41. For the view that serious social interests and alignments lay at the origin of at least some faction fighting, see Paul E.W. Roberts, 'Caravats and Shanavests: Whiteboyism and Faction Fighting in East Munster, 1802-11' in Samuel Clark and James Donnelly, Jr. (eds.), *Irish Peasants: Violence and Political Unrest 1780-1914* (Manchester, 1983), pp. 64-101. Faction fights continued long after this in some parts of the country, most notably in Cappawhite, county Tipperary, an area which Father Mathew never seems to have visited on his crusade, although his mother came from there. Seamus Fitzgerald, *Cappawhite and Doon* (Pallaskenry, c.1983), p. 89.

15   Halls, *Ireland*, i, p. 245.

16   Fr. Augustine, *Footprints*, pp. 110-157; Halls, *Ireland*, i, pp. 33-46, 253, 281, 310, 321, iii, pp. 59-61; Kohl, *Ireland*, pp. 65-7, 125, 93-109, 167-70, 189, 193, 219, 248-9, 251-2. His last two references were to Wicklow, and suggest there was great enthusiasm for Father Mathew's work there, an impression confirmed by Elizabeth Smith's journal entry on the shops in Blessington in late 1840 no longer selling whiskey. *Journals . . . Smith*, p. 21; Nicholson, *Ireland's Welcome*, pp. 90, 94, 140; Bretherton, 'Irish Temperance Movement', p. 300. Kearney has also confirmed that 'towns in the south became focal points of the teetotal endeavour'. Kearney, 'Father Mathew', p. 171.

17   Taking an account of Lee's arguments that the 1841 census was an underestimation and Mokyr's view that 'the regional variation in the degree of under-numeration was not too large', I have taken the census of 1841 to represent the actual population of the various counties as it was two years earlier, i.e. in 1839. Joseph Lee, 'On the Accuracy of the Pre-Famine Irish Censuses' in Goldstrom and Clarkson, *Irish Population*, p. 54, and Mokyr, *Why Ireland Starved*, p. 32; Kohl, *Ireland*, p. 219; for Father Mathew in Wexford see J. Glynn, 'The Catholic Church in Wexford Town' in *The Past: the organ of the Ui Cinsealaigh Historical Society*, No. 15 (1984), pp. 42-3.

18 Crampton quoted *S.C. . . . Crime,* p. 286; Hoppen, *Elections, Politics and Society,* p. 369; J.W. Hurst, 'Disturbed Tipperary 1831-60' in *Eire-Ireland,* ix (1974), p. 54; Keegan, *Diary,* p. 33; *Nen. Guar.,* 8 June 42.

19 For Baker, P.R.O. (L.) H.O. 100 187 (395); *Nen. Gaz.,* 22 June, 42; Maguire, *Father Mathew,* p. 15.

20 Michael Beames, *Peasants and Power* (Brighton, 1983), pp. 78-9, 85, 90; Hoppen, *Elections, Politics and Society,* p. 385; for the background to Scully's murder, see his brother's evidence to Devon Commissioners, *Comm . . . Land in Ireland,* Part iii, pp. 903-910; the police abstracts of the two outrages in 1841 are in P.R.O. (L.) H.O. 45 175 (3).

21 Hurst, 'Disturbed Tipperary', p. 58.

22 For the wide variety of outrages unconnected with land see *Abstract . . . outrages . . . Tipperary,* pp. 309-37.

23 The number of murders and manslaughters in Tipperary for each year from 1839 to 1845 were: 164, 90, 56, 44, 46, 47, 66.

24 *Nen. Guar.,* 7 May 42; *Comm . . . Land in Ireland,* Part ii, p. 504.

25 *D.E.P.,* 3 Mar. 40, 7 June 42; *Free Jour.,* 17 Nov. 40.

26 *Bal. Her.,* 22 June 41; *Lon. T.M.,* 9 Aug. 46.

27 *Tip. Vin.,* 12 Jan., 26 Feb., 12 Apr. 45 (for meetings), 19 Mar. 45 (for resolution).

28 *Tipp. Vin.,* 13 Apr. 44.

29 *D.E.M.,* 6, 8, 13 June 42; *Mor. Her.,* 5 July 42.

30 A couple of days earlier the *Guardian* had been complaining that murder in Tipperary was not looked on with the horror that it ought. 'It is some time excused, other times palliated — but more frequently justified.' *Nen.Guar.,* 4, 8 June 42.

31 *Nat.,* 27 May 43; *Cork Ex.,* 5 Jan. 44; Hansard lxiii, pp. 964-73; the *Guardian* felt the number of priests who were actively opposed to outrages were few compared to those who said nothing. *Nen. Guard.,* 4 June 42.

32 J. Venedey, *Ireland and the Irish during the Repeal Year,* trans. W.B. McCabe (Dublin, 1844), p. 138.

33 O'Brien, *Drummond,* p. 284; *Week. Free.,* 2 Aug. 45; *Mor. Chron.,* 6 Nov. 45; *Pil.,* 15 Dec. 45.

CHAPTER 5: TEETOTALLERS AND REPEALERS

1 T. Mooney, *A History of Ireland from Earliest Times to the Present* (Boston, 1846), p. 1,566.

2 For the bishops and Repeal see O. MacDonagh, 'The Politicization of the Irish Catholic Bishops, 1800-1850' in *Historical Journal,* xviii, No. 1, p. 47. Higgins and MacHale both approved of the pledge, though not of Father Mathew. The influence of the clergy in promoting temperance is discussed more fully in Chapter 7.

3 *Lim. Rep.*, 10 Dec. 39; *Lim. Stan.*, 24 Dec. 39, 19 Jan. 40; *D.E.M.*, 3 Jan., 20 Mar. 40; G.A. Hayes-McCoy, *A History of Irish Flags from Earliest Times* (Dublin, 1979), pp. 42-5, 125.

4 *D.E.M.*, 18 Mar. 40; *Wat. Mail.*, 21 Mar. 40.

5 T.R. Bansha, county Tipperary, Charleville and Macroom, county Cork, Kenmare, county Kerry and Corofin, county Clare; *West. Guar.*, 28 July 40.

7 T.R. Abbeyleix, Queen's County, Arthurstown, county Wexford, Newport, county Tipperary and Corofin, county Clare. Venedey noted the 'consolatary proverb' in 1843, 'Oh, if we had not got drunk at the battle of Ross.' Venedey, *Ireland*, p. 171.

8 *Tim.*, 26 Mar. 40; *D.E.P.*, 28 Mar. 40. For a more favourable attitude towards Father Mathew's work from the London press see *Mor. Chron.*, 6 Feb., 24 Mar. 40. The *Dublin Evening Post*, from December 1839, emphasised the moral rather than the political nature of the temperance 'revolution'. *D.E.P.*, 14 Dec. 39. This was perhaps appropriate for what was a 'Castle Newspaper' for most of the decade. See Brian Inglis, *The Freedom of the Press in Ireland 1784-1841* (London, 1954), p. 207.

9 *Sligo Jour.*, 26 June 40; *Con. Jour.*, 25 June, 23 July 40; *Gal. Adv.*, 27 June 40.

10 Hansard lii, pp. 1311-12, liii, pp. 552-53. The authority on Irish flags has given 1848 as the date when the tricolour was accepted as a national symbol. Hayes-McCoy, *Irish Flags*, p. 143. That Normanby should feel obliged to deny the presence of the tricolour at the Carlow procession might be considered evidence that the symbol had gained acceptance earlier. Father Maher, 'an old incorrigible advocate of temperance', admitted he was one of the priests who led the parade. He was active in O'Connell's election campaign in Carlow the following year. Daniel O'Connell to Christopher FitzSimon, 18 and 19 Jun. 1814, Maurice O'Connell (ed.), *The Correspondence of Daniel O'Connell* (Dublin 1978), vii, pp. 93, 95. As well as Normanby and Lord Fortescue (the Lord Lieutenant), the Irish Chief Secretary Lord Morpeth was also impressed by the movement, having, in the course of a speech in the House of Commons in 1840, praised its good results and bore further witness to the benefits it had brought about on the occasion of his retirement as Chief Secretary the following year. Hansard li, p. 950; J.J. Caskin (ed.), *The Vice Regal Speeches and Addresses, Lectures and Poems of the Earl of Carlisle, K.G.* (Dublin,1866), p. xx. The respect was mutual: Father Mathew kept a 'life-sized bust of Lord Morpeth' in his house in Cove Street. J.F. Maguire, *Father Mathew*, p. 123.

11 Father Mathew to Rev. Philip Carpenter, n.d. (709), Mathew Draft Correspondence (Q); *D.E.P.*, 20 Oct. 42.

12 *Cork Ex.*, 1 Sept. 64.

13 *Wat. Chron.*, 12 Dec. 39; Haughton, *A Plea for Teetotalism*, p. 228;

Thackeray, *Irish Sketch Book,* p. 62; Fr. Mathew to S.C. Hall, n.d. (83), Mathew Draft Correspondence (Q); Maguire, *Father Mathew,* pp. 13-14; James McGlashen, 'Father Mathew' in *Dublin University Magazine,* xxxiii (1849), p. 705; Bretherton, 'Irish Temperance Movement', p. 283; *Gal. Vin.,* 21 Jan. 46.

14 For Galway see Kerrigan, 'Temperance and Politics'; *D.E.P.,* 19 Mar., 1 Sept. 40, 18 Mar. 43; for Cootehill, Fr. Augustine, *Footprints,* p. 193; *Tipp. Vin.,* 9 Apr. 45.

15 *Mor. Chron.,* 24 Mar. 40; *Gal. Adv.,* 25 Apr., 30 May 40; *Con. Jour.,* 4 Jun. 40.

16 *Lim. Stan.,* 6 Apr. 40; *D.W.H.,* 6 June 40.

17 Hansard lv, pp. 590-91. Westmeath informed the House a few weeks later that all he had meant was that the Lord Lieutenant should have approved of the pledge in his personal rather than in his official, capacity. Hansard lv, pp. 859-60. The Marquis of Londonderry, who approved of sobriety and order as much as Westmeath, refused to grant a piece of land for a temperance hall in Newtownards because, like Wellington, he thought assemblies of teetotallers 'only create terror'. *Tim.,* 29 Aug. 1840; *Con. Jour.,* 23 Jul., 24 Sep. 1840.

18 *West Guard.,* 16 July, 40; *D.E.P.,* 28 Jul., 25 Aug. 40; *D.E.M.,* 28 Aug. 40; *Mayo Con.,* 15 Sep. 40.

19 *Lon. T.M.,* Aug. 40; Daniel O'Connell to Archbishop MacHale, 8 April and 16 July 1840, O'Connell, *Correspondence,* vi, pp. 320, 346; Daniel O'Connell to T.R. Ray, printed *Con. Jour.,* 16 July 40; *Mayo Mer.,* 1 Aug. 40; *Conn. Jour.,* 6, 20 Aug. 40.

20 *D.E.P.,* 1 Sep. 40; *Kil. Jour.,* 17 Oct. 40.

21 *Conn. Jour.,* 20 Mar., 19 Sept. 40; Father Mathew to Thomas O'Connell, quoted Bretherton, 'Irish Temperance Movement', p. 276; Father Mathew to John Russel, n.d. (123), Mathew Draft Correspondence (Q).

22 Oliver MacDonagh, *The Emancipist,* Daniel O'Connell 1830-47 (London, 1989), p. 183. For Cork Temperance Institute see McCarthy, *Story,* pp. 36-42; for reading and the poor, Justin McCarthy, *Irish Recollections* (London, n.d.), p. 11; *Conn. Jour.,* 4 June, 13 Aug. 40. For opposition to halls, Father Mathew to Edward Bullen, n.d. (13), Mathew Draft Correspondence (Q). Father Mathew's efforts to abolish night work for bakers was widely acknowledged, as in Galway in 1842, when he received an address of thanks from the operative bakers of the town for his exertions, 'and soliciting their continuance'. *Gal. Vin.,* 14 Sept. 42.

23 *The Repealer Repulsed! A correct narrative of the Repeal Invasion of Ulster: Dr. Cooke's challenge and Mr. O'Connell's declinature, tactics and flight* (Belfast 1841), p. 46; *Free. Jour.,* 20 Mar. 41; *Sligo Jour.,* 19 Mar. 41; *S. Rep.,* 17 Apr. 41.

24 *S. Rep.,* 22 Apr. 41; Father Mathew quoted Fr. Augustine, *Footprints,* p. 196.

25 *Br. T.A.*, 15 Dec. 41; Gwynn, *O'Connell*, p. 248; MacIntyre, *Liberator*, p. 265; Maguire, *Father Mathew*, p. 234. For a full report on the Cork procession see *S. Rep.*, 29 Mar. 42. From the time of the Cork procession, Norman has written, it became 'difficult to distinguish repeal and temperance themes in the speeches heard at public meetings'. Edward Norman, *A History of Modern Ireland* (London, 1971), p. 75.

26 Hansard lxiii, pp. 1424-25; *D.E.M.*, 6 June 42; Daniel O'Connell to John O'Connell, 29 April 1840, O'Connell, *Correspondence*, vi, p. 326. Anonymous, 'The Temperance Reformation' in *Dublin Monthly Magazine*, Jan.-June 1842, p. 168.

27 *Nat.*, 28 Jan. 43; Venedey, *Ireland*, p. 176. For how the *Nation* was influenced by Father Mathew's success see Mary Helen Thuente, 'The Folklore of Irish Nationalism' in Thomas E. Hackey and L. McCaffrey (eds.), *Perspectives in Irish Nationalism* (Lexington, Kentucky, 1989), p. 55.

28 Kohl, *Ireland*, pp. 95, 189; Maguire, *Father Mathew*, p. 233; Malcolm, 'Temperance and Irish Nationalism', p. 77; for O'Connell's early admiration for Father Mathew's work see his letter to Richard Moore, 29 Nov. 1839, *Correspondence*, vi, p. 287; F. Guizot, *An Embassy to the Court of St. James in 1840* (London, 1862), pp. 137-8; *Pil.*, 23 Aug. 43; Venedey, *Ireland*, p. 40.

29 *D.E.P.*, 18 Apr. 43; *D.E.M.*, 17 Apr. 43.

30 *Wat. Chron.*, 25 Jan. 42; Father Mathew to Mr. Aston, n.d., Mathew Draft Correspondence; *S. Rep.*, 29 Mar. 42; for Tipperary bands, *Nen. Gaz.*, 22 May 41; *Tipp. Vin.*, 8 Jan. 45; for Buckingham, *Temp. Rec.*, Nov. 42; for music, *Dublin Monthly Magazine*, Oct. 42. Maguire confirmed that Father Mathew had no ear for music. Maguire, *Father Mathew*, p. 175. Kohl, *Ireland*, p. 162. Globe Lane 'was celebrated during the great temperance movement of Father Mathew for the excellence of its band'. R. D(ay), 'Sketches of Cork. By W. Roe' in *Journal of the Cork Historical and Archaeological Society*, viii, 2nd series (1902), p. 152.

31 His letter was printed, for example, in *Wat. Mir.*, 10 Oct. 42 and *Clare Jour.*, 13 Oct. 42.

32 Father Mathew to William West, n.d. (1742); Father Mathew to Edward Bullen, n.d. (33); Father Mathew pointed out that temperance bands sometimes attended 'the July Anniversary processions in Ulster, and I'm not to be censured on that account'. Father Mathew to Thomas Beaumont. All Mathew Draft Correspondence (Q).

33 Venedey, *Ireland*, p. 34; *Nat.*, 27 May 43. Elsewhere in his book, Venedey drew attention to the fact that O'Connell had been able to get people to stop drinking at the Clare election in 1828, and his translator corrected him by pointing out that the earliest 'experiment made upon the abstinence of the people, was at the Waterford election of 1826'. Venedey,

Ireland, p. 171. Sir Charles Gavan Duffy, *Young Ireland: A fragment of Irish History 1840-45* (London, 1896), p. 167; Sean O'Faolain thought the three men might have been joking. S. O'Faolain, *King of the Beggars* (Dublin, 1980 edn.), p. 297.

34 K. Inglis, 'Father Mathew's Statue: the Making of a Monument in Cork', in O. MacDonagh and W.F. Mandle (eds.), *Ireland and Irish Australia* (London, 1986), p. 127; Gregg is quoted in Venedey, *Ireland*, pp. 173-4; anonymous letter to Sir James Graham, 23 June 1843, P.R.O. (L.) H.O. 100 257 (211). The Orange order had been dissolved in 1836 and was not formally reconstituted until 1846. H. Senior, 'The Early Orange Order' in T. Desmond Williams (ed.), *Secret Societies in Ireland* (Dublin, 1973), p. 73.

35 *Circular addressed by order of the Irish government to the county inspectors of the constabulary force with the several answers received from these officers* (1843); *Circular addressed by order of the Irish government to the stipendiary magistrates in Ireland, with the several answers received from these officers* (1843). Liverpool Record Office, Papers of the Earl of Darby, Box 34. The replies as they relate to the role of Catholic clergy in the Repeal movement have already been explored in Kerr, *Peel*, pp. 82-6.

36 *Constabulary*, pp. 2, 5, 8, 9, 15, 22, 36, 46.

37 *Constabulary*, pp. 3, 6, 13, 17-19, 29, 40, 41, 49, 54. Father Mathew had not visited Derry up to this time. Fr. Spratt, the leading figure in the temperance movement in Dublin, was a follower of O'Connell. As in 1840, the bands' uniforms and drill were seen by Tory newspapers as suggesting something sinister. See *Gal. Stan.*, 30 Jun. 1843. The report from the Sub Inspector at Arthurstown three years earlier noted the movement there had a 'political leaning' and the Tory newspaper for Wexford town had proclaimed around the same time that Ribbonism and teetotalism were 'clearly one and the same thing', *Wex. Con.*, 11 Apr. 40. The reply from the Wexford County Inspector of Constabulary is echoed in a quotation in Karl Miller's recent book, although the source of the quotation is not clear: "the poor . . . peasants got it into their heads that surely God, through the means of his servant in making them a sober people, was thus preparing the country for that national uprising which they supposed would be imminent should O'Connell's parliamentary tactics fail". Kirby Miller, *Emigrants and Exiles*. Ireland and the Irish Exodus to North America (Oxford, 1988 edn.), p. 241.

38 *Magistrates*, pp. 9, 11, 19, 84, 93-105, 107.

39 *Magistrates*, pp. 9, 31, 44, 72. For Ribbonmen and Repeal see L.M. McCaffrey, *Daniel O'Connell and the Repeal Year* (Kentucky, 1966), p. 187. The moderate Tory newspaper in Cork ceased to support Father Mathew's work in Cork when it saw teetotallers at this time 'marshalled in O'CONNELL'S processions, and we were significantly reminded that they had

acquired the virtue for want of which their fathers failed in '98'. *Cork. Con.,* 9 May 46.

40 *Magistrates,* pp. 53, 54, 60, 84, 88, 91. The Magistrate who saw no connection between the two movements in Athlone was Mr. H. French, brother of Lord French, who had provided Father Mathew with a carriage when he was in Ahascragh, county Galway, in 1840. *Con. Jour.,* 28 May 1840. Lord French was one of the six 'Repeal' magistrates arrested when the Lord Chancellor of Ireland, Sir Edward Sugden, was carried away with enthusiasm following Peel's speech in the Commons in May 1840, saying that the Government would do everything to preserve the Union. L.M. McCaffrey, *Repeal Year,* pp. 60-62.

41 Sir Robert Peel to Lord Eliot, 4 Nov. 1843; Lord Eliot to Sir Robert Peel, 18 Nov. 1843, British Library, Peel Papers, Add. MS. 40480.

42 Temperance was given some credit for the calm that prevailed at O'Connell's arrest: see *Tyr. Her.,* 8 Feb. 1844; for sobriety on his release, see *Temp. Rec.,* Oct. 1844. For accusations of 'Popery' in London see Kerrigan, 'London Teetotalism', p. 108.

43 Kerr, *Peel,* p. 349. Father Mathew wrote that he was 'sincerely interested in the success of the New Colleges'. Father Mathew to Hon. Richard Pennefather, n.d. (993), Mathew Draft Correspondence (Q).

44 Theobald Mathew to Sir Robert Peel, 27 June 1845, Peel Papers, Add. MS. 40569; Father Mathew to Dr. John Sheil, printed *Gal. Mer.,* 26 Apr. 1845; Theobald Mathew to Sir Robert Peel, 23 July 1845, Peel Papers, Add. MS. 40571.

45 Gwynn, *O'Connell,* pp. 75-8; John O'Connell to Bishop Maginn, 8 May 1847, printed Thomas D'Arcy McGee, *A Life of the Rt. Rev. Edward Maginn* (New York, 1857), pp. 142, 157. See also Richard Davis, *The Young Ireland Movement* (Dublin, 1987), pp. 82-144.

46 Daunt, *A Life,* p. 56; K.B. Nowlan, *Charles Gavan Duffy and the Repeal Movement* (Dublin, 1963), p. 12.

47 C.G. Duffy, *The Use and Capacity of Confederate Clubs* (Dublin, 1847), p. 5; C.G. Duffy, *My Life in Two Hemispheres* (London, 1898), p. 67.

48 *Cork Ex.,* 21 Apr. 47, 16 Feb. 48; *S. Rep.,* 26 Jan. 39; Gwynn, *O'Connell,* pp. 124-25, 202. O'Connell himself was of course a supporter of Father Mathew's work but he could hardly be called a personal friend. When O'Connell died in 1847 Father Mathew sent a letter to his son expressing his love for O'Connell, but the sincerity of this could be doubted. The letter was written in his secretary's handwriting. 'Letters and Documents Relating to the Irish Capuchin Province', pp. 53-4. Capuchin Archives.

49 *Con. Jour.,* 2 Jul. 40; *I.L.N.,* 4 Sept. 47; for O'Brien, Father Mathew to John B. Sheil, printed *D.E.P.,* 31 Aug. 44; Fr. Augustine, *Footprints,* p. 477. O'Brien kept his promise, at least up to 1848. *The Prosecuted Speeches*

of William Smith O'Brien, M.P., and Thomas Francis Meagher . . . (Broadsheet, British Library).

50 Murphy, 'Ennis Temperance Society', p. 88; *Nen. Gaz.*, 22 May 41; S.P.A., *The Life and Letters of John Martin. With Sketches of . . . John Kenyon, and other 'Young Irelanders'* (1893), p. 44; *Un. Ir.*, 12 Feb. 48. There is no mention of his support for temperance in his biography. L. Fogarty, *Father John Kenyon: a Patriot Priest of '48* (Dublin, n.d.); *Cork Ex.*, 19 Apr. 48, 19 May, 15 June 48.

51 C.G. Duffy, *Young Ireland: a fragment of Irish History 1840-1850* (London, 1880), pp. 264, 289; McGee, *Maginn*, pp. 146-7; A. Brady, *Thomas D'Arcy McGee* (Toronto, 1925), p. 23.

52 John Mitchel, *The Last Conquest of Ireland (Perhaps)* (Glasgow, 1876 edn.), p. 180; *S. Rep.*, 1 June 48. Lord Cloncurry was one of the leading magistrates who resigned in protest against the removal of Repealers from the magistracy in 1843. MacDonagh, *The Emancipist*, p. 233.

53 *Nat.*, 27 May, 22 July 48; Fogarty, *Kenyon*, p. 120; S.P.A., *Martin . . . Kenyon*, p. 204; Father Mathew's letter is quoted, Inglis, 'Father Mathew's Statue', p. 126.

54 *Free. Jour.*, 21 Feb. 49; some of Father Mathew's testimony, with that of Bishop Blake and William Carleton, was poorly received by Mitchel, then in Bermuda *en route* for Australia, seeing testimony for Duffy's peaceful character and his denial of responsibility for some of the *Nation* articles as a sort of betrayal, 'all very wretched work'. John Mitchel, *Jail Journal* (London, 1983 edn.), pp. 105-6. Duffy's defence tactics earned him the nickname 'Give-in Duffy'. Davis, *Young Ireland*, p. 165. For Father Mathew and slavery see Colm Kerrigan, 'Irish Temperance and U.S. Anti-Slavery: Father Mathew and the Abolitionists' in *History Workshop*, 31 (1991), pp. 105-119.

CHAPTER 6: REASONS AND SUPERSTITIONS

1 Kohl, *Ireland*, p. 102.

2 Larkin, 'Devotional Revolution', p. 637; Maguire, *Father Mathew*, p. 112; T.R. Gort, county Galway; Norman, *Modern Ireland*, pp. 74-5. Converts coming forward to tell of their transition from the misery of drunkenness to the joys of sobriety had been common at English temperance gatherings for some time. Longmate, *Waterdrinkers*, p. 70.

3 Anne Taylor, *Visions of Harmony. A study in Nineteenth Century Millenarianism* (Oxford, 1987), p. 11; James S. Donnelly, Jr., 'Pastorini and Captain Rock: Millenarianism and Sectarianism in the Rockite Movement of 1821-4' in Clark and Donnelly, Jr. (eds.), *Irish Peasants*, pp. 104-5; Patrick O'Farrell, 'Millenialism, Messianism and Utopianism in Irish History' in *Anglo-Irish Studies*, ii (1976), p. 49. On the social interpretation

of millenarianism see E.P. Thompson, *The Making of the English Working Class* (Penguin, 1984 edn.), p. 130 and J.F.C. Harrison, *The Second Coming. Popular Millenarianism 1780-1850* (London, 1979), pp. 218-226.

4   E.J. Hobsbawm, *Primitive Rebels*. Studies in Archaic Forms of Social Movement in the 19th and 20th Centuries (Manchester, 1977), pp. 57-8; *Con. Jour.*, 2 July 40; *Kerry E.P.*, 29 Dec. 40; *Temp. Rec.*, Feb. 43; Grant, *Impressions*, ii, pp. 235-6.

5   *Con. Jour.*, 2 July 40; Father Mathew to Rev. James Clarke, n.d. (1593), Mathew Draft Correspondence (Q); *Nat.*, 28 Jan. 43; Venedey, *Ireland*, p. 175; William Carleton, *Art Maguire; or, The Broken Pledge: a narrative* (Dublin, 1845), pp. 158-60; *B.F.T.I.*, 29 Feb. 40.

6   *Wat. Chron.*, 21 Dec. 39; Carleton, *Art Maguire*, pp. 161-62.

7   Sir James O'Connor, *History of Ireland 1798-1924* (London, 1925), i, p. 302; 'To the Landlords, Rate Payers, and Poor Law Commissioners of Ireland' (handbill), P.R.O. HO 100 257 (213); Hall, *Retrospect*, p. 502.

8   Temperance certificates are in N.L.I. MS. 10731; *D.E.P.*, 6 Feb. 40.

9   *Cork Stan.*, 23 July 38; Birmingham, *Memoir*, pp. 19-20.

10   *Wat. Chron.*, 14 Dec. 39; T.R. Skibbereen and Kinsale, county Cork.

11   T.R. Ennis, Ennistymon and Tulla, county Clare, Mountmellick, Queen's County, Dungarvan, county Waterford, Outerard (Oughterard), county Galway. Sister Mary Francis Clare, *Father Mathew*, pp. 146-53. In Dublin, at around the time the Temperance Reports were being written, Father Mathew said that the pledge did not bind people for life and that anyone wishing to resign could so do by writing to him in Cork to have their names removed from the register, *D.E.P.*, 7 Apr. 40.

12   T.R. Corofin, county Clare, Clonmel, county Tipperary, Dingle, county Kerry.

13   T.R. Dunmore, county Kilkenny; *Free Jour.*, 18 Nov. 40; Father Mathew to Many Shackleton, 4 Aug. 1841, MS. 5055, N.L.I.; Maguire, *Father Mathew*, pp. 141, 365. For the view that the pledge was looked on as something lucky, 'The price paid for certain blessings in prospect' see Richard Webb to William Lloyd Garrison, 28 Nov. 1841, printed *Lib.*, 24 Sept. 41.

14   *Nen. Gaz.*, 25 May 41; *Cork Ex.*, 1 July 46; *Wat. Chron.*, 27 Jan. 42.

15   Bretherton, 'Irish Temperance Movement', p. 275; *Tab.*, 15 July 43; *I.L.N.*, 5 Aug., 16 Sept. 43; *Times*, 23 Aug. 43; Fr. Augustine, *Footprints*, pp. 320-28.

16   *Free. Jour.*, 2 Apr. 40; *Wat. Chron.*, 25 Jan. 42; *Argus* reprinted *Wat. Chron.*, 24 Mar. 42; *Temp. Rec.*, Aug. 45; Father Mathew to William Morris, n.d. (748); Father Mathew to Thomas Beggs, 22 July 1847 (2060), Mathew Draft Correspondence (Q).

17   *Lim. Chron.*, 14 Dec. 39; *Free. Jour.*, 17 Nov. 40; *Clare Jour.*, 6 Oct. 42. For evidence of decline, *Cork Ex.*, 31 Jan. 42 and *Wat. Chron.*, 19 Mar. 42.

18 T.R. Enniscorthy and Arthurstown, county Wexford, Bruff, county Limerick, Mount Bellew Bridge and Gort, county Galway; John Allen Krout, *The Origins of Prohibition* (New York, 1925), p. 188; *Mor. Chron.*, 28 Aug. 43.

19 *Cork. Con.*, 22 Oct. 39; T.R. Rathkeale, county Limerick; *Nen. Gaz.*, 22 May 41.

20 Kohl, *Ireland*, p. 64; Halls, *Ireland*, i, pp. 279-80; W.G. Wood-Martin, *Traces of the Elder Faiths of Ireland*. A folklore sketch: a handbook of Irish pre-Christian traditions (London, 1902), i, p. 72, ii, pp. 87-115; Lady Wilde, *Ancient cures, charms and usages of Ireland* (London, 1890), pp. 77, 110, 161; E. Estyn Evans, *Irish Folk Ways* (London, 1988 edn.), p. 298; Philip Dixon Hardy, *The Holy Wells of Ireland* (Dublin, 1836), pp. 35-6; Sir William Wilde, *Irish Popular Superstitions* (Dublin, 1979 edn.), pp. 28-30. For the ancient origin of Irish superstitions see also James Bonwick, *Irish Druids and Old Irish Religions* (1986, reprint of 1894 edn.), pp. 79 ff. Devotions at many holy wells continued into the present century, as at Tullaghan, county Sligo. Maire MacNeill, *The Festival of Lughnasa*. A Study of the Survival of the Celtic Festival of the Beginning of Harvest (Dublin, 1982 edn.), i, pp. 113-117. For the excitement associated with miracles among the poor in nineteenth century France, see Judith Devlin, *The Superstitious Mind*. French Peasants and the Supernatural in the 19th century (London, 1987).

21 Wood-Martin, *Elder Faiths*, ii, p. 318; Daniel Murray, *A Pastoral Address to the Catholic Clergy and Laity of the Diocese of Dublin announcing the Miraculous Cure of Miss Mary Stuart* (Dublin, 1823), pp. 4-5; Anonymous, *Miracles Mooted*. An Inquiry into the Nature and Object of Miracles, generally, and of the Recent Irish Miracles (Dublin, 1823), p. 12; Anonymous, *An Exposure of the late Irish Miracles* (Dublin, 1823), p. 4; Connolly, *Priests and People*, p. 116; *New Catholic Encyclopedia* (Washington, 1967), xiii, p. 817.

22 Croker, *Researches;* David O. Croly, *An Essay religious and political on ecclesiastical finance, as regards the Roman Catholic church in Ireland, interspersed with other matters not irrelevant to the subject* (Cork, 1834), p. 67; Lady Gregory, *Visions and Beliefs in the West of Ireland* (New York, 1920), ii, p. 287; Irish Folklore Commission, MSS. Iml. 259, p. 306 (Waterford), Iml. 84, p. 300 (Waterford), Iml. 32, pp. 196-7 (Kerry), Iml. 107, p. 683 (Cork) and Iml. 107, p. 279 (Wexford); Connolly, *Priests and People*, pp. 117-18; Sean O'Suilleabhain, *Irish Folk Custom and Belief* (Dublin, n.d.), p. 60. For Cavanagh see *Mayo Con.*, 22 Sept. 40 and *Ir. Ecc. Jour.*, Dec. 40. For contemporary French peasants' expectations of spiritual help for practical services from their priests see Edward Berenson, *Populist Religion and Left Wing Politics in France 1830-1852* (Princeton, 1984), p. 60.

23 Kohl, *Ireland*, p. 67.

24 O'Brien quoted in Fr. Mathew Russell, 'The Memory of Father Theobald Mathew' in *The Irish Monthly*, Jan. 1902, p. 10; Pope Gregory's opinion is in Dr. Paul Cullen to Father Mathew, 10 October 1841; printed Peadar MacSuibhne, *Paul Cullen and his contemporaries, with their letters from 1820-1902* (Naas, 1962), ii, p. 9. For Father Mathew's view see his letter to Dr. Kirby, 5 May 1842 (copy in Mathew Draft Correspondence). Two pamphlets published in 1840 confirm this view was held from an early date, one referring to it in the title, and the other in expressing the conviction that Father Mathew's work was 'from God': Anonymous, *The Life of the Very Rev. T. Mathew, with a correct account of his miraculous labours in favour of teetotalism in the city of Dublin* (Dublin, 1840), and Miley, *Will Teetotalism Last?*, p. 19.

25 Mathew, *Father Mathew*, p. 37; Tynan, *Father Mathew*, p. 39; Rogers, *Father Mathew*, p. 44; T.R. Ballickmoyler, Queen's county, and Ballinasloe, county Galway.

26 Quin, 'Temperance Movement', p. 470; Mathew, *Father Mathew*, p. 38.

27 T.R. Loughrea, county Galway. At around the same time the *Mail* reported that Father Mathew had almost cured a boy of blindness, but the boy was later seen being led away by two people, *D.E.M.*, 25 Mar. 40. For a fake miracle at Roscrea see *D.E.M.*, 25 Mar. 40, and for one at Castletown Delvin see *West. Guar.*, 16 July 40.

28 *Wat. Chron.*, 29 Jan. 42.

29 *Lim. Chron.*, 8 Jan. 42; *Lim. Rep.*, 11 Jan. 42.

30 John Hamilton, *Sixty Years Experience as an Irish Landlord* (London, 1894), pp. 199, 201.

31 *D.E.M.*, 4 Dec. 39, 3 Jan. 40; *Tipp. Con.*, 20 Dec. 39.

32 *Free Jour.*, 31 Mar. 40; *D.E.P.*, 31 Mar., 2 Apr. 40; Allen, 'Early Temperance Struggles', p. 65; *D.E.M.*, 1 Apr. 40.

33 Edwards, quoted MacSuibhne, *Paul Cullen*, ii, p. 14; Kohl, *Ireland*, p. 66; Halls, *Ireland*, i, p. 43. Harriet Martineau quoted a similar letter to that received by the Halls and considered Father Mathew to have been 'dallying' with superstition. Harriet Martineau, *Biographical Sketches* (London, 1869), p. 302. T.R. Arthurstown, county Wexford; *D.E.M.*, 9 Mar. 40.

34 Hamilton, *Irish Landlord*, p. 203; Jonathan Simpson, *Annals of my Life, Labours, and Travels* (Belfast, 1895), p. 76.

35 Letter to Father Mathew, writer unidentified, 29 Aug. 1840, Mathew Draft Correspondence; *Cork Con.*, 7 Nov. 44. For O'Connell see Mary Helen Thuente, 'Violence in Pre-Famine Ireland: the Testimony of Irish Folklore and Fiction' in *Irish University Review*, xv (1985), pp. 145-46.

36 *Ir. Ecc. Jour.*, 30 Aug. 42.

37 T.R., City of Waterford; Hugh J. Nolan, *The Most Reverend Francis Patrick Kenrick, Third Bishop of Philadelphia* (Washington, 1948), p. 415.

38 *Ireland's Own,* 10 Apr. 1954; *Nen. Guar.,* 4 Apr. 40; *Sligo Jour.,* 16 Oct. 40.
39 T.R. Arthurstown, county Wexford. 'The Roman Catholics think Father Mathew a person gifted by the Deity, with supernatural and miraculous powers — one who could, as if by magic, heal the sick, who could, in short, raise them from the dead.' *Gal. Adv.,* 25 Apr. 40. It is of interest that one contemporary, John Blake Dillon, believed that Father Mathew had 'effected a great reformation, without the aid of law or superstition, by the mere majesty of virtue'. Quoted in Brendan O'Cathoir, *John Blake Dillon: Young Irelander* (Dublin, 1990), p. 18.
40 *The Monthly Visitor and Friend of Ireland,* i, Part 2 (1842). For four articles on the origin of the scapular see *Irish Ecclesiastical Record,* May 1901, Feb., Mar., Apr. 1904. *Mayo Con.,* 25 Aug. 40. For contemporary Protestant criticism of the scapular see Anonymous, 'Roman Catholic Devotion — The Order of Carmel and the Scapular of Dr. Stock' in *Dublin University Magazine,* lxxxvii (1840), pp. 284-94.
41 T.R. Arthurstown, county Wexford, Cahir, county Tipperary, Kilfinnane, county Limerick, Dunmore, county Galway, Abbeyleix, Queen's County; Kohl, *Ireland,* p. 106; W.R. Le Fanu, *Seventy Years of Irish Life.* Being Anecdotes and Reminiscences (London, 1896 edn.), p. 122; H. McManus, *Sketches of the Irish Highlands* (London, 1863), pp. 182-83. For similar magical powers attributed to the seals used by the English prophetess, Joanna Southcott, see Harrison, *The Second Coming,* p. 93.
42 Maguire, *Father Mathew,* pp. 528, 530-31; Lady Wilde, *Ancient Legends, mystic charms, and superstitions of Ireland* (London, 1887), ii, p. 292.
43 Sister Mary Frances Clare, *Father Mathew,* pp. 87-93. The author herself claimed to have witnessed a statue move at Knock and to have had a knee complaint cured there. William O'Malley, *Glancing Back.* 70 Years Experience and Reminiscences of Pressman, Sportsman and Member of Parliament (London, 1933), pp. 2, 8-9. Maguire, *Father Mathew,* p. 534; 'Statement signed by the Bishop of Cork, Most Rev. Dr. O'Callaghan, in presence of V. Rev. Fr. Aloysius OFM, Provincial of the Irish Capuchins; Cork, 6 Aug. 1914', in Capuchin Archives.
44 Lysaght, *Father Mathew,* p. 45; Dr. Channing quoted S.R. Wells, *Father Mathew, the Temperance Apostle: his character and biography* (New York, 1867), p. 14.

CHAPTER 7: THE CATHOLIC CLERGY

1 Father Mathew to Dr. Kirby, 25 Feb. 1842, transcript in Capuchin Archives.
2 Father J.G. Lyons to Father Mathew, 5 Aug. 1840, Letters to Father Mathew.
3 *D.E.P.,* 19 Oct. 39; *Cork Con.,* 22 Oct. 39; *S. Rep.,* 24 Oct. 39.
4 Sir Archibald Alison, *History of Europe from the Fall of Napoleon in 1815*

to the Accession of Louis Napoleon in 1852 (Edinburgh, 1858), vii, p. 64. See also McCaffrey, *Repeal Year,* p. 23. Hoppen, *Elections, Politics and Society,* p. 199; Malcolm, *Ireland Sober,* p. 123.

5   *Wex. Ind.,* 1 Apr. 40; T.R. Oulart, county Wexford; for Keating see Lambert McKenna, S.J., *Life and Work of Rev. James Aloysius Cullen, S.J.* (London, 1924), p. 305. Fr. Augustine's view is in his *Footprints,* p. 335. Malcolm refers to Keating's 'reservations about the crusade', but gives no reasons for them. Malcolm, *Ireland Sober,* p. 123.

6   Hugh O'Reilly, *Father Mathew: his Life and Labours* (Newry, 1889), p. 13; *Wat. Chron.,* 29 Sept. 42.

7   *Mayo Con.,* 30 June 40; Fr. Augustine, *Footprints,* p. 195; Desmond Bowen, *Paul Cardinal Cullen and the Shaping of Modern Irish Catholicism* (Dublin, 1983), p. 183; *Nat.,* 14 Jan. 43; *D.E.P.,* 29 Sept. 40.

8   *Catholic Directory for 1842,* p. 271; Fr. Augustine, *Footprints,* p. 194; W. Maziere Brady, *The Episcopal Succession in England, Scotland and Ireland* (Rome, 1876), i, p. 322; *Cork Ex.,* 1 Sept. 47; *Free. Jour.,* 27 Jan. 49.

9   *Gal. Vin.,* 24 Jan. 46; Birmingham, *Memoir,* p. 75; Ullathorne, *Cabin Boy,* p. 195; *S. Rep.,* 29 Mar. 43.

10 Hoppen, *Elections, Politics and Society,* p. 199; Malcolm, *Ireland Sober,* p. 124; T.R. Cahir, county Tipperary; *Free. Jour.,* 5 Dec. 44; *Rules and Regulations of St. Paul's Total Abstinence Society* (Thurles, 1845). I am grateful to Father C. O'Dwyer of St. Patrick's College, Thurles, for providing me with a copy of this item. Slattery was a contributor to the Mathew Relief Fund. *Cork Ex.,* 7 Feb. 45.

11 *Nen. Gaz.,* 22 June 42. Higgins' letter to Cullen is quoted in Bowen, *Cullen,* p. 83. For teetotallers from Ardagh diocese retaking pledge at Kilbeggan, *Free. Jour.,* 3 Apr. 41; Kerr, *Peel,* p. 8. For Father Mathew's visit to Bishop Kennedy's diocese in May 1840 see Flan Enright, 'Father Mathew visits the Wells and Killaloe 1840' in *The Other Clare,* vii (1983), p. 55. For 'the wholehearted support of the priests' in part of the diocese see Murphy, 'Father Mathew . . . South-West Clare', p. 11. Rev. R. Davys to Father Mathew, 12 Aug. 1840, Letters to Father Mathew.

12 Father Mathew to Dr. Cullen, 20 Sept. 41, transcript in Mathew Draft Correspondence. Cullen's reply is in MacSuibhne, *Paul Cullen,* ii, pp. 9-11. *Con. Jour.,* 17 Dec. 40; *Temp. Rec.,* June 43. The Resident Magistrate in Tuam confirmed in 1843 that 'the movement had not taken place to any extent' in his district because of MacHale's opposition, *Magistrates,* p. 48.

13 Bowen, *Cullen,* p. 82; Elizabeth Malcolm, 'The Catholic church and the Irish temperance movement, 1838-1901' in *Irish Historical Studies,* xxiii (May 1982), p. 2; *Tuam H.,* 28 Mar., 30 May 40; *Mayo Con.,* 25 Aug. 40; *Gal. Adv.* 27 Mar. 41; *Gal. Vin.,* 14, 17 July 41; Theobald Mathew to A.

O'Connell, 5 July 1841, A. O'Connell to Theobald Mathew, 7 July 1841, both printed Fr. Augustine, *Footprints*, pp. 206-208. John Forbes, *Memorandums made in Ireland in the Autumn of 1852* (London, 1853), i, p. 246.

14 Fr. Augustine, *Footprints*, pp. 191, 195, 222; *S. Rep.*, 22 Oct. 39, 4 Apr., 25 May 41; *Free. Jour.*, 18 Mar. 41; Bowen, *Cullen*, pp. 185-86. For opposition from farmers and manufacturers in the North, see *S. Rep.*, 16 Feb. 41.

15 *Gal. Vin.*, 21 Jan. 46; *Gal. Mer.*, 24 Jan. 46.

16 T.R. Enniscorthy, county Wexford, Kilfinnane, county Limerick, Abbeyleix, Queen's County, City of Limerick, Corofin, county Clare; *Gal. Adv.*, 29 Aug. 40.

17 *Wat. Chron.*, 14 Dec. 39; Richard Allen to E.C. Delevan, 19 Nov. 1839, printed *Jour. Am. Temp. U.*, Feb. 40; *B.F.T.I.*, 7 Mar. 40; *D.E.P.*, 31 Mar. 40.

18 Birmingham, *Memoir*, pp. 75-6. Notable omissions from Birmingham's list are the Dublin city priests and Father Foley of Youghal, who by this time was estimated to have given the pledge to 100,000 people, *Free. Jour.*, 18 Apr. 40. For Meath, *Wat. Chron.*, 29 Sept. 42; for Killaloe, *Nen. Gaz.*, 22 June 42; T.R. Waterford City, Rathkeale, county Limerick and Outerard (Oughterard), county Galway.

19 Birmingham *Memoir* (1841 edn.), p. vii; *S. Rep.*, 3 Sept. 40; *Br. T.A.*, 1 Mar., 15 July 41; *Bal. Her.*, 22 Jan. 41.

20 Malcolm, *Ireland Sober*, p. 125; Hannah Maria Wigham, *A Christian Philanthropist of Dublin* (London, 1886), p. 44; Father Mathew to Dr. Kirby, 5 May 1842, transcript in Mathew Draft Correspondence; *Nen. Gaz.*, 22 June 42; *Jour. Am. Temp. Un.*, Dec. 42.

21 Venedey, *Ireland*, p. 175; Kohl, *Ireland*, p. 94. Grant, however, writing around the same time, complained of the hostility Father Mathew had encountered from priests. Grant, *Impressions*, ii, p. 239.

22 *S. Rep.*, 8 Apr. 41; *Nen. Guar.*, 4 Mar. 40; Birmingham, *Memoir*, p. 37. *Nat.* 25 Mar. 43; Mac Suibhne, *Cullen*, ii, p. 11. While Cullen did not believe the charges against Father Mathew, but for other reasons, as Bretherton has pointed out, the disciplinarian Cullen could not have been happy with Father Mathew: 'His independent ways must have caused Cullen great concern, and he might serve as a symbol to all those members of the clergy and laity who resented strong episcopal control and the growing presence of Rome in the affairs of the Irish Church.' Bretherton, 'Irish Temperance Movement', pp. 292-3.

23 *Tipp. Vin.*, 20 Mar. 44; *Temp. Rec.*, Jan. 44; Lillian Lewis Shiman, *Crusade against Drink in Victorian England* (London, 1988), pp. 65-6; W.R. Lambert, *Drink and Sobriety in Victorian Wales c.1820-c.1890* (Cardiff, 1983), p. 126. For all his efforts to accommodate Protestants, he had to admit in 1846 that there were 'not fifty Protestants united with us'. Father Mathew

to James Haughton, n.d., but c.Nov. 1846 (1622), Mathew Draft Correspondence (Q).

24   Lambert, *Drink and Sobriety*, pp. 64, 122; Harrison, *Drink and the Victorians*, pp. 179-80; Shiman, *Crusade against Drink*, pp. 63-4; Roberts, *Nineteenth Century Germany*, p. 23.

25   Theobald Mathew to Dr. Kirby, 5 May 1842, transcript in Mathew Draft Correspondence; *Temp. Rec.*, Jan. 44.

26   *Free Jour.*, 14 Jan. 46; *D.W.R.*, 21 Feb. 46; Peter O'Dwyer, *Father John Spratt. Beloved of Dublin's Poor* (Dublin, 1971), pp. 44-5; Father Mathew to Mr. Duff, 27 June 1846 (1090), Mathew Draft Correspondence (Q); Father Mathew to Dr. James Nagle, 1 Oct. 1846, quoted Fr. Augustine, *Footprints*, p. 408; Father Mathew to Mr. Duff, 24 Nov. 1846 (1093), Mathew Draft Correspondence (Q).

CHAPTER 8: CONCLUSION

1   *Br. Temp. H.*, March 45; *Temp. Chron.*, Nov., Dec. 45. For his effect on Blessington in 1840, *Journals . . . Smith*, p. 21.

2   Lord Cloncurry to Sir Robert Peel, 7 Nov. 1845, *Report of the Mansion House Committee on the Potato Disease* (Dublin, 1846), p. 6; 'Copy of the Report of Dr. Playfair and Mr. Lindley on the present state of the Irish Potato Crop and on the Prospect of approaching Scarcity' in *Potatoes* (Ireland), p. 33; *Tip. Vin.*, 31 Dec. 45. Father Mathew distributed cheap flax seeds to farmers, but, though the Belfast Flax Society recommended the cultivation of flax in parts of Ireland hit by the potato famine, they did not respond to Father Mathew's proposal for extending it in Tipperary in 1848. Montague Gore, *Suggestions for the Amelioration of the Present state of Ireland* (Dublin, 1847), p. 39; Fr. Augustine, *Footprints*, pp. 463, 475.

3   *Cork Con.*, 9 May 46.

4   *Gal. Vin.*, 21 Jan. 46. The charity he preached for was the Breakfast Institute in Lombard Street. See L.H. Walker, *One Man's Famine. One Man's Tribute to Bro. Paul James O'Connor on his Centenary: 17 April 1979* (Galway, n.d.), p. 104. Hewetson's comments on Father Mathew are from a letter to Trevelyan, Secretary of the Treasury, which is quoted Maguire, *Father Mathew*, p. 372; for Indian meal, *Cork Con.*, 17 Feb. 46, *Cork Ex.*, 16 Feb., 5 Mar. 46, Maguire, *Father Mathew*, p. 422.

5   Father Mathew to Mr. Trevelyan, 22 Dec. 1846, *Commissariat*, pp. 425-26; Father Mathew to Mr. Trevelyan, 14 July 1847 (417), Mathew Draft Correspondence (Q).

6   *Cork Ex.*, 2 Sept., 28 Dec. 46, 5, 8 Feb., 3, 24 Mar. 47. Schoolchildren in Cork, given food by charitable organisations, often smuggled it out of school under their clothes for those starving at home, S(arah) A(tkinson), *Mary Aikenhead: her life, her work and her friends* (Dublin, 1882), p. 401.

7   *Cork Ex.*, 13, 29 Oct., 17, 24 Nov., 6, 17 Dec. 47, 12 Jan., 16 Feb. 48. He later attributed the low attendance at temperance hall meetings to the fee of 1d. or 2d. which continued to be charged, *Cork Ex.*, 9 May 49. There was a substantial decrease in the numbers arrested for drunkenness in the cities of Cork, Waterford and Limerick between 1845 and 1847, *Drunkenness ... 1841 to 1851*, pp. 300-301.

8   Maguire, *Father Mathew*, pp. 446-7.

9   Mokyr, *Why Ireland Starved*, p. 266; S.H. Cousens, 'Regional death rates in Ireland during the great famine from 1846 to 1851' in *Population Studies*, xiv (1960), pp. 70-73; S.H. Cousens, 'The regional variation in mortality during the great Irish famine' in *Proceedings of the Royal Irish Academy*, 63 (1963), pp. 133-4.

10 James J. Donnelly, Jr., 'Excess Mortality and emigration' in W.E. Vaughan (ed.), *A New History of Ireland* (Oxford, 1989), v, p. 352.

11 For Skibbereen, Cecil Woodham-Smith, *The Great Hunger: Ireland 1845-9* (London, 1968 edn.), pp. 161-4; for Nenagh, Rev. John Gleeson, *History of the Ely O'Carroll Territory* (Dublin, 1915), p. 192; for Claddagh, W. Dillon, 'The "Claddagh" Ring' in *Journal of the Galway Archaeological and Historical Society*, iv (1905-6), p. 13. Revisiting the Claddagh in 1852, the Halls found it 'much deteriorated'. Mr. & Mrs. S.G. Hall, *Hand-Books for Ireland: The West and Connemara* (London, 1853), p. 31.

12 *Cork Ex.*, 9 Feb. 49; Father Mathew to Mr. Allen, 30 June 1847 (1278), Mathew Draft Correspondence (Q). Miller has noted that even when hunger eased in the early 1850s demoralisation was caused by the evictions. Miller, *Emigrants and Exiles*, p. 299.

13 S.H. Cousens, 'Regional Patterns of Emigration during the Great Irish Famine, 1846-51' in *Transactions of the Institute of British Geographers*, 28 (1960), pp. 121, 128, 133. The population of the province of Munster, where Father Mathew's work was probably most influential, had a 22.5% population decline between 1841 and 1851, against a national average of 19.9%. The figure for Connaught was 28.8%, Joseph Lee, *The Modernisation of Irish Society 1848-1918* (Dublin, 1981 edn.), p. 2.

14 Kearney, 'Apostle of Modernisation', p. 175.

15 Malcolm, *Ireland Sober*, p. 147; Hall, *Retrospect*, p. 502. For the view that detections for illicit distillation can be 'an uncertain index of the output of poteen' see K.H. Connell, 'Illicit Distillation' in *Irish Peasant Society* (Oxford, 1968), p. 42.

16 *Cork Ex.*, 9 Feb. 49.

17 Kearney, 'Apostle of Modernisation', pp. 172-3; Malcolm, *Ireland Sober*, p. 145.

18 *Lim. Chron.*, 5 Dec. 39.

19 *Lim. Chron.*, 14 Jan. 42.

20 *Table ... Committed or bailed*, p. 180.

21 *Cork Ex.*, 4 Sept., 11 Oct., 4, 23 Dec. 50, 5, 7, 28 Mar., 7, 30 May, 7, 14 July, 17, 31 Oct. 51; Father Mathew to Richard Dowden, 22 Nov. 1850, printed *Cork Ex.*, 20 Dec. 50. Dr. Spratt, Richard Allen and James Haughton were active in the temperance cause in Dublin in the 1850s. J.S. Buckingham, *History and Progress of the Temperance Reformation* (London, 1854), p. 523.

22 *Cork Ex.*, 23 Aug., 6 Sept., 50. Fr. Augustine's view was that, having had long discussions in finding agreement on the colleges, the bishops 'were loath to introduce another subject which would excite further differences of opinion'. Fr. Augustine, *Footprints*, p. 336.

23 Forbes, *Memorandums*, i, p. 150, ii, pp. 26, 45, 262. For Killarney tee-totallers emigrating, *Cork Ex.*, 31 Jan. 51.

24 McKenna, *Life of Cullen*, pp. 340-46.

25 *Cork Ex.*, 18 Dec. 54.

26 McKenna, *Life of Cullen*, pp. 304-5; Fr. Augustine, *Footprints*, pp. 325-6.

27 Fr. Augustine, *Footprints*, p. 562; A.W. Hutton, *Cardinal Manning* (London, 1894), p. 161; J. Bennet, *Father Nugent of Liverpool* (Liverpool, 1949), pp. 107-108; *Porcupine*, 4 May 72; E.S. Purcell, *Life of Cardinal Manning* (London, 1895), ii, pp. 594-5.

28 Malcolm, *Ireland Sober,* p. 317; Cullen quoted John J. Dunne, *The Pioneers* (Dublin, 1981), p. 23; Maguire, *Father Mathew*, pp. 259-63; McCarthy, *Story*, p. 36. Father Mathew's sympathy with the drunkard was a characteristic of teetotal reformers in England and America, many of whom were themselves reformed drunkards. While Father Mathew had never been a drunkard — the story Kohl heard in Kerry that he had been one as a schoolboy is almost certainly untrue — it is possible that he believed he was capable of becoming one, a belief fuelled perhaps by the knowledge that some of the Mathews had in fact done so. A more significant factor in determining his sympathy for the drunkard was his experience of work-ing among the poor in Cork which was looked at in Chapter 2, an experience that gave him not only a knowledge and understanding of the poor but also a genuine love for them. Harrison, *Drink and the Victorians*, p. 115; Kohl, *Ireland*, p. 125.

29 Letter to Bullen quoted Fr. Augustine, *Footprints*, p. 531.

30 *Cork Ex.*, 17 Feb. 43. The song was written by Daniel Casey. See *Gems of the Cork Poets* (Cork, 1883), pp. 269-70.

31 Kohl, *Ireland*, pp. 102-103.

32 D. Holland, quoted Fr. Augustine, *Footprints*, p. 560; Father Mathew to Dr. Spratt, n.d. (938), Father Mathew to John Russell, 5 Sept. 1846 (952), Mathew Draft Correspondence (Q); Maguire, *Father Mathew*, p. 428.

33 *S. Rep.*, 13 June 48; Father Mathew to Col. Sherbourne, 7 April 1849, N.L.I. Ms. 15297; *N.Y.D.T.*, 7 July 49.

34 Father Mathew to G.W. Carr, 8 Dec. 1839, Miscellaneous Letters, Friends Library, Dublin.

35 *Cork Ex.*, 17 Oct. 56.

36 *Cork Con.*, 9 Dec. 56; *Times*, 11 Dec. 56; *Cork Ex.*, 10 Dec. 56; Haughton, *Memoir*, p. 37; S.C. Hall, *A Book of Memories of great men and women of the age, from personal acquaintance* (London, 1871), p. 409.

37 *Cork Ex.*, 15 Dec. 56.

Bibliography

1. MANUSCRIPT SOURCES

British Library, London:
    Peel Papers
    Papers of Joseph Sturge, M.P.

Capuchin Archives, Dublin:
    Father Mathew Draft Correspondence
    Letters to Father Mathew

Cork Archives Institute:
    Day Papers

Liverpool Record Office:
    Papers of the 14th Earl of Darby

National Library of Ireland, Dublin:
    Mathew Papers
    Minutes of St. Peter's Vestry, Cork city

Public Record Office, London:
    Return of Outrages (Ireland)
    Return of Offences before magistrates (Ireland)

State Paper Office, Dublin:
    Temperance Reports
    Magistrates' Diaries

University College, Dublin:
    Irish Folklore Commission

2. BRITISH PARLIAMENTARY PAPERS (with abbreviations used in notes.)

Fifth Report of the Commissioners of Inquiry into the Collection . . . of the Revenue in Ireland (Fifth Exc. Comm.) 1823 (270) vii

Report from the Select Committee on Inquiry into Drunkenness (S.C. Drunkenness) 1834 (559) viii

Seventh Report of the Commissioners of Inquiry into the Excise Establishment (Seven Ex. Comm.) Pt. I, 1834 xxv, Pt. II, 1835 xxx

First Report of the Commissioners . . . to inquire into the Municipal Corporations in Ireland (Municipal Corporations) 1835 xxvii

First Report from Commissioners for Inquiring into the Condition of the Poor in Ireland (First Poor Inq.) 1835 (369) xxxii

225

Third Report . . . Poorer classes in Ireland (Third Poor Inq.) 1836 (35) xxx

Fifth Report . . . Poor in Ireland (Fifth Poor Inq.) 1839 (239) xx

Spirit Licences (Ireland) 1837-8 (717) xlvi

Report from the Select Committee of the House of Lords Appointed to Inquire into the State of Ireland in Respect of Crime (S.C. . . . Crime) 1839 (486) xii

Abstract of Returns Relating to Infirmaries, Fever Hospitals and Dispensaries in Ireland (Fever and Dispensaries) 1840 (59) xlviii

Resolutions passed by the Board of Guardians in Ireland, relative to the Suppression of Mendicity (Medicity) 1840 (168) xlviii

Report of the Commissioners Appointed to take the Census of Ireland, for the Year 1841 (Census 1841) 1843 (504) xxiv

An Abstract of the Aggregate Number of Persons committed for Criminal Offences (Abstract . . . Criminal Offences) 1841 (345) xviii

Report from Select Committee on the Spirit Trade (Ireland) 1842 (338) xiv

Spirits (Ireland) 1843 (73) li

Evidence taken before Her Majesty's Commission of Inquiry into the State of the Law and Practice in respect to the Occupation of Land in Ireland (Comm. . . . Land in Ireland) Pt. II 1845 (616) xx, Pt. III 1845 (657) xxi

Abstract of Police Reports of some of the principal outrages in the County of Tipperary in the year 1845 (Abstract . . . Outrages . . . Tipperary) 1846 (710)

Potatoes (Ireland) 1846 (28) xxxvii

Comparative Table showing the Number of persons Committed or Bailed in each County and Ireland for each of the last seven years, and the result of proceedings (Table . . . committed or bailed) 1846 (696) xxxv

Return of the Total Number of Gallons of Spirits distilled and charged with duty . . . 1800-1845 (Spirits . . . 1800-1845) 1846 (361) xliv

Correspondence . . . relating to the Measures adopted for the Relief of the Distress in Ireland. Board of Works Series (Board of Works) 1847 (764) l

Correspondence relating to the Measures adopted for the Relief of the Distress in Ireland. Commissariat Series (Commissariat) 1847 li

Fourteenth Report from the Select Committee on Poor Laws (Fourteenth Poor Laws) 1849 (572) xv

Table showing the Number of Persons Committed for Trial (Table . . . Committed for Trial) 1851 liv

Licensed Distillers (Ireland) (Lic. Dist. Ire.) 1851 (369) l

Abstract of Return of the Number of Persons taken into Custody for Drunkenness and Disorderly Conduct in each City and Town in the United Kingdom, in each Year 1841 to 1851 (Drunkenness . . . 1841 to 1851) 1852-3 (531) lxxxi

Report from the Select Committee of the House of Lords, appointed to

consider the consequences of extending the Function of the Constabulary in Ireland to the Suppression or Prevention of Illicit Distillation (S.C. Constab.) 1854 (53) x

Report of the Commissioners Of Inland Revenue on the duties under their Management for the Year 1856 to 1859 . . . and complete Tables of Accounts of the Duties from their first imposition (Rev. Comm. Tables) 1870 (C.82) xx

3. NEWSPAPERS AND PERIODICALS (with abbreviations used in notes. All dates of newspapers cited in the notes are for the nineteenth century unless otherwise stated.)

Athlone Sentinel (Ath. Sen.)
Ballyshannon Herald (Bal. Her.)
Boston Herald (Bos. Her.)
Bristol Temperance Herald (Br. Temp. Her.)
British and Foreign Temperance Intelligencer (B.F.T.I.)
British Temperance Advocate and Journal (Br. T.A.)
Clare Journal (Clare J.)
Connaught Journal (Con. Jour.)
Cork Constitution (Cork Con.)
Cork Examiner (Cork Ex.)
Cork Standard (Cork Stan.)
Dublin Evening Mail (D.E.M.)
Dublin Evening Post (D.E.P.)
Dublin Weekly Herald (D.W.H.)
Dublin Weekly Regigter (D.W.R.)
Father Mathew Record (Fr. M. Rec.)
Freeholder (Free.)
Freeman's Journal (Free. Jour.)
Galway Advertiser (Gal. Adv.)
Galway Mercury (Gal. Mer.)
Galway Patriot (Gal. Pat.)
Galway Standard (Gal. Stan.)
Galway Vindicator (Gal. Vin.)
Hibernian Temperance Journal (Hib. Temp. J.)
Illustrated London News (I.L.N.)
Irish Ecclesiastical Journal (Ir. Ecc. Jour.)
Irish Railway Telegraph (I.R.T.)
Irish Temperance Chronicle (Ir. Temp. Chron.)
Irish Temperance and Literary Gazette (I.T.L.G.)
Irish Temperance League Journal (I.T.L.J.)
Irish Times (Ir. Tim.)

Journal of the American Temperance Union (J. Am. Temp. U.)
Kerry Evening Post (Kerry E.P.)
Kerry Examiner (Kerry Ex.)
Kilkenny Journal (Kil. Jour.)
Leeds Mercury (Leeds M.)
Liberator (Lib.)
Limerick Chronicle (Lim. Chron.)
Limerick Reporter (Lim. Rep.)
Limerick Standard (Lim. Stan.)
London Teetotal Magazine (Lon. T. M.)
London Teetotaller and General Temperance Intelligencer (L.T.G.T.I.)
Mayo Constitution (Mayo Con.)
Mayo Mercury (Mayo Mer.)
Morning Chronicle (Mor. Chron.)
Morning Herald (Mor. Her.)
Nation (Nat.)
National Intelligencer (Nat. Int.)
National Temperance Advocate and Herald (N.T.A.H.)
Nenagh Gazette (Nen. Gaz.)
Nenagh Guardian (Nen. Guar.)
New York Daily Tribune (N.Y.D.T.)
New York Herald (N.Y. Her.)
Pilot (Pil.)
Sligo Journal (Sligo Jour.)
Southern Reporter (S. Rep.)
Statesman and Dublin Christian Record (Statesman)
Sunday Press (Sun. P.)
Tablet (Tab.)
Temperance Chronicle (Temp. Chron.)
Temperance Penny Magazine (Temp. Penny Mag.)
Temperance Recorder (Temp. Rec.)
Temperance Register (Temp. Reg.)
Temperance Worker (Temp. Work.)
Times
Tipperary Constitution (Tipp. Con.)
Tipperary Free Press (Tipp. F.P.)
Tipperary Vindicator (Tipp. Vin.)
Tuam Herald (Tuam Her.)
Tyrawly Herald (Tyr. Her.)
United Irishman (Un. Ir.)
Waterford Chronicle (Wat. Chron.)
Waterford Freeman (Wat. Free.)

Waterford Mail (Wat. M.)
Waterford Mirror (Wat. Mir.)
Westmeath Guardian (West. Guar.)
Wexford Conservative (Wex. Con.)
Wexford Independent (Wex. Ind.)

4. BOOKS, ARTICLES AND PAMPHLETS

Adams, William Forbes, *Ireland and Irish Emigration to the New World from 1815 to the Famine* (New Haven, 1932)

Akenson, Donald H., *The Irish Education Experiment*. The National System of Education in the nineteenth century (London, 1970)

Alison, Sir Archibald, *History of Europe from the Fall of Napoleon in 1815 to the Accession of Louis Napoleon in 1852* (Edinburgh, 1857)

Allen, Richard, 'Early Temperance Struggles' in Frederick Sherlock (ed.), *Fifty Years Ago, or Erin's Temperance Jubilee* (Belfast, 1879), 64-66

Almquist, Eric L., 'Pre-Famine Ireland and the Theory of European Proto-industrialization: Evidence from the 1841 Census' in *Journal of Economic History*, xxxix (1979), 699-718

Annual Report of the House of Recovery . . . of the City of Cork for the year 1826 (Cork, 1827)

Anonymous, *An Accurate Report of the Very Rev. Theobald Mathew, in Dublin, in the Cause of Temperance* (Dublin, 1840)

Anonymous, *The Life of the Very Rev. T. Mathew . . .* (Dublin, 1840)

Anonymous, 'Roman Catholic Devotion — The Order of Carmel and the Scapular of Dr. Stock' in *Dublin University Magazine*, lxxxvii (1840), 284-94

Anonymous, 'The Temperance Reformation' in *Dublin Monthly Magazine*, Jan.-June 1842, 156-168

Anonymous, *The South of Ireland and her Poor* (London, 1843)

Anonymous, *Life of the Very Reverend Theobald Mathew, the Great Apostle of Temperance* (Boston, 1844)

Anonymous, 'A few of Ireland's Temperance Worthies' in Sherlock, *Fifty Years Ago*, 106-126

Anonymous, 'Rev. Theobald Mathew' in Charles A. Read (ed.), *The Cabinet of Irish Literature* (Dublin, 1880), iii, 117-121

A(tkinson), S(arah), *Mary Aikenhead: her life, her work and her friends* (Dublin, 1882 edn.)

Augustine, Father, *Footprints of Father Theobald Mathew, OFM Cap: apostle of temperance* (Dublin, 1947)

Augustine, Father, *Edmund Rice and Theobald Mathew* (Dublin, 1944)

Bales, Robert F., 'Attitudes towards Drinking in the Irish Culture' in David J. Pittman and Charles R. Snyder (eds.), *Society, Culture and Drinking Patterns* (New York, 1962), 157-87

Barnard, Alfred, *The Whiskey Distillers of the United Kingdom* (London, 1887)
Barnard, Alfred, *The Noted Breweries of Great Britain and Ireland* (London, c.1890)
Barrett, James R., 'Why Paddy Drank: The Social Importance of Whiskey in Pre-Famine Ireland' in *Journal of Popular Culture*, xi (1977), 155/17-165/27
Barrow, G.L., *The Emergence of the Irish Banking System 1820-45* (Dublin, 1975)
Barrow, John, *A Tour Round Ireland, through the sea-coast counties in the autumn of 1835* (London, 1836)
Bassett, George Henry, *The Book of County Tipperary* (Dublin, 1889)
Battersby, W.J., 'Biographical Sketch of Very Rev. T. Mathew' in *Catholic Directory 1841* (Dublin, 1840)
Beames, M.R., 'Rural Conflict in Pre-Famine Ireland: Peasant Assassinations in Tipperary 1837-1847' in *Past and Present*, lxxxi, 75-91
Beames, Michael, *Peasants and Power.* The Whiteboy Movements and their Control in Pre-Famine Ireland (Brighton, 1983)
Begley, Archdeacon John, *The Diocese of Limerick.* From 1691 to the Present Time (Dublin, 1938)
Bence-Jones, Mark, 'Thomastown Castle, County Tipperary' in *Country Life*, 2 Oct. 1969
Bennet, J., *Father Nugent of Liverpool* (Liverpool, 1949)
Berenson, Edward P., *Populist Religion and Left-Wing Politics in France 1830-1852* (Princeton, 1984)
Bianconi, M. O'C. and S.J. Watson, *Bianconi, King of the Irish Roads* (Dublin, 1962)
Bicheno, J.E., *Ireland, and its economy* (London, 1830)
Binns, Jonathan, *The Miseries and Beauties of Ireland* (London, 1837)
(Birmingham, Rev. James), *Memoir* (of Theobald Mathew) (1840)
Birmingham, Rev. James, *A Memoir of the Very Rev. Theobald Mathew . . .* (Dublin, 1840). The New York, 1841, edition of this book contains additional material.
Bonwick, James, *Irish Druids and Old Irish Religions* (London, 1894)
Bowen, Desmond, *The Protestant Crusade in Ireland, 1800-1870* (Dublin, 1978)
Bowen, Desmond, *Paul Cardinal Cullen and the Shaping of Modern Irish Catholicism* (Dublin, 1983)
Brady, A., *Thomas D'Arcy McGee,* (Toronto, 1925)
Brady, W. Maziere, *The Episcopal Succession in England, Scotland and Ireland* (Rome, 1876)
Breathnach, Seamus, *The Irish Police from earliest times to the present day* (Dublin, 1974)
Broderick, John F., *The Holy See and the Irish Movement for the Repeal of the Union with England 1829-1847* (Rome, 1951)

Broeker, Galen, *Rural Disorder and Police Reform in Ireland 1812-36* (London, 1970)

Buckingham, James Silk, *History and Progress of the Temperance Reformation* (London, 1854)

Buckley, M.B., *The Life and Writings of Rev. Arthur O'Leary* (Dublin, 1868)

(Burgoyne, Sir John), *Ireland in 1831.* Letters on the state of Ireland (London, 1831)

Burke, Sir Bernard, . . . *Peerages of the British Empire* (London, 1883)

Burke, Helen, *The People and the Poor Law in Nineteenth Century Ireland* (Littlehampton, 1987)

Burke, S.H., *The Rise and Progress of Father Mathew's Temperance Mission* (London, 1885)

Burns, Dawson, *Temperance History* (London, 1889-91)

Burns, Dawson, *Pen-Pictures of Temperance Notables* (London, 1895)

Carleton, William, *Art Maguire; or, the Broken Pledge* (Dublin, 1847)

Carleton, William, *The Black Prophet* (Shannon, 1972 edn.)

Carlyle, Jane, *A New Selection of Her Letters.* Arranged by Trudy Bliss (London, 1949)

Casteleyn, Mary, *A History of Literacy and Libraries in Ireland* (Aldershot, 1984)

Cavour, Count, *Thoughts on Ireland: its present and its future.* Trans. W.B. Hodgson (London, 1868)

Channing, William E., *An Address on Temperance* (Boston, 1837)

Chatterton, Lady, *Rambles in the South of Ireland during the Year 1838* (London, 1839)

Cobbett, William, *Cobbett in Ireland,* ed. Denis Knight (London, 1984)

Cologan, W.H., *Father Mathew: the Apostle of Temperance* (London, 1890)

Connell, K.H., *The Population of Ireland 1750-1845* (Oxford, 1950)

Connell, K.H., *Irish Peasant Society.* Four Historical Essays (Oxford, 1968)

Connolly, S.J., *Priests and People in Pre-Famine Ireland 1780-1845* (Dublin, 1985 edn.)

Connolly, S.J., 'Marriage in pre-Famine Ireland' in Art Cosgrove (ed.), *Marriage in Ireland* (Dublin, 1985), 78-98

Coombes, Rev. James, 'Europe's First Total Abstinence Society' in *Journal of the Cork Historical and Archaeological Society,* lxxii (1967), 52-57

Corish, Patrick, J., *The Irish Catholic Experience.* A Historical Survey (Dublin, 1985)

Cousens, S.H., 'Regional death rates in Ireland during the Great Famine from 1846 to 1851' in *Population Studies,* xiv (1960), 55-74

Cousens, S.H., 'The regional pattern of emigration during the Great Irish Famine' in *Institute of British Geographers, Transactions and Papers,* 28 (1960), 119-34

Cousens, S.H., 'The regional variation in mortality during the Great Irish Famine' in *Proceedings of the Royal Irish Academy,* 63 (1963), 127-49

Critchley, T.A., *A History of Police in England and Wales* (London, 1978 edn.)

Croker, T. Crofton, *Researches in the South of Ireland* (London, 1824)

Croly, Rev. David O., *An Essay religious and political on ecclesiastical finance* . . . (Cork, 1834)

Crotty, Raymond, *Irish Agricultural Production: its Volume and Structure* (Cork, 1966)

Cullen L.M., *The Emergence of Modern Ireland 1600-1900* (London, 1981)

Cullen, L.M., *An Economic History of Ireland since 1660* (London, 1981 edn.)

Cusack, Sister Mary Francis Clare, *The Life of Father Mathew*. The People's Soggarth Aroon (Dublin, 1874)

Cuthbert, Fr., *The Capuchins: a contribution to the history of the counter-reformation* (London, 1928)

D'Alton, Ian, *Protestant Society and Politics in Cork 1812-1844* (Cork, 1980)

Danaher, Kevin, *The Year in Ireland* (Cork, 1972)

D'Arcy, Fergus A., 'The decline and fall of Donnybrook Fair: moral reform and social control in mid-nineteenth century' in *Saothair*, 13 (1988), 7-21

Daunt, William J. O'Neill, *Ireland and her Agitators* (Dublin, 1845)

Daunt, William J. O'Neill, *A Life Spent for Ireland*. Selections from his Journals, edited by his daughter (Shannon, 1972 edn.)

Davis, Richard, *The Young Ireland Movement* (Dublin, 1987)

De Beaumont, Gustave, *Ireland: Social, Political and Religious*, Ed. W.C. Taylor (London, 1839)

Denvir, John, *The Life Story of an Old Rebel* (Shannon, 1972 edn.)

De Tocqueville, Alexis, *Journeys to England and Ireland*. Trans. George Lawrence and K.P. Meyer (London, 1958)

Devlin, Judith, *The Superstitious Mind. French Peasants and the supernatural in the 19th century* (Yale, 1987)

Donnelly, James S., *The Land and the People of Nineteenth-Century Cork* (London, 1975)

Donnelly, James S., Jr., 'Pastorini and Captain Rock: Millenarianism and Sectarianism in the Rockite Movement of 1821-4', in Samuel Clark and James S. Donnelly, Jr. (eds.), *Irish Peasants. Violence and Political Unrest 1780-1914* (Manchester, 1983), 102-139

Donnelly, James S., Jr., 'Excess Mortality and Emigration' in W.E. Vaughan (ed.), *A New History of Ireland* (Oxford, 1989), 350-56

Downes, William Mac Namara, *Temperance Melodies for the Teetotallers of Ireland* (Cork, 1843)

Drake, Michael, 'Marriage and Population Growth in Ireland, 1750-1845' in *Economic History Review*, 2nd series, xvi (1963), 301-313

Dublin Almanac (Dublin, 1838-1839)

Duffy, Charles Gavan, *The Use and Capacity of Confederate Clubs* (Dublin, 1847)

Duffy, Charles Gavan, *Young Ireland. A fragment of Irish History 1840-1850* (London, 1880)

Duffy, Sir Charles Gavan, *Young Ireland. A fragment of Irish History 1840-45* (London, 1896)

Duffy, Sir Charles Gavan, *My Life in Two Hemispheres* (London, 1898)

Duffy, Susan Gavan, 'Father Theobald Mathew, O.S.F.C. 1791-1856' in *A Roll of Honour: Irish Prelates and Priests of the last century* (London, 1905), 107-152

Dunlop, John, *The Philosophy of Artificial and Compulsory Drinking Usages in Great Britain and Ireland* (London, 1839)

Dunne, John J., *The Pioneers* (Dublin, 1981)

Edgar, John, *The evils, cause and cure of drunkenness* (Belfast, 1830)

Edgar, John, *On The Advantages of Temperance Societies* (London, c.1833)

Enright, Flan, 'Father Mathew visits the Wells and Killaloe 1840' in *The Other Clare*, vii (1983), 55-6

Evans, E. Estyn, *The Personality of Ireland: habitat, heritage and history* (Cambridge, 1973)

Evans, E. Estyn, *Irish Folk Ways* (London, 1988 edn.)

F., H., 'Father Mathew' in *The Munster Journal*, Oct. 1890

Fair, T. Wilson, 'The Dublin Total Abstinence Society' in Sherlock, *Fifty Years Ago*, 74-77

Fitzpatrick, David, *Irish Emigration 1801-1921* (Dublin, 1984)

Fitzpatrick, William John, *The Life, Times and Correspondence of the Right Rev. Dr. Doyle, Bishop of Kildare and Leighlin* (Dublin, 1861)

Fogarty, L., *Fr. John Kenyon: A Patriot Priest of '48* (Dublin, n.d.)

Forbes, John, *Memorandums made in Ireland in the Autumn of 1852* (London, 1853)

Fraser, James, *Guide Through Ireland* (Dublin, 1838)

Freeman, T.W., *Pre-Famine Ireland. A Study in Historical Geography* (Manchester, 1957)

Freeman, T.W., 'Irish Towns in the Eighteenth and Nineteenth Centuries' in R.A. Butlin (ed.), *The Development of the Irish Town* (London, 1977), 101-38

Fry, Elizabeth and Joseph John Gurney, *Report Addressed to the Marquess Wellesley, Lord Lieutenant of Ireland, respecting their late visit to that country* (London, 1827)

Gailey, Alan, 'Changes in Irish rural housing' in Patrick O'Hanagan, Paul Ferguson and Kevin Whelan (eds.), *Rural Ireland 1600-1900: Modernisation and change* (Cork, 1987), 86-103

Gaskin, J.J. (ed.), *Viceregal Speeches and Addresses, Lectures and Poems of the Late Earl of Carlile, K.G.* (Dublin, 1866)

Gatrell, V.A.C. and T.B. Hadden, 'Criminal Statistics and their interpretation' in E.A. Wrigley, *Nineteenth Century Society: Essays in the use of quantitative methods for the study of social data* (Cambridge, 1972), 336-96

Gleeson, Rev. John, *History of the Ely O'Carroll Territory* (Dublin, 1915)

Glynn, Jarlath, 'The Catholic Church in Wexford Town 1800-1858' in *The Past*. The Organ of the Ui Cinsealaigh Historical Society, xv (1984), 5-53

Goldstrom, J.M., 'Irish Agriculture and the Great Famine' in J.M. Goldstrom and L.A. Clarkson (eds.), *Irish Population, Economy, and Society* (Oxford, 1981), 155-171

Gore, Montague, *Suggestions for the Amelioration of the Present State of Ireland* (Dublin, 1847)

Grant, James, *Impressions of Ireland and the Irish* (London, 1844)

Gregory, Lady, *Visions and Beliefs in the West of Ireland* (New York, 1920)

Guizot, F., *An Embassy to the Court of St. James* (London, 1862)

Gwynn, Dennis, *Daniel O'Connell: The Irish Liberator* (London, 1930)

Gwynn, Dennis, *Young Ireland and 1848* (Cork, 1949)

Gwynn, Stephen, *Saints and Scholars* (London, 1929)

Haliday, Charles, *An Inquiry into the influence of the excessive use of spirituous liquors in producing crime, disease, and poverty in Ireland* (Dublin, 1830)

Hall, Mr. & Mrs. S.C., *Ireland: its scenery, and character* (London, 1841-3)

Hall, Mr. & Mrs. S.C., *Hand-Books for Ireland: The West and Connemara* (London, 1853)

Hall, Mr. & Mrs. S.C., *Hand-Books for Ireland: The South and Killarney* (London, 1853)

Hall, Mrs. S.C., *Sketches of Irish Character* (London, n.d.)

Hall, Mrs. S.C., *Lights and Shadows of Irish Life* (London, 1838)

Hall, S.C., *A Book of Memories of great men and women of the age, from Personal acquaintance* (London, 1871)

Hall, S.C., *Retrospect of a long life: from 1815-1883* (London, 1883)

Hamilton, John, *Sixty years experience as an Irish Landlord* (London, 1894)

Hardy, Philip Dixon, *The Holy Wells of Ireland* (Dublin, 1836)

Harrison, Brian, *Drink and the Victorians. The Temperance Question in England 1815-1872* (London, 1971)

Harrison, Brian, *Dictionary of British Temperance Biography* (Coventry, 1973)

Harrison, J.F.C., *The Second Coming*. Popular Millenarianism 1780-1850 (London, 1979)

Haughton, James, *A Plea for Teetotalism and the Maine Liquor Law* (London, 1855)

Haughton, Samuel, *Memoir of James Haughton . . .* (Dublin, 1877)

Hayes-McCoy, Gerard Anthony, *A History of Irish Flags from Earliest Times* (Dublin, 1979)

Henry, James, *Essays on Intemperance . . .* (Dublin, 1830)

Hibernian Temperance Society, *Appeal . . . to all Persons interested in the real welfare of Ireland* (Dublin, c.1830)

Hibernian Temperance Society, *Paper A, Paper B* (Dublin, 1830)

Hibernian Temperance Society, *Proceedings of the First annual general meeting* . . . (Dublin, 1830)

Hobhouse, Henry, *Seeds of Change.* Five plants that transformed mankind (London, 1985)

Hobsbawm, E.J., *Primitive Rebels. Studies in Archaic Forms of Social Movement in the 19th and 20th Centuries* (Manchester, 1959)

Hoppen, K. Theodore, *Elections, Politics and Society in Ireland 1832-1885* (Oxford, 1984)

Hughes, Archbishop John, *A Lecture on the Antecedent causes of the Irish Famine in 1847* (New York, 1847)

Hughes, T. Jones, 'The Estate System of Landholding in Nineteenth Century Ireland' in William Nolan (ed.), *The Shaping of Ireland: The Geographical Perspective* (Cork, 1986), 137-50

Hurst, J.W., 'Disturbed Tipperary 1831-60' in *Eire-Ireland*, ix (1974), 44-59

Hurst, Michael, *Maria Edgeworth and the Public Scene* (London, 1969)

Inglis, Brian, *The Freedom of the Press in Ireland 1784-1841* (London, 1954)

Inglis, Henry D., *A Journey Throughout Ireland during the Spring, Summer and Autumn of 1834* (London, 1838 edn.)

Inglis, Ken, 'Father Mathew's Statue: The Making of a Monument in Cork' in Oliver MacDonagh and W.F. Mandle (eds.), *Ireland and Irish Australia. Studies in Cultural and Political History* (London, 1986), 119-36

Isichei, Elizabeth, *Victorian Quakers* (Oxford, 1970)

James, Father, 'Secret of Theobald Mathew — Capuchin' in *The Capuchin Annual*, 1956-7, 111-115

Johnson, James, *A Tour in Ireland* (London, 1844)

Kearney, H.F., 'Fr. Mathew: apostle of Modernisation' in Art Cosgrove and Donal McCartney (eds.), *Studies in Irish History Presented to R. Dudley Edwards* (Dublin, 1979), 164-175

Keegan, John, *A Young Irishman's Diary (1836-1847)* (Privately printed 1928)

Keenan, Desmond, *The Catholic Church in Nineteenth Century Ireland* (Dublin, 1983)

Kerr, Donal A., *Peel, Priests and Politics.* Sir Robert Peel's Administration and the Roman Catholic Church in Ireland, 1841-1846 (Oxford, 1984 edn.)

Kerrigan, Colm, 'Temperance and the Irish in West Ham' in *Essex Journal*, xvii (1982), 20-22

Kerrigan, Colm, 'Father Mathew and Teetotalism in London, 1843' in *London Journal*, xi (1985), 107-114

Kerrigan, Colm, 'Father Mathew in Limerick' in *North Munster Antiquarian Journal*, xxvii (1985), 62-69

Kerrigan, Colm, 'The Social Impact of the Irish Temperance Movement, 1839-1845' in *Irish Economic and Social History*, xiv (1987), 20-28

Kerrigan, Colm, 'Temperance and Politics in Pre-Famine Galway' in *Journal of the Galway Archaeological and Historical Society*, 43 (1991) 82-94

Kerrigan, Colm, 'Irish Temperance and U.S. Anti-slavery: Father Mathew and the Abolitionists' in *History Workshop*, 31 (1991), 105-119

Killeen, W.D., *Memoir of John Edgar, D.D., L.L.D.* (Belfast, 1867)

Kohl, J.G., *Travels in Ireland* (London, 1844)

Krout, John Allen, *The Origins of Prohibition* (New York), 1925

Lambert, W.R., *Drink and Sobriety in Victorian Wales c.1820 - c.1895* (Cardiff, 1983)

Langan, Thomas, *Life and Times of Father Mathew. Apostle of Temperance* (Dublin, 1889)

Larkin, Emmet, 'The Devotional Revolution in Ireland, 1850-75' in *American Historical Review*, lxxii (1972), 625-52

Lee, Joseph, *The Modernisation of Irish Society 1848-1918* (Dublin, 1981 edn.)

Lee, Joseph, 'Capital in the Irish Economy' in L.M. Cullen (ed.), *The Formation of the Irish Economy* (Cork, 1969), 53-63

Lee, Joseph, 'The Dual Economy in Ireland 1800-1850' in T. Desmond Williams (ed.), *Historical Studies*, viii (1971), 191-201

Lee, Joseph, 'On the Accuracy of the Pre-Famine Irish Censuses' in Goldstrom and Clarkson, *Irish Population*, 37-56

Le Fanu, W.R., *Seventy Years of Irish Life*. Being Anecdotes and Reminiscences (London, 1896 edn.)

Letter of the Right Reverend Dr. Doyle on Temperance Societies with an answer of James Henry, M.D. (Dublin, 1840)

Lewis, George Cornwall, *Local Disturbances in Ireland and on the Irish Church Question* (London, 1836)

Lewis, Samuel, *A Topographical Dictionary of Ireland* (London, 1837)

Logan, William, *Early Heroes of the Temperance Reformation* (Glasgow, 1873)

Longmate, Norman, *The Waterdrinkers. A History of Temperance* (London, 1968)

Lowery, Robert, *Robert Lowery: Radical and Chartist*. Edited by Brian Harrison and Patricia Hollis (London, 1979)

Lynch, Patrick, and John Vaizey, *Guinness's Brewery in the Irish Economy 1759-1876* (Cambridge, 1960)

Lyons, J.B., *Scholar and Sceptic. The career of James Henry, M.D. 1798-1876* (Dublin, 1985)

Lysaght, Moira, *Fr. Theobald Mathew OFM Cap: the Apostle of Temperance* (Dublin, 1983)

Macardle, T. Callan, and Walter Callan, 'The brewing industry in Ireland' in William P. Coyne (ed.), *Ireland: Industrial and Agricultural* (Dublin, 1902), 451-93

McCaffrey, Lawrence John, *Daniel O'Connell and the Repeal Year* (Lexington, 1966)

McCarthy, Justin, *The Story of an Irishman* (London, 1904)

McCarthy, Justin, *Irish Reminiscences* (London, n.d.)

MacDonagh, Oliver, 'The Politicization of the Irish Catholic Bishops, 1800-1850' in *Historical Journal*, xviii (1975), 37-53

MacDonagh, Oliver, *The Union and its aftermath* (London, 1977 edn.)

MacDonagh, Oliver, *States of Mind. A Study of Anglo-Irish Conflict 1780-1980* (London, 1983)

MacDonagh, Oliver, *The Hereditary Bondsman. Daniel O'Connell 1775-1829* (London, 1988)

MacDonagh, Oliver, *The Emancipist. Daniel O'Connell 1830-47* (London, 1989)

McDowell, R.B., *Public Opinion and Government Policy in Ireland 1801-1845* (London, 1952)

MacErlaine, J.C., *Whither Goest Thou? Or was Father Mathew right?* (Dublin, 1910)

McGee, Thomas D'Arcy, *A Life of the Rt. Rev. Edward Maginn* (New York, 1857)

McGlashan, James, 'Father Mathew' in *Dublin University Magazine*, cxcviii (1849), 694-706

McGuire, E.B., *Irish Whiskey* (Dublin, 1973)

MacIntyre, Angus, *The Liberator. Daniel O'Connell and the Irish Party 1830-47* (London, 1965)

McKenna, Lambert, *Life and work of Rev. James Aloysius Cullen, S.J.* (London, 1924)

McKernan, Anne, 'In Search of the Irish Town: Re-discovery of a Source for Bandon, Cork' in *Bandon Historical Journal* (1985), 23-36

McManus, Henry, *Sketches of the Irish Highlands* (London, 1863)

MacNeill, Maire, *The Festival of Lughnasa* (Oxford, 1962)

MacSuibhne, Peadar, *Paul Cullen and his contemporaries, with their letters from 1820-1902* (Naas, 1962)

Madden, Daniel Owen, *Ireland and its Rulers Since 1829* (Dublin, 1843)

Magee, Malachy, *1,000 years of Irish Whiskey* (Dublin, 1980)

Maguire, John Francis, *Father Mathew: a biography* (London, 1863)

Maguire, J(ohn) F(rancis), 'The Life and Labours of Father Mathew' in *Irish Penny Readings* (Dublin, 1879), III, 121-26

Maguire, W.A., *Living Like a Lord*. The Second Marquis of Donegall (Belfast, 1984)

Malcolm, Elizabeth, 'Temperance and Irish Nationalism' in F.S.L. Lyons and R.A.J. Hawkins (eds.), *Ireland Under the Union: Varieties of Tension* (Oxford, 1980), 69-114

Malcolm, Elizabeth, 'The Catholic Church and the Irish Temperance Movement, 1838-1901' in *Irish Historical Studies*, xxiii (1982), 1-16

Malcolm, Elizabeth, 'Popular Recreation in Nineteenth-century Ireland' in Oliver

MacDonagh, W.F. Mandle and Pauric Travers (eds), *Irish Culture and Nationalism, 1750-1950* (London, 1983), 40-55

Malcolm, Elizabeth, 'Bibliography of Drink and Temperance in Ireland' in *Alcohol and Temperance History Group Newsletter*, Autumn 1983, 8-10

Malcolm, Elizabeth, *Ireland Sober, Ireland Free: Drink and Temperance in Nineteenth-Century Ireland* (Dublin, 1986)

Mansergh, Nicholas, *Ireland in the age of Reform and Revolution* (London, 1940)

Marmion, Anthony, *The Ancient and Modern History of the Maritime Ports of Ireland* (London, 1855)

Martineau, Harriet, *Biographical Sketches* (London, 1876)

Mathew, Rev. David, 'Father Mathew's Family: The Mathews of Tipperary' in *The Capuchin Annual*, 1956-7, 143-152

Mathew, Rev. David, 'Father Theobald Mathew' in *Irish Ecclesiastical Record*, lxxxvii (1957), 81-90

Mathew, Frank, *Father Mathew. His Life and Times* (London, 1890)

M(athew), J.C., 'Mathew, Theobald (1790-1856)' in *Dictionary of National Biography* (London, 1894), xxxvii, 32-4

Maxwell, Constantia, *The Stranger in Ireland. From the Reign of Elizabeth to the Great Famine* (Dublin, 1979 edn.)

Meyler, Walter Thomas, *Saint Catherine's Bells: an autobiography* (London, 1868-70)

Miley, Rev. John, *Will Teetotalism Last?* (Dublin, 1840)

Miller, David, 'Irish Catholicism and the Great Famine, in *Journal of Social History*, ix (1975), 81-98

Miller, Kerby A., *Emigrants and Exiles* (Oxford, 1988 edn.)

Mitchell, B.R., *European Historical Statistics 1750-1975* (London, 1981 edn.)

Mitchell, B.R., and P. Deane, *Abstract of British Historical Statistics* (Cambridge, 1962)

Mitchel, John, *Jail Journal* (London, 1983 edn.)

Mitchel, John, *The Last Conquest of Ireland (Perhaps)* (Glasgow, 1876 edn.)

Mokyr, Joel, *Why Ireland Starved. A Quantitative and Analytical Study of the Irish Economy 1800-1850* (London, 1983)

Mooney, Thomas, *A History of Ireland from its first settlement to the Present Time* (Boston, 1846)

Morewood, Samuel, *A Philosophical and Statistical History . . . of Inebriating Liquors* (Dublin, 1838)

Mulhall, Michael G., *The Dictionary of Statistics* (London, 1899 edn.)

Murphy, Fr. Ignatius, 'Catholic Education: Primary Education' in Patrick J. Corish (ed.), *A History of Irish Catholicism* (Dublin, 1971), v, 1-52

Murphy, Fr. Ignatius, 'Pre-Famine Passenger Services on the Lower Shannon' in *North Munster Antiquarian Journal*, xvi (1973-4), 70-83

Murphy, Fr. Ignatius, 'Father Mathew, Apostle of Temperance, in South-West Clare' in *The Other Clare*, ix (1985), 5-12

Murphy, Fr. Ignatius, 'Ennis Temperance Society, 1835-1839' in *North Munster Antiquarian Journal*, xxvii (1985), 88-89

Murphy, Maura, 'The Working Class of Nineteenth Century Cork' in *Journal of the Cork Historical and Archaeological Society*, lxxxv (1980), pp. 26-51

Murphy, Maura, 'The Economic and Social Structure of Nineteenth Century Cork' in David Harkness and Mary O'Dowd (eds), *The Town in Ireland: Historical Studies, xiii* (Belfast, 1981), 125-154

Nessan, Fr., 'The Total Abstinence Movement' in *The Capuchin Annual*, 1956-7, 129-137

Nicholson, Mrs. A., *Ireland's Welcome to the Stranger* (London, 1847)

Noel, Baptist Wriothesley, *Notes on a Short Tour through the Midland Counties of Ireland in the summer of 1836* (London, 1837)

Nolan, Hugh J., *The Most Reverend Francis Patrick Kenrick, Third Bishop of Philadelphia* (Washington, 1948)

Nolan, William, *Fassadinin: Land, Settlement and Society in Southeast Ireland 1600-1850* (Dublin, 1979)

Norman, Edward, *A History of Modern Ireland* (London, 1971)

Nowlan, K.B., *Charles Gavan Duffy and the Repeal Movement* (Dublin, 1963)

Nowlan, K.B., 'The Catholic Clergy and Irish Politics in the Eighteen Thirties and Forties' in *Historical Studies*, ix (Belfast, 1974)

O'Brien, John B., 'Agricultural Prices and Living Costs in Pre-Famine Cork' in *Journal of the Cork Historical and Archaeological Society*, lxxxii (1977), 1-10

O'Brien, John B., *The Catholic Middle Classes in Pre-Famine Cork* (Dublin, 1979)

O'Brien, John B., 'Glimpses of Entrepreneurial Life in Cork, 1800-1870' in *Journal of the Cork Historical and Archaeological Society*, xc (1985), 150-58

O'Brien, R. Barry, *Thomas Drummond: Under Secretary in Ireland 1835-40: Life and Letters* (London, 1889)

O'Cathoir, Brendan, *John Blake Dillon, Young Irelander* (Dublin, 1990)

O'Connell, Maurice, *The Correspondence of Daniel O'Connell*, vi and vii (Dublin, 1978)

O'Connell, William D., 'Three Documents Relating to Father Mathew' in *Journal of the Cork Historical and Archaeological Society*, xlvi (1941), 63-67

O'Connor, John, *History of Ireland 1798-1924* (London, 1925)

O'Cuiv, Brian, 'Irish Language and Literature 1691-1845' in T.W. Moody and W.E. Vaughan (eds.), *Eighteenth Century Ireland 1691-1800* (Oxford, 1986), 374-423

O'Dea, Lawrence, 'The Fair at Donnybrook' in *Dublin Historical Record*, xv (1958-9), 11-20

O'Donnell, Patrick, *The Irish Faction Fighters of the 19th Century* (Dublin, 1975)

O'Donoghue, D.J., *Sir Walter Scott's Tour in Ireland in 1825* (Glasgow, 1905)

O'Dwyer, Peter, *Father John Spratt. Beloved of Dublin's Poor* (Dublin, 1971)

O'Fearghail, Fergus, *St. Kieran's College, Kilkenny 1782-1982* (Kilkenny, 1982)

O'Flanagain, Peadar, 'Pre-Famine Westport 1825-1845' in *Cathair-na-Mart*, iii (1983), 39-49

O'Flynn, James, *The Present State of the Poor, with outlines of a Plan of General Employment* (London, 1835)

O'Faolain, Sean, *King of the Beggars* (Dublin, 1980 edn.)

O'Farrell, Patrick, 'Millenialism, Messianism and Utopianism in Irish History' in *Anglo-Irish Studies*, ii (1976), 45-68

O'Haire, Fr., *The Very Rev. Theobald Mathew and the Temperance Cause* (Dublin, 1883)

O'Higgins, Rachel, 'Irish Trade Unions and Politics' in *Historical Journal*, iv (1961) 208-17

Olivier, J.H., *Vie du Père Mathew* (Saint Dizier, 1878)

O'Mahony, Fr. James, 'Theobald Mathew (1790-1856)' in F.J. Sheed (ed.), *The Irish Way* (London, 1932)

O'Malley, William, *Glancing Back. 70 Years Experience and Reminiscences . . .* (London, 1933)

O'Neill, Kevin, *Family and Farm in Pre-Famine Ireland. The Parish of Killashandra* (Madison, 1984)

O'Neill, Timothy P., *Life and Tradition in Rural Ireland* (London, 1977)

O'Neill, Timothy P., 'The Catholic Church and Relief of the Poor 1815-1845' in *Archivium Hibernicum*, xxxi (1973), 132-45

O'Reilly, Fr. Bernard, *John MacHale Archbishop of Tuam. His Life, Times, Correspondence* (New York, 1890)

Osofsky, Gilbert, 'Abolitionists, Irish Immigrants, and the Dilemmas of Romantic Nationalism' in *American Historical Review*, lxxx (1975), 889-912

O'Suileabhain, Amblaoibh, *The Diary of Humphrey O'Sullivan*. Trans. Rev. M. McGrath (London, 1936)

O'Suilleabhain, Sean, *Irish Folk Custom and Belief* (Dublin, n.d.)

O'Tuathaigh, Gearoid, *Ireland Before the Famine 1798-1848* (Dublin, 1972)

O'Tuathaigh, Gearoid, *Thomas Drummond and the Government of Ireland 1835-41* (Dublin, 1978)

O(tway), C(harles), *A Tour Through Connaught* (Dublin, 1839)

Palmer, Stanley H., *Police and Protest in England and Ireland 1780-1850* (Cambridge, 1988)

Parliamentary Gazetteer of Ireland, 1843-44 (Dublin, 1844)

Pearson, Geoffrey, *Hooligan: A History of Respectable Fears* (London, 1983)

Pettit, S.F., *This City of Cork 1700-1900* (Cork, 1977)

(Prince Puckler-Muskau), *Tour in England, Ireland and France in the years 1826,*

1827, 1828 and 1829 . . . in a series of letters (Philadelphia, 1833)

Proceedings of the Cork Literary and Scientific Society during . . . 1837-8 (Cork, 1838)

Pupil of the School, *Visit of the Apostle of Temperance to the Christian Brothers School, North Richmond Street, Dublin* (Dublin, 1843)

Purcell, E.S., *Life of Cardinal Manning* (London, 1895)

(Quin, M.J.), 'Temperance Movement in Ireland' in *The Dublin Review*, viii (1840), 448-484

Raymond, Raymond James, 'A Reinterpretation of Irish Economic History (1730-1850)' in *Journal of European Economic History*, xi (1982), 651-64

The Repealer Repulsed! A correct narrative of the Rise and Progress of the Repeal Invasion of Ulster: Dr. Cooke's Challenge and Mr. O'Connell's declinature, tactics and flight (Belfast, 1841)

Report of the Mansion House Committee on the Potato Disease (Dublin, 1846)

Roberts, James S., *Drink, Temperance and the Working Class in Nineteenth Century Germany* (London, 1984)

Roberts, Paul E.W., 'Caravats and Shanavests: Whiteboyism and Faction Fighting in East Munster, 1802-11' in Clark and Donnelly (eds.), *Irish Peasants*, 64-101

Rogers, Fr. Patrick, 'Father Theobald Mathew, OFM Cap.: A Centenary Memoir' in *Capuchin Annual*, 1938, 213-95

Rogers, Fr. Patrick, 'Father Mathew: a biography' in *Bonaventura*, Spring 1939, 178-195

Rogers, Fr. Patrick, *Father Theobald Mathew: apostle of Temperance* (Dublin, 1943)

Ronan, Myles, *An Apostle of Catholic Dublin* (Dublin, 1944)

Rose, R.B., 'John Finch, 1784-1857: A Liverpool Disciple of Robert Owen' in *Transactions of the Historic Society of Lancashire and Cheshire*, cix (1957), 159-84

Rushe, Desmond, *Edmund Rice: the man and his times* (Dublin, 1981)

Russell, Matthew, 'The Memory of Father Theobald Mathew' in *The Irish Monthly*, Jan. 1902, 1-14

Salaman, Redcliffe N., *The History and Social Influence of the Potato* (Cambridge, 1949)

Samuel, Raphael, 'The Roman Catholic Church and the Irish Poor' in Roger Swift and Sheridan Gilley (eds.), *The Irish in the Victorian City* (London 1985), 267-300

Sheil, John Barclay, *History of the Temperance Movement in Ireland* (Dublin, 1843)

Sherlock, Frederick, *Illustrious Abstainers* (London, 1879)

Sherlock, Frederick, *Ann Jane Carlile: a temperance Pioneer* (London, 1897)

Shiman, Lillian Lewis, *Crusade against Drink in Victorian England* (London, 1988)

Simpson, Jonathan, *Annals of my Life, Labours and Travels* (Belfast, 1895)
Slater, I., *National Commercial Directory of Ireland* (Manchester, 1846)
Smith, Elizabeth, *The Irish Journals of Elizabeth Smith 1840-1850*. Edited David Thomson and Moyra McGusty (Oxford, 1980)
Smyth, George Lewis, *Ireland: Historical and Statistical* (London, 1844-9)
S(tanislaus), Fr., 'Father Mathew and Temperance' in *The Capuchin Annual*, 1930, 162-68
Stivers, Richard, *A Hair of the Dog. Irish Drinking and American Stereotypes* (London, 1976)
Strauss, Erich, *Irish Nationalism and British Democracy* (London, 1951)
Sullivan, A.M., *New Ireland. Political Sketches and Personal Reminiscences of Thirty Years of Irish Public Life* (Glasgow, 1877)
Taylor, Anne, *Visions of Harmony. A Study in Nineteenth Century Millenarianism* (Oxford, 1987)
Thackeray, W.M., *The Irish Sketch Book; and Notes of a Journey from Cornhill to Grand Cairo* (London, 1869 edn.)
Thom's Irish Almanac and Official Directory . . . for the Year 1847 (Dublin, 1847)
Thompson, H.S., *Ireland in 1839 and 1869* (London, 1870)
Thuente, Mary Helen, 'Violence in Pre-Famine Ireland: the Testimony of Irish Folklore and Fiction' in *Irish University Review*, xv (1985), 129-47
Thuente, Mary Helen, 'The Folklore of Irish Nationalism' in Thomas E. Hackey and L. McCaffrey (eds.), *Perspectives in Irish Nationalism* (Lexington, 1989), 42-60
Tobias, J.J., *Crime and Industrial Society in the 19th Century* (London, 1967)
Trollope, Anthony, *An Autobiography* (Oxford, 1980 edn.)
Tuke, James H., *A Visit to Connaught in the autumn of 1847* (London, 1848)
Tynan, Katharine, *Father Mathew* (London, 1908)
Ua Ceallaigh, Sean, *Beatha an athar Tioboid Maitiú* (Dublin, 1907)
Ullathorne, Archbishop, *From Cabin Box to Archbishop* (London, 1941)
Urwick, William, *The Life and Letters of William Urwick, D.D., of Dublin*. Edited by his son (London, 1870)
Vaughan, W.E. & A.J. Fitzpatrick (eds), *Irish Historical Statistics: Population 1821-1971* (Dublin, 1978)
Venedey, J., *Ireland and the Irish during the Repeal Year* (Dublin, 1844)
Walsh, Brendan, 'A Perspective on Irish Population Patterns' in *Eire-Ireland*, iv (1969), 3-21
Walsh, Fr. T.J., 'Father Mathew in Cork' in *The Capuchin Annual*, 1956-7, 116-24
Wells, S.R., *Father Mathew, the Temperance Apostle: his character and biography* (New York, 1867)
Whelan, Kevin, 'The Famine and Post-Famine Adjustment' in Nolan (ed.), *The Shaping of Ireland*
Wigham, Hannah Maria, *A Christian Philanthropist of Dublin* (London, 1886)

Wilde, Lady, *Ancient legends, mystic charms, and superstitions of Ireland* (London, 1887)

Wilde, Lady, *Ancient cures, charms and usages of Ireland* (London, 1890)

Wilde, William, *Irish Popular Superstitions* (Dublin, 1979 edn.)

Wilderspin, Samuel, *Early Discipline Illustrated, or, the Infant System progressing and successful* (London, 1840 edn.)

Wills, James and Freeman Wills, 'The Very Rev. Theobald Mathew' in *The Irish Nation: its History and Biography* (1875)

Wilson, George, *Alcohol and the Nation* (London, 1940)

Windele, J., *Historical and descriptive notices of the City of Cork and its vicinity . . .* (Cork, 1839)

Winskill, P.T., *The Comprehensive History of the Rise and Progress of the Temperance Reformation* (Warrington, 1881)

Winskill, *The Temperance Movement and its Workers* (London, 1892)

Wood-Martin, W.G., *Traces of the elder faiths of Ireland* (London, 1902)

Woodham-Smith, Cecil, *The Great Hunger. Ireland 1845-9* (London, 1962)

5. THESES, TYPESCRIPTS, etc.

Bretherton, George Cornelius III, 'The Irish Temperance Movement 1829-47', Ph.D., Columbia University, 1978

Martin, W.R., 'William Martin', typescript, in Friends Library, London

Nessan, Fr., 'Notes on Intemperance in Ireland', typescript, in Capuchin Archives, Dublin

Pike, William, 'Information about Thomastown and Father Mathew' typescript, in Capuchin Archives, Dublin

Shaw, H.B.F. (later Fr. Nessan, OFM Cap.), 'The Life and Times of Fr. Theobald Mathew', M.A. Thesis, University College, Cork, 1939

Index

Aghada, 53
Abbeyleix, 109, 151, 161
Allen, Richard, 68, 73, 147, 162
America, 131, 165, 172-3, 178, 183
Anti-slavery movement, 27, 32, 178
Anti-spirits (Moderation) movement, 26-30, 33, 46-8, 50-51
Antrim, 97, 124
Aran Islands, 151
Ardmore, 70, 78, 142, 155
Armagh, 160
Arthurstown, 141, 150
Athlone, 76, 121, 123, 126, 148, 158
Augustine, Fr., 4-5, 50, 155, 180

Ballickmoyler, 86
Ballina, 74, 155, 179
Ballinasloe, 74, 172
Ballingarry, 131
Ballintemple, 77, 179
Ballymahon, 147, 150
Ballyshannon, 103, 163
Ballyvaughan, 175
Ballyvourney, 53
Bandon, 15, 164
Bansha, 109
Bantry, 31
Beggars, 11, 14, 43, 77
Belfast, 20, 33, 46, 56, 127, 135, 160, 166
Belmullet, 154
Bianconi, Charles, 38, 60-1
Birmingham, Fr., 1, 54, 56, 61, 63, 65, 130, 137, 156, 162
Blackpool, 139
Blackrock, 35
Blake, Fr., (later Bishop), 28, 34, 130, 155
Blarney, 53
Blessington, 168
Borrisokane, 1, 61, 130, 157, 172
Boston, 129
Boyle, 82
Bretherton, George C., 34, 54, 97
Breweries, 23, 42, 47-8, 90

Browne, Bishop (of Galway), 35, 116, 155
Browne, Bishop (of Kilmore), 156, 175
Bruff, 86
Buckingham, James Silk, 78, 122, 134
Bunmahon, 74
Buttevant, 136-7

Cahir, 60, 61, 68, 151, 157
Callan, 74
Caltra Repeal Meeting, 123
Cantwell, Bishop, 155
Carlisle, Earl of, see Lord Morpeth
Carlisle, Jane Anne, 27-8
Carlow, 15, 17, 60, 63, 72, 97, 111, 147
Carr, G.W., 27-9, 52, 137, 184
Carrickmacross, 124, 160
Carrick-on-Suir, 71, 74
Carrigaline, 53
Carrigtwohill, 53, 179
Cashel, 61, 67, 116
Castlebar, 32, 114, 116, 122, 124
Castleblaney, 160
Castlecomer, 138
Castleconnell, 126
Castletown Delvin, 109
Castletownsend, 31
Cavan, 12
Channing, William, 21-2, 152
Charleville, 73, 109
Claddagh, 62, 67-8, 110-11, 174
Clare, 10, 56, 58, 99, 141, 173, 175
Clare, Sister Mary Francis (M.F. Cusack), 3, 138, 152
Clifden, 73, 110, 134, 175
Clonakilty, 31, 46
Cloncurry, Lord, 26, 68, 130
Clonmel, 32, 60, 65, 68, 71, 74, 77, 100-2, 138, 157
Clontarf Repeal Meeting, 127
Cloyne, 53
Cobh, 53
Coen, Bishop, 63, 156
Coleraine, 32

245

Connaught, 11, 16, 61-2, 162
Connemara, 29, 62, 129
Cootehill, 28, 113, 160
Cork, 1, 20-1, 27, 39-56, 73-4, 77, 79-82,
    84, 97, 108, 118-9, 124-5, 127, 129, 137,
    140, 142, 144, 152, 157, 160, 163, 168, 178,
    180, 182, 184-5
Corofin, 109, 138, 161
Crampton, Judge, 26, 27, 30, 34, 118
Crime and Temperance, 86-7, 90-106
Crolly, Archbishop, 159-60
Crotty, Bishop, 161
Cullen, Dr. (later Cardinal), 158, 164, 179
Cullen, Fr., 179-81, 184

Daunt, John O'Neill, 41, 128
Davis, Thomas, 21, 119-20, 129, 135
Denvir, Bishop, 159-60
Denvir, John, 66, 181
Derry, 156, 172
Dingle, 47, 72, 138
Distillers, 20, 42, 46, 69-71
Donegal, 16, 32, 146, 148, 163
Donnybrook Fair, 71-2
Douglas, 179
Dowden, Richard, 46, 48, 73, 178-9, 184
Doyle, Bishop, 20, 28
Drogheda, 15, 29, 34, 166
Drummond, Thomas, 19, 95-6, 106
Dublin, 2, 6, 15, 20, 26, 28, 33, 34, 46,
    63-4, 71-3, 75-6, 77-8, 80-82, 84, 89-90,
    97-9, 108, 111, 119, 121, 124, 139, 141,
    143, 147, 162, 172
Duffy, Charles Gavan, 119, 123, 128-31
Dungarvan, 67, 125
Dunkerrin, 82, 85
Dunscombe, Rev., 46-8, 154

Edgar, Dr. John, 20, 26, 27, 29, 33, 86,
    97
Egan, Bishop, 156-7
Ennis, 33, 35, 78, 86, 138, 157
Enniscorthy, 76-7, 141, 155, 161
Enniskillen, 108, 113, 164

Faction fights, 95-7
Famine, 8, 106, 128, 130, 168-9, 170-5,
    183
Feeney, Bishop, 155

Fermanagh, 163
Finch, John, 29, 32-6, 48, 56, 61
Finglas, 84, 166
Foley, Fr., 55, 75, 161
Foran, Bishop, 60, 78, 149, 155, 177-8
French, Bishop, 156

Galway, 17, 32, 58, 62-3, 67, 69, 75-6,
    82-4, 89-91, 99, 110, 113-18, 124, 127, 150,
    155, 159, 161, 170, 173, 175, 177, 179
Glanmire, 53, 179
Glendore, 31
Glengall, Lord, 61, 66, 68, 105, 126
Golden, 169
Gort, 61-2, 72, 90, 142
Granard, 115
Gregory XVI, Pope, 145, 153

Hall, S.C. and A.M., 20, 64, 68, 97, 112,
    136-7, 147, 175, 184-5
Haly, Bishop, 156
Haughton, James, 27, 33, 70, 72, 80, 84,
    112, 130, 163, 184
Hibernian Temperance Society, 25, 27-9,
    33, 56
Hierarchy and Temperance, 107, 154-61,
    166
Higgins, Bishop, 157-8, 183
Hockings, John, 35, 50-2, 63
Holyhead, 46

Inglis, Ken, 123
Inishowen, 172

Josephian Society, 40, 49

Kanturk, 86
Kearney, H.F., 6-7, 175-7
Keating, Bishop, 155
Kenmare, 109
Kenrick, Bishop, 149, 165
Kennedy, Bishop, 35, 130-1, 157, 162
Kenyon, Fr., 35, 86, 101, 129-31
Kernan, Bishop, 156
Kerry, 42, 58, 97, 99, 144, 173, 175
Kildare, 60, 63
Kilydysart, 72, 74
Kilfeacle, 100

Kilfinnane, 150, 161, 172
Kilkee, 56
Kilkenny, 38-9, 82, 86, 97, 116, 124, 127, 138
Killala, 116
Killaloe, 74
Killarney, 172, 179
Kilrush, 56, 61, 77, 97, 157, 174, 182
King's County, 60, 99, 124-5
Kingstown, 84
Kinsale, 137, 178
Kinsealy, 84
Kinsella, Bishop, 96, 156
Kirby, Dr., 163, 165
Knockmahon, 68
Kohl, J.G., 10-11, 14, 16, 56, 68-70, 72, 75, 77, 82, 97, 120, 122, 132, 134, 142, 144, 147, 151, 164, 182-3

Landsdowne, Marquis of, 68, 74
Lane, Denny, 129
League of the Cross, 180-1
Lehenagh, 151
Leitrim, 124, 126, 163
Letterkenny, 156, 163
Limerick, 6, 55, 57-60, 64-5, 68-9, 78, 80, 87, 97, 108, 114, 124, 126, 137, 141, 146, 148, 151, 172-3, 175, 177-8
Lismore, 86, 136
Liverpool, 180-1
Livesey, Joseph, 32, 33
London, 5-6, 70, 80-1, 127, 140
Londonderry, 32, 124
Longford, 63, 83, 124, 158, 172
Lorrha, 102
Loughrea, 62-3, 69, 75, 90, 118, 145-6
Louth, 16
Lucan, 103

McCarthy, Justin, 52, 66, 73-4, 181
McCurdy, Robert, 33-4, 135-6, 162
McGettigan, Bishop, 156
McGlashan, James, 112
MacHale, Archbishop, 16, 116, 158-9, 164, 173
McKenna, James, 48-50, 52, 73, 79, 81-2
McLaughlin, Bishop, 156
Macroom, 109
Maginn, Bishop, 130, 156

Maguire, John Francis, 2, 22, 41, 49-50, 54, 93, 120, 138, 151-2, 171, 181, 183
Mahony, Fr. ('Father Prout'), 46, 49
Malcolm, Elizabeth, 6-7, 54, 72, 81-2, 120, 155, 157, 175-7
Manning, Cardinal, 180-1, 184
Martin, William, 46-8, 50, 52-3
Mathew, Anne (née Whyte), 38
Mathew, Charles, 126-7
Mathew, Fr. (later Archbishop) David, 37-8
Mathew, Lady Elizabeth, 2, 37-8, 79
Mathew, Francis (Lord Llandaff), 37-8, 100
Mathew, Frank, 3
Mathew, 'Grand George', 37
Mathew, James, 38
Mathew, Fr. Theobald: childhood and youth, 37-9, 112; priest in Cork, 39-42; adopts temperance, 49-50; his anti-sectarianism, 41, 104, 111-2, 164; his conservatism, 112-3; his debts, 2, 79-80, 183; and Famine relief, 170-5; and Indian meal, 170-1; and cheap bread, 171-2; his death, 184; his burial, 185; his statue, 184
Mayne, Alexander, 27
Maynooth, 17, 39, 87, 127, 134
Mayo, 58, 62, 124, 173
Meath, 63
Mechanics Institute: Cork, 45; Galway, 62, 76, 117-8
Midleton, 35, 53
Millenarianism and Temperance, 133-6
Miracles, 3, 59-60, 143-50, 182
Mitchel, John, 130
Moate, 158
Moira, 160
Mohill, 126
Monaghan, 111, 124, 160
Morpeth, Lord, 1, 19, 64, 72, 95
Mountmellick, 74
Mulgrave, Earl, see Marquis of Normanby
Mullingar, 115, 124
Munster, 16
Murray, Archbishop, 39, 143, 155
Murphy, Bishop, 51, 156-7
Navan, 140, 149
Nenagh, 61, 65, 67-8, 71, 77, 81-2, 84-5, 100-3, 105, 113, 122, 157, 162-5, 174

Nessan, Fr., 5
Newcastle, 175
Newport, 67, 115
New Ross, 27, 29, 31, 46, 148
Newry, 32, 116, 155, 160
Newspapers and Temperance, 1, 5, 54,
 75-6, 83, 88, 104, 122-3, 139, 176
Newtown Hamilton, 125
New York, 183
Nicholson, Asenath, 41, 97
Normanby, Marquis of, 19, 33, 105, 111
Nugent, Fr., 180-1, 184

O'Brien, William Smith, 129-30, 145
O'Connell, Daniel, 1, 7, 18-19, 33, 45,
 100, 103, 105, 107, 110, 114, 116-130,
 140, 148, 157, 160
O'Connell, Fr., 28, 34, 64, 81, 83, 159
O'Connell, John, 48-9, 53
O'Donnell, Bishop, 161
Oldcastle, 115
Olden, Roger, 48-9
Olivier, J.H., 3
Omagh, 125, 172
Oranmore, 110
O'Regan, Fr., 178-9
Oughterard, 138, 162
Oulart, 155

Pallas Green, 72, 77
Parsonstown, 34, 35, 81
Passage, 53, 179
Peel, Sir Robert, 1, 106, 119, 126-8
Philadelphia, 149, 165
Pioneer Total Abstinence
 Association, 179
Portlaw, 29, 32, 34, 55, 77
Portumna, 63, 72, 90
Preston, 30-2
Priests and Temperance, 28, 34-6, 82,
 153-4, 161-6, 179-80
Proselytism and Temperance, 28, 34-5,
 47-9, 154

Quin, Michael, 38, 145
Queen's County, 60, 124, 173

Rathcloheen, 38, 61
Rathcormack, 53

Rathkeale, 55, 126, 162
Repeal, 1, 6-7, 18-19, 45, 105, 107-127,
 132-3, 139, 154, 164, 181
Repeal Reports, 1, 123-6, 176
Riverstown, 53
Roche, Fr., 83-4, 110, 113-4, 161
Roe, George, 69-71, 121
Rogers, Fr. Patrick, 4
Roscommon, 62, 99, 121, 124, 126
Roscrea, 61, 65, 68, 85, 104
Rosscarbery, 31, 46
Rostrevor, 29
Ryan, Bishop, 58, 155

Sandyford, 116, 166
St. Joseph's Cemetery, 40, 152, 185
Savings Banks, 77-8
Scanlan, Fr., 61, 84, 164
Sedwards, Jeffrey, 31
Shiel, John Barclay, 28
Shinrone, 125
Silvermines, 101
Skibbereen, 31-2, 46, 86, 137, 174
Slattery, Archbishop, 157
Sligo, 15, 21, 33, 34, 110, 118, 155, 172,
 179
Spirits, 20-5, 30, 87-90, 170, 176
Spratt, Dr., 17, 28, 33, 34, 64, 71-2, 76,
 130, 166, 183
Steele, Tom, 103, 105
Strabane, 32, 172
Stratford, 142
Swindelhurst, Thomas, 32

Tabuteau, Joseph, 67, 85
Tara Repeal Meeting, 123
Teetotal Movement: origins, 30-34; in
 Cork, 48; in Dublin, 63
Temperance Bands, 73, 79, 83, 117, 119,
 121-3
Temperance Certificates, 81-2, 136
Temperance Medals, 55, 59-60, 62, 77,
 79-80, 150-1, 153, 156, 158-9, 163
Temperance Pledge: wording of, 65; as a
 'vow', 138-40; taken when drunk, 141-2;
 breaking it, 83-5, 138-9; dispensations
 from, 140, 165; and Protestants, 65, 164;
 and religion, 84, 163-5, 180; and
 revivalism, 133; and superstition, 137-8;

Temperance Pledge (cont.)
and landlords, 68; and employers, 64, 68; and gentry, 66; and secret societies, 104; and women, 66; and children, 66-7; and social pressure, 73-4; and publicans, 68, 70
Temperance Processions, 63, 84-5, 108, 110-11, 114-16, 177
Temperance Reports, 1, 4-7, 53, 55, 57, 65, 67-8, 72, 86, 88, 109-10, 119, 123, 134-5, 151, 161-2, 165-6, 176-8. For particular Reports see under place names.
Temperance Societies, 34, 64, 72-3, 117-8, 137; and welfare schemes, 78-9; and politics, 103, 116-8, 124-6. For particular Societies see under place names.
Thackeray, W.M., 21, 41, 112
Thomastown, 37-8, 100
Thurles, 53, 61, 65, 67, 72, 85, 157
Thurles, Synod of, 179
Tipperary, 58, 61, 65, 74-5, 85, 100-106, 124-5, 129, 157, 173 175
Toomyvara, 77, 130, 139, 142
Tralee, 134
Trevelyan, Charles, 171
Tuam, 83, 159
Tullamore, 125
Tynan, Katherine, 3

Ua Ceallaigh, Sean, 4
Ullathorne, Archbishop, 40, 51, 79, 156-7
Ulster, 10, 11, 33, 83, 113, 130, 164, 173
Urwick, Dr., 28, 30, 108

Varian, Isaac, 129-30
Volkes, Major, 65, 67

Wallscourt, Lord, 129
Waterford, 32, 55, 57-8, 60-61, 65-6, 68-9, 74, 78-9, 120-1, 124-5, 139, 144, 146, 162, 177-8
Webb, James, 71
Webb, Richard, 27
Wellington, Duke of, 18, 108
Westmeath, 109, 124
Westport, 20, 159, 179
Wexford, 31, 32, 60, 63, 76, 89, 99, 108-9, 124-5, 144, 146
White, R.G., 33
Whitegate, 53
Wicklow, 11, 60, 63
Wiseman, Dr., 140

Young Ireland, 6-7, 128-31
Yore, Fr., 34, 72
Youghal, 53